CARDINAL CONSALVI

The Wyatts

Royal Residences

The Dukes of Norfolk

Georgian Model Farms

The Latest Country Houses

The Architecture of Northern England

CARDINAL CONSALVI
1757–1824

John Martin Robinson

ST. MARTIN'S PRESS
NEW YORK

© John Martin Robinson 1987

All rights reserved. For information, write:
Scholarly & Reference Division,
St. Martin's Press, Inc., 175 Fifth Avenue, New York, NY 10010

First published in the United States of America in 1987

Printed in Great Britain

ISBN 0-312-01297-7

Library of Congress Cataloging-in-Publication number:

CIP applied for

Contents

List of Plates

Acknowledgments

The Rt Revd the Bishop of Arundel and Brighton; His Excellency Archbishop Luigi Barbarito, Apostolic Pro-Nuncio to the United Kingdom of Great Britain; Mr Peter Barber of the Department of Manuscripts, British Library; Mr and Mrs Christopher Brown; The Rt Revd Mgr Charles Burns of the Archivio Segreto at the Vatican; The Revd Philip Caraman, S.J.; Mr Peter Chevako; The Courtauld Institute; The Revd Ronald Creighton-Jobe; Mr Peter Day, Keeper of the Devonshire Collections; His Grace The Duke of Devonshire and the Trustees of the Chatsworth Settlement; The Durham County Archivist; Lady Maureen Fellowes; Mr Brian Fothergill; Mr J. C. G. George, Kintyre Pursuivant of Arms; Mr St. John Gore; The Earl of Harewood and the West Yorkshire Archives Service; Professor Francis Haskell; The Revd Raglan Hay-Will; Mrs Dyveke Helsted, Director of the Thorwaldsen Museum, Copenhagen; Mr Charles Hind; Mr Hugh Honour; Mr Peter Howell; Hon Hubert Howard; The Conservateur of the Musée Ingres at Montauban; The Rt Revd Mgr John Kennedy, Rector of the Venerable English College, Rome; Mrs I. H. Kenrick of the Royal Commission on Historical Manuscripts; Mr John Kenworthy-Browne; Miss Jane Langton, Registrar of the Royal Archives at Windsor Castle; Mr James Lees-Milne; Signor Maurizio Lodi-Fé; Mr Jonathan Mennell; The Rt Revd Mgr Josef Metzler, Prefect of the Vatican Library; Sir Oliver Millar;

His Grace the Duke of Norfolk; The Archivist, Archives of Propaganda Fidei, Rome; The Archivist, Public Record Office of Northern Ireland; Mr Ian Scott; Mr Denys Sutton; Mrs Rosella Szamocki; Mr Henry Tempest; Mr David Wakefield; Mrs Margaret Windsor; Mr Thomas Woodcock, Somerset Herald of Arms. Quotations from the Royal Archives at Windsor Castle are reproduced by gracious permission of Her Majesty The Queen, and from the Vatican Archives by permission of The Cardinal Prefect of the Vatican Library.

Preface

THE visitor to Chatsworth in Derbyshire may be surprised to find a handsome marble bust of Cardinal Consalvi by Bertel Thorwaldsen in a ground-floor corridor outside the chapel. How did it get there, and why? The visitor might be even more surprised to learn that the bust is a replica of the one on Consalvi's cenotaph in the Pantheon in Rome, and that that memorial in turn was paid for largely by the Cavendish family. The story behind this is an interesting one, and is explored in the following pages. I was inspired to write this book by the bust at Chatsworth and also the magnificent full-length portrait of Consalvi by Sir Thomas Lawrence in the Waterloo Chamber at Windsor Castle when, to my surprise, I discovered that there was no proper biography of Consalvi in any language, let alone in English. It seemed to me extraordinary that such an influential and amiable figure should have been neglected by historians and writers and I determined to fill the gap.

Consalvi was one of the leading statesmen and diplomats of early-nineteenth-century Europe, an international figure comparable with Metternich or Talleyrand. He was greatly admired by his contemporaries. Stendhal, for instance, described him as 'the greatest statesman in Europe, because the only honest one'. He was among the most formidable opponents of Napoleon's regime; and he was largely responsible for saving the temporal power of the papacy in the aftermath of the French Revolution;

through his diplomatic skill in negotiating a system of concordats between the Catholic states of Europe and the Holy See, he laid the foundations for the ultramontane revival of the papacy in the nineteenth century. He did much to embellish the city of Rome, enlarging the museums, restoring ancient monuments, laying out the Piazza del Popolo and the gardens on the Pincio. His internal reforms of the government of the Papal States fell short of his own aims and were largely dismantled by his successors in the years before the states of the Church were subsumed into the united kingdom of Italy, but deserved success. His constancy of purpose, kindness of heart, devotion to duty, courage, wisdom and personal integrity, contributed a note of grandeur to the early-nineteenth-century papacy.

A biography of Consalvi might have been best written by a German or Austrian, because much of the recent historical research into eighteenth-century Italy has been published in German. Italian historians are, it seems, too weighed down by Risorgimento propaganda still to take a detached view of their own recent past; while the English have been equally hampered by inherited prejudice. Nevertheless, as the unfolding story will, I hope, make clear, there is good historical reason for an Englishman to attempt a biography of Consalvi, and this encouraged me to embark on one, though I am not an expert on papal or Italian history as such. I hope, nevertheless, that a tribute to an Anglophile Italian from an Italophile Englishman will not be judged too severely by the *zelanti*.

John Martin Robinson

Beckside House
Barbon
via Carnforth, Lancashire
July 1986

Introduction

BEFORE plunging into the story proper it is necessary to set the context and to explain for the benefit of the non-specialist reader something of the political evolution and character of the state over which Consalvi ruled as papal secretary of state, although anybody who knows the history of the papacy between the Renaissance and Pio Nono may well wish to ignore this Introduction.

For centuries the pope fulfilled two roles. On the one hand, as head of the Catholic Church and the successor to St Peter he enjoyed a universal spiritual authority, on the other he was an Italian secular prince, the sovereign of the Papal States in the middle of the Italian peninsula. Consalvi's career has to be seen primarily in the context of the secular political, or temporal, aspect of the papacy, not the religious. He was, as Daniel O'Connell later remarked, 'a secular cardinal'.

The Roman Church had enjoyed extensive territorial possessions from very early times, but the papal monarchy as such only emerged in the eighth century to fill the vacuum in central Italy caused by the withdrawal of Byzantine influence from the West. The popes, shorn of the protection of the Greek emperors, put themselves under the protection of the Frankish princes and assumed direct responsibility for the defence of Rome and the surrounding area in the face of the advancing Lombard invasions in northern Italy. Thus a form of temporal sovereignty was established, and the neighbourhood of Rome came to be seen as a special domain consecrated to St Peter. To this nucleus of papal territory was added the exarchate of Ravenna and other districts of central Italy, conquered from the Lombards by Pepin and Charlemagne. Further territorial expansion occurred in the following centuries and was accompanied by the development of a highly centralized political organization under the control of the pope. The papal monarchy reached its zenith in the thirteenth century when, in addition to direct rule over central Italy and many other territories the popes enjoyed feudal overlordship over most of the rest of Italy including Naples and Sicily.

During the residence of the papacy at Avignon in the fourteenth century, and the subsequent Great Schism, the Papal States fell into chaos but control was re-established by a succession of worldly fifteenth-century pontiffs who put the aggrandizement of their secular princedom and the enrichment of their own families before their religious duties with a single-mindedness which amounted to a systematic secularization of the papacy and culminated in the reign of Alexander VI (Borgia) who did his best to appropriate the whole of the Church's lands in central Italy to the Borgia family. The Papal States were restored in the form they retained down to the nineteenth century by Alexander VI's successor, Julius II (della Rovere), a forceful and violent ruler who established a strong and independent papacy free from foreign domination. In a series of brilliant military campaigns which he led himself, dressed in full armour, he reconquered the whole of Romagna, as well as Bologna and Perugia. His aim was to make the papacy the chief power in Italy by a combination of force of arms and the patronage of the arts. In Rome he encouraged the most notable artists of the age to embellish the city, Michelangelo above all, and he began the enormous project for rebuilding St Peter's on an unsurpassed scale that was to occupy the papacy for the next hundred years. The foundation stone of the new basilica was laid on 18 April 1506.

Julius II's political policies were continued by his successors, Italian Renaissance princes and lavish patrons of the arts who pursued an energetic, reformist, expansionist programme in the temporal sphere, as in the spiritual. Leo X (Medici) refounded Rome University in 1513 and employed Raphael to decorate the Vatican. Paul III built the Palazzo Farnese, revived the Carnival and made Rome the centre of a brilliant social life. Paul IV in the 1550s took severe action to suppress lawlessness and opened war on the brigands who infested the countryside. Gregory XIII, who reigned from 1572–85, established the secretary of state as the chief minister of the papal administration, and built the Quirinal Palace which for the next three centuries became the chief papal residence in place of the low-lying and old-fashioned Vatican. The greatest of all the sixteenth-century popes, in secular terms, was Sixtus V (Felice Peretti) who reigned from 1585–90. A Franciscan of humble origins, the son of a Dalmatian peasant, he was energetic, forceful, single-minded. He made the Papal States the safest and best-governed country in Europe. Lawlessness was extirpated and the surviving bandits repressed with ruthless efficiency – over 1,000 were publicly executed. The financial system was reorganized, and a new, strictly ordered central administration established; it was made up of fifteen permanent congregations of cardinals, six of which dealt with the temporal government and nine with religious affairs. Sixtus encouraged agriculture and commerce, promoted a scheme for converting the Colosseum into a woollen factory and commenced the draining of the Pontine Marshes with the aid of 2,000 workmen. He made Rome into a magnificent baroque city, the most impressive capital in Europe. He was the first modern town planner and laid out a network of long, ruler-straight streets and vistas, embellished with obelisks at the principal intersections, to connect the seven great basilicas. He also created a new water supply, the Aqua Felice, to serve twenty-seven new fountains and public washhouses. He built up a large financial reserve with four million scudi in gold stored in the Castel S. Angelo, making the pope one of the richest monarchs in Europe as well as one of the most powerful.

The seventeenth-century popes were equally distinguished: energetic reformers, adventurous diplomats and lavish patrons of the arts. Under Urban VIII (Barberini) St Peter's was completed and consecrated in 1626, Bernini employed to adorn Rome, a new fortified port created at Civitavecchia and the papal summer residence established at Castel Gandolfo. The incorporation of the duchy of Urbino in 1631 saw the completion of the territorial expansion of the papal states, while the Treaty of Westphalia in 1648 marked the high-water mark of the Counter-Reformation with much of Europe restored to the Catholic fold; only some small peripheral countries like England, Holland, Scandinavia and a few German principalities remaining officially Protestant.

The second half of the seventeenth century, however, saw the international power of the papacy beginning to wane in the face of the French ambitions of Mazarin and Louis XIV. Internally, too, there were signs of decay, with increasing financial problems facing the papal government. The 'age of glory' left behind a grievous legacy of debt caused partly by extravagant artistic and architectural projects but more by the results of nepotism and the enrichment of successive papal families out of the public treasure. The Aldobrandini, the Borghesi, the Lodovisi and the Barberini had all carved out huge estates for themselves and built luxurious palaces out of the proceeds of the sale of government offices, bonds, and annuities at ruinous rates. Twenty years after the fall of the Barberini, Alexander VII claimed that they alone had burdened the state with 483,000 scudi of annual interest. By the late seventeenth century 85 per cent of the state's income was being swallowed up in interest charges. To remedy this, recourse was had to higher taxation which in turn sparked off lawlessness, banditry and highway robbery, and damaged trade and commerce.

Thus the papacy entered the eighteenth century seriously in debt at home and with greatly decreased political prestige abroad. The Treaty of Utrecht in 1713 effectively marked the end of papal pretensions to great-power status. Clement XI (1700–21) saw his nuncio excluded from the treaty negotiations, while the lay signatories disposed of Sicily, and even Parma and Piacenza with cynical disregard for papal claims to overlordship of those territories. The Bourbon conquest of Naples set at nought papal claims to feudal sovereignty there. At every subsequent treaty and settlement of European boundaries in the eighteenth century the papacy was ignored and snubbed. The rise of new and non-Catholic great powers, Britain, Prussia and Russia, further made papal claims irrelevant and relegated its political aspirations to a sideshow, just as the intellectual movements of the day seemed to undermine its spiritual authority.

By the middle of the eighteenth century the political prestige of the papacy had sunk to its lowest level for centuries. The rationalist and nationalist spirit of the age had scant sympathy for an institution whose claims were irrational and international. Even the Catholic powers were set on curtailing the influence of the pope within their domains. Joseph II of Austria, for example, introduced a series of fundamental 'Gallican' reforms ('Josephism') aimed at bringing the Church within his territories under state control and curtailing the powers of the pope. The decline of the papacy was vividly shown up in 1773 when Clement XIV bowed to the pressure of the 'Enlightened' Catholic monarchs and disbanded the Jesuit order against his will.

The internal affairs of the Papal States were hardly less unhappy, as the country plunged further into spiralling economic decline and administrative chaos. Even Romagna (the 'Legations'), the richest part of the Papal States, suffered a serious decline in population and prosperity. Ferrara, for instance, when absorbed into the Papal States in 1598 had enjoyed a high, perhaps an artificially high, level of prosperity, but by the eighteenth century its population had shrunk by two thirds. Large areas of good land, including most of the Campagna, had been reduced to rough grazing by their absentee landlords, descendants of grasping sixteenth- and seventeenth-century papal nephews, who neglected their large estates. Economic decline in late seventeenth- and eighteenth-century Italy was not, of course, confined to the Papal States. The whole of Italy, regardless of governments, faced increasing economic difficulties caused by, among other things, shifting trade routes. But within the Papal States the economic problems were exacerbated by bad government, high taxation and debasement of the currency, and under the pious and unworldly Benedict XIII (1724–30) there was a complete temporary collapse of the papal finances provoked by gross maladministration.

The papacy reached the end of the eighteenth century seriously impoverished and burdened with debt. Though successive popes had attempted economic reform and tried to encourage trade and agriculture, all were hampered by the chaotic and corrupt administration. However, these papal attempts to stimulate economic development in the eighteenth century were allied to a concern for the cultural development of Rome, the patronage of artists, the enlargement of museums, the establishment of artistic competitions and new university chairs, and the government was rewarded with more success on this front than on the financial one. Despite the political and economic decay of the papacy, Rome maintained its pre-eminence as the artistic capital of Europe and the chief objective of all Grand Tourists from the North, who found the city impoverished but graced with an incomparable artistic and architectural heritage and an easy-going international social life: operas, the Carnival, horse races, hunting, fireworks and endless parties.

The population of the Papal States in the later eighteenth century was about three million souls (equivalent to that of modern Yorkshire), most of whom were employed in agriculture, backward and uneducated. But the 'higher classes', as Consalvi himself demonstrated, were as well educated as any in Europe. The Papal States possessed seven universities, of which those at Rome and Bologna enjoyed international reputations. And, far from teaching just Latin and theology, as has sometimes been alleged, they had up-to-date departments of law, surgery, astronomy, mathematics and chemistry, at a time when England, for instance, had only two universities and a medical system constrained by ordinances of Henry VIII restricting anatomical research to one corpse a year! The problem in the Papal States was that unless they pursued a clerical career there was little for ambitious, educated young men to do. The government was entirely in clerical hands with no lay officials, and there were no representative institutions, not even nominated ones. The pope was a paternalist absolute monarch. His states were under the jurisdiction of bishops, of whom there were a great many, and a series of clerical governors resident in all the principal towns and cities, including Rome; they were responsible for local administration and answerable to various congregations of cardinals in the Roman curia. The system was chaotic in the extreme and varied from province to province and town to town. Everywhere there were entrenched privileges, jealously protected local immunities and independent traditions which effectively prevented all attempts at reform or control from the centre. Some areas were semi-independent feudal fiefs under the umbrella of the great Roman noble families, rather like smaller-scale versions of the princely states within British India, while elsewhere there were communes which retained some of the privileges of independent city states. The deleterious effect of the feudal privileges of the aristocracy and the ancient municipal privileges of the cities on the government administration was further exacerbated by extravagant clerical privileges. None of the clergy, who formed a not insubstantial proportion of the population, paid any taxes.

Consalvi, a Roman noble with a legal education, as a matter of course pursued a clerical administrative career. He inherited a system still in need of radical reform. At home, the papal finances were on the verge of bankruptcy with the currency debased by inflationary paper money; the economy strangled by myriad local customs duties and excessive and inequitable taxes; agriculture and commerce languishing with much of the land uncultivated. Abroad, the papacy's influence had been undermined by the rising tide of secularism and atheism, as well as by the expanding claims of individual national governments to control the Church in their own realms independently of the pope. Consalvi's achievement in restoring the supranational prestige of the papacy through his diplomatic activity has to be judged against the dismal history of decline over the previous century. Likewise his internal reforms of the administration and finances of the Papal States have to be seen in the context of the consistent failures of his immediate predecessors.

I

The *ancien régime*

ERCOLE Consalvi was born in Rome on 8 June 1757 and baptized in S. Lorenzo in Damaso, a little church of ancient foundation tucked into one corner of the magnificent Renaissance Palazzo della Cancellaria. His father was the Marchesino Giuseppe Consalvi, while his mother, Claudia, was the daughter of Count Ludovico Carandini of Modena. His paternal ancestors came from the papal town of Toscanella in the province of Viterbo, to the north of Rome, and his grandfather, 'Giovane' Gregorio, had been created a marchese in 1755 by Pope Benedict XIV, not long before Ercole was born. His family was, however, an old one, long settled at Toscanella. Their original name was Brunacci and they claimed descent from the Counts Brunacci of Pisa. Although this could not be proved, they were able to trace the tree of their descent from the early sixteenth century and the family had served as *gonfalonieri*, or magistrates, and officers in the army during successive centuries. Consalvi's ancestors were equivalent to English landed gentry, untitled nobility living quietly on their own property at Toscanella and performing the public duties of their rank. In origin they were similar to the Farnese who had risen from the same area.

The family's ascent to greater importance in the eighteenth century was due to a series of lucky inheritances through marriages to heiresses in the three generations leading up to

Consalvi's father. His great-great-grandfather Gregorio had married Livia Pioja from another noble family of Toscanella. His great-grandfather, Francesco Felix, had married Julia Antonia Consalvi, and it was the death of her two brothers, Artibal and Ercole, without issue that left her son 'Giovane' Gregorio (Consalvi's grandfather) the heir to the Consalvi property. The Consalvi were a 'noble and ancient house' of Toscanella and like the Brunacci could prove their descent from the sixteenth century, but they were much better off and this inheritance was important in enabling Consalvi's grandfather to establish himself at Rome and to enter the ranks of the titled nobility. Under the terms of the will of his uncle Ercole, who died on 18 January 1735, 'Giovane' Gregorio exchanged the name and arms of Brunacci for those of Consalvi. He moved from Toscanella to Rome and bought a family burial vault in the church of S. Marcello in the Corso, one of the most fashionable in the city. In this way he marked his rise from the provincial nobility to a higher status.

The Marchese 'Giovane' Gregorio Consalvi himself married Maria Angela Perti, and on the death of her first cousin without issue the Perti estates near Rome also passed to the Brunacci-Consalvi. Ercole Consalvi's own mother's family, the Carandini of Modena, were distinguished and had filled high office in church and state, producing two cardinals, one of whom, Cardinal Filipo Carandini, was Consalvi's uncle and a clever judicial and financial administrator in the Roman curia, where his policies foreshadowed those of his nephew. It is likely that Consalvi inherited his brains and administrative abilities from his mother's family.[1]

Ercole Consalvi was the eldest of four brothers and one sister; the latter and the third brother died as babies, but Ercole and two of his younger brothers, Gian Domenico and Andrea, survived infancy. He was only six years old when his father died, on 26 May 1763, of a fever at the early age of twenty-five, and was buried in the new family vault at S. Marcello. His mother, as was the custom, went back to live with her father, Count Gian Ludovico and her brother Monsignor (later Cardinal) Filipo

Carandini at their house in Rome, taking with her only a dowry of 100 scudi* a year from the Consalvi property. Ercole and his two surviving brothers were left in the house of their grandfather, the marchese, but he in turn died three years later in 1766. Under the terms of his will he appointed an influential cleric, Cardinal Negroni, as the guardian of his three little grandsons. Andrea Negroni was a Roman noble and a powerful member of the curia under successive popes from Benedict XIV to Pius VI. Among other posts, he was chancellor, auditor, or private secretary, to the pope, Secretary of Briefs and Cardinal Protector of the Ospizio di S. Michele a Ripa. In leaving his three little grandsons to the care of this influential personage, the marchese was doing his best to provide them with a useful protector and to give them an auspicious start in life. So it was to prove in the long run, but their guardian's first decision had unhappy consequences. This was his selection of a school for them. Not unnaturally, he chose his own old school, the college for noble youths at Urbino run by the Scolopi, the nickname for the 'Congregation of the Holy Name of Mary', an Italian religious order which ran schools, namely, the Congregazione del Santissimo Nome di Maria eretta nel Collegio di Nobili di Padri delle Scuole Pie di Urbino. Ercole, now Marchese Consalvi, and his younger brothers, Andrea and Gian Domenico, were duly enrolled there in September 1766.[2]

They spent four and a half years in that place, and hated it. Ercole studied grammar, humanities and rhetoric. There was nothing wrong with this academic grounding, but the college was run on extremely harsh lines. The prefect, in particular, was a brutal sadist who used to beat his young charges in their nightshirts with a heavy leather strap for the transgressions of the day. As a result of ill-treatment, Consalvi's youngest brother became sick and his knee started to swell in a grotesque manner. As soon as they heard this, their mother and uncle had the boys taken away from Urbino and brought back to Rome. There Gian Domenico underwent a surgical operation on his knee, but it was unsuccessful and he died aged only twelve. This was very

*There were approximately four scudi to the English pound.

upsetting for Consalvi who, as the eldest of the semi-orphans, was particularly close to his younger brothers. Their guardian, after this set-back, began to look around more warily for another school for his surviving charges and was considering the Nazarine College in Rome (also run by the Scolopi) when good fortune intervened in a way, and from a source, which was to colour all Consalvi's future career and outlook.[3]

Cardinal Negroni had been at one stage the auditor to HRH Cardinal Henry Benedict Stuart, Bishop of Frascati, Duke of York and younger brother of Bonnie Prince Charlie. Born in 1725 at the Palazzo Muti in Rome, the second son of Prince James Edward Stuart, the 'Old Pretender', and Princess Clementina Sobieska, he had entered the Church as a young man being created a cardinal and Bishop of Frascati. He bought the palace of La Rocca there, redecorated it and lived in great state with countless servants in royal livery. Rich, pious and stupid, he kept out of politics and devoted himself to running his diocese, entertaining English visitors, and listening to music, of which he was very fond.

In 1770 Cardinal York, as he was usually called, was in the process of reopening the diocesan college at Frascati which had reverted into his hands prior to the suppression of the Jesuits by Pope Clement XIV. The Cardinal-Duke was anxious to make his college the best in the Papal States, and to this end he largely rebuilt it, created a splendid library to which he gave many English as well as Latin and Italian books, added a concert hall, a theatre for masques and oratorios, set up a printing press, and attracted the best teachers he could find. 'Though he was not himself either learned or endowed with great abilities, he knew the value of both.'[4] He naturally wanted to fill his new college with suitable young pupils, and hearing that Negroni was seeking a school for his two charges he asked that they be placed at Frascati where they would be under his own special protection. Negroni could hardly refuse, and Ercole and Andrea matriculated at Frascati in July 1771. In Consalvi's own words: 'From that moment to the last hour of his life Cardinal York showered favours and friendship on me.'[5] Early impressions often run deep. Consalvi, recently transferred from the grim Dotheboys atmosphere of Urbino to the civilized amenities of Frascati and entrusted to the care of a kindly royal patron, must have been strongly affected by the near-miraculous transformation in his circumstances. There can be little doubt that the extreme partiality for England and the English which he displayed all through his life can be traced initially to the kindness and favour shown to him at the age of fourteen by the brother of the *de jure* King of England. For, though Cardinal York had been born in Rome and spent his life on the Continent, he spoke English as his first language and never properly mastered Italian, being more fluent in French. He saw himself as an Englishman, and so did everybody else. Anecdotes were circulated about his exiguous Italian. Once, while being shown the sights in Rome and wishing to tip the guide, he asked his chamberlain how much. The latter suggested a *zeccino* (a gold piece). Thinking the diminutive '-ino' implied a small coin, the Cardinal-Duke replied, 'I think that too little. Give him a *grosso*.' (2p.)[6]

Consalvi remained at Frascati for five and a half years and there studied rhetoric, philosophy, logic, metaphysics, mathematics (including algebra, geometry and trigonometry) and theology. His exercise books with lecture notes (in Latin) for the years 1772 and 1773 still survive and give an impression of his precocious talents.[7] He had the good luck to have excellent teachers at Frascati, in maths and philosophy in particular, and they provided him with a sound academic grounding. As well as his main studies, he also pursued his own more artistic interests, including poetry and music. While a student at Frascati he became a member of the Arcadia, the famous poetic society of Rome, taking the bucolic name of Floridante Erminiano, and writing ambitious verse in Latin and Italian. Even more than poetry, however, music was the great passion of his life. At Frascati he played the violin, and it was his skill as a musician as much as any of his other qualities which won Cardinal York's regard. In Cardinal Wiseman's words: 'Let not the reader be startled if he hears, that it was rather by the ornamental than by the useful arts that the future statesman captivated the good Duke bishop's affections. It is said to have been his skill and graces in a musical performance which first attracted this notice.'[8]

Towards the end of his time at Frascati, Consalvi contracted an illness after which he recuperated at his mother's house in Rome. While resting there, and dreamily contemplating his future prospects, he first conceived the ambition to play a great part in public affairs. Though he always claimed that he had never aspired to become a statesman or actively sought high office, from Frascati onwards he nursed a quiet faith in his own destiny. The latent consciousness of power, of energy and of the perseverance which is essential to successful achievement in any field, seems first to have come to Consalvi while he was convalescing. It is expressed in a long poem which he wrote to celebrate his return to his studies, a typical eighteenth-century classical effusion, beginning: '*Me che riporto alle belle arti, e ai dolci Industri studi desioso il piede . . .*'

> 'Me, – who recall my willing steps, to tread
> Once more the course of studious toil, relieved
> By noble arts; who lure from dreamy flights
> The thoughts and fancies which, with rapid strokes,
> Imagination artist-like creates; –
> Me smiling greet, and tenderly embrace,
> Pallas! the friend and only soothing stay,
> Or rather certain joy of him, whose lips
> The Nine who dwell on the Parnassian hill
> Were first to moisten with their purest milk.
>   Put by thine aegis, lay aside the spear
> That arms thy hand with terror, and afrights
> The timid heart that dwells in gentle breast.
> Tritonian Goddess! – Daughter of great Jove! –
> Bestow thine aid; the path whereon I tread
> Make smooth and straight; my yearnings bear on high.
> With thee propitious I will haste along,
> And cheerful wipe my moist and pallid brow.
> If, when on either side I look for thee,
> I see thee, Goddess! more than is thy wont,

Regard me kindly, with a gracious eye,
And on thy rosy lips a cheerful smile;
That smile alone, yet more a soothing word,
Will still my panting heart, and give me breath.
  Then come, indeed, with gruff and sidelong gaze,
From the rough caverns, 'neath her beetling brows,
And with her hollow cheeks and sallow skin,
Hard-fisted and hard-minded, cheerless Toil;
And threaten me with long and weary watch
By night, and straining breathless work by day.
For, by thee guided, I will make but light
Of cramping labour, and of anguish dire.
That Dame unjust, with strength and patience armed
I will defy; with adamantine breast
Will bend her head, and yoke her to my car.
  Yes, I will reach the goal, which sweet Desire,
Most noble offspring, as she boasts, of Hope,
Points to, with flattering look that wins my heart.
There – oh, I know it! – honour, glory, wealth,
Await me, goad and prize to honest deeds.
Certain is this my lot: this is the web
Woven for me in heaven's unfailing loom.
  But stay – dream I, perchance? or does some God
Benignant whisper to me happy truths?
No, no, I dream not; full soon shall I know it,
When all shall see me, by fair Fortune's love,
Pass through the days which Fate unsparing spins
On her eternal distaff for my destiny,
Joyful, contented with myself; for then
Far other shall I be than now I am.'[9]

The frank avowal of a desire for future honour, glory and
wealth is a striking illustration of his youthful confidence. While
honour and glory were indeed to be his, in his days of power he
was to eschew accumulation of wealth and be content with his
own family patrimony and the basic salaries of his various official
employments. He was in fact relatively well-off on his own

account, independent of any official salaries. As well as the Consalvi family property at Toscanella, from which he derived the rent and other net income, he was also to inherit, in January 1788, from his cousin Anna Maria Perti, her estate as well. The income from this included the rent from houses in Rome, Albano and Tivoli and vineyards at Albano, Castel Gandolfo and close to Rome, outside the Porta Pia. They produced a gross income of between 13,000 and 15,000 scudi a year, though a proportion was always ploughed back to pay for repairs, planting new vines and suchlike. Consalvi ran his properties well and liked to keep them in good condition, the woodwork painted a smart shade of green. He had a resident agent at Toscanella, Alberto Parisani, a distant relation who had been appointed to look after the family property by Consalvi's grandfather some years before Ercole was born, and who was solely responsible for their maintenance and administration during the years of Consalvi's minority, though in the end it was to turn out that the complete and unquestioning trust which the family had in him was misplaced.[10]

Consalvi left Frascati in September 1776, aged nineteen and, with his brother Andrea, went up to the Academy for Noble Ecclesiastics in Rome, recently founded by the new pope, Pius VI. He remained there for six years, reading law and history under the tutelage of a celebrated professor and ex-Jesuit, the Abate Zaccaria. He had decided to follow his guardian and his uncle into the papal curia, and read at the Academy those subjects which would be the best introduction to a legal or administrative career. Zaccaria was responsible for instilling in him that clarity and integrity of thought which always distinguished his conduct though Consalvi distanced himself from his tutor's extreme reactionary views. He prospered at the Academy and was chosen to give a Latin address to the pope in the Vatican on Ascension Day 1780, a daunting task but one which he carried off well, with learned references to the Old and New Testaments and the writings of St Augustine and St Leo.[11] It was the first occasion on which he came to the direct notice of the reigning pontiff. He left the Academy with distinction in October 1782 and was awarded a pension of fifty scudi, receiving his doctorate of Canon and Civil Law two years' later, on 9 July 1784.[12]

A word might be said about the quality of Consalvi's education, particularly as much has been written about the backward educational facilities in the Papal States in the eighteenth and early nineteenth centuries. Consalvi was at least as well educated as contemporary English statesmen, and higher education in the Papal States compared very favourably with that in eighteenth-century England. It may be that Consalvi himself benefited from the new colleges founded in the aftermath of the suppression of the Jesuits (who had hitherto run the educational system in the Papal States) but far from being taught just Latin and theology, he received a balanced education which left him fluent in French and an accomplished musician and poet, as well as lawyer, historian and practical man of affairs.

The papacy was an absolute monarchy with its own political state made up of several provinces. The nucleus was the 'patrimony of St Peter' around Rome itself, the origins of which were lost in the mists of the Dark Ages, but which the medieval popes claimed had been given to the Church by Constantine when he moved the capital of the Roman Empire to Constantinople. Extending beyond the patrimony to the north and east as far as the Po and the Adriatic were the further provinces of Umbria, the Marches and the Legations which had been acquired piecemeal over a long period and finally secured by Julius II's military activity in the early sixteenth century. There was also Avignon and the Venaissin in France, purchased in the thirteenth and fourteenth centuries, and the independent enclaves of Benevento and Ponte Corvo deep within the Kingdom of Naples, which had been acquired by the Church in the Middle Ages as the result of an exchange of lands with the emperor. This conglomerate principality provided the pope with the funds, status and political independence necessary to sustain his religious role as head of the Church. Both the government of the Catholic Church and the administration of the pope's Italian state were carried on through the body of judicial and administrative institutions known collectively as the curia, a name derived ultimately from the senate of ancient Rome. In many ways the eighteenth-century curia did not much differ from the courts of other contemporary European monarchies, though of course the theocratic element was more pronounced in Rome than, say, in Madrid, Vienna or Versailles.

The papal court was divided into two parts, the pope's religious household known as his 'capella' (chapel), and his civil household or 'familia' (family). It was this latter, composed of cardinals, prelates and lesser officials, which assisted with the administrative, judicial and legislative functions of the papacy and in which Consalvi was to pursue his career. He never became a priest and did not even take minor orders as a deacon until he was made a cardinal in 1800. If this sounds odd, it should be remembered that throughout eighteenth-century Europe, and not just in the Papal States, there were classes of men, other than parish clergy, who wore clerical dress. Even in Protestant England, for example, the dons of Oxford and Cambridge were not allowed to marry and had to be in Holy Orders, while the monarch was anointed as a priest with holy oil at his coronation. So, in the Papal States clever young men followed administrative or judicial careers in the curia dressed as clergy, living ostensibly celibate lives, but never becoming fully-fledged priests. They were known collectively as the *prelatura* and made up a large part of the pope's *familia* or civil household. They were entitled to wear violet-coloured ecclesiastical dress and to be called Monsignor like bishops; they had jurisdictional powers but no priestly functions. It was this special administrative class, recruited chiefly from the educated Roman nobility, into which Consalvi was drawn, almost as a matter of course, when he aspired to a career in public affairs when his education was completed.

His official career began when he was nominated a Camerero Segreto, or private chamberlain, to the pope on 20 April 1785. This was the lowest rung on the ladder of the curia, and involved the undemanding task of hanging around in the papal ante-chamber to receive those admitted to audience. Despite its humdrum character it provided a great opportunity for a young man like Consalvi, with good looks, courteous manners, a good mind, a sound academic training and powerful connections. It was not long before he was appointed a Domestic Prelate to the pope with the courtesy title of Monsignor. When he became a monsignor, Consalvi relinquished his marquessate to his younger brother Andrea who now became the Marchese Consalvi in accordance with Roman practice. The two brothers remained close to each other. When they had first left the Academy they shared lodgings together in the Casino Colonna, but now Consalvi moved into an apartment of his own at the Palazzo della Cancellaria, which was Cardinal York's official residence in Rome. There can be little doubt that the Cardinal-Duke was responsible for Consalvi being appointed a prelate so expeditiously and for obtaining for him a position in the curia in the first place. At the Palazzo della Cancellaria he was often to be seen in the Cardinal-Duke's rooms, as was noted by a succession of foreign visitors who came to pay their respects to the *palazzo*'s royal occupant. It was after all just a short walk for Consalvi across the courtyard to visit his benefactor and protector. The Cancellaria was to be his home for sixteen years and he left it only to move into the papal palace itself on the Quirinal. He also kept the little house at Frascati, rented from Barbara Panizza, where he had lodged as a student. He continued to spend his holidays there in the hot summer months, and in January. At Frascati, too, he was a frequent guest of Cardinal York's at the episcopal palace, and the old man came to depend more and more on his company.

As well as the relaxed vacations at Frascati, Consalvi also took the opportunity to travel and to see other countries. In the autumn of 1782, between leaving the Academy and entering the curia, he had taken an extended holiday in Naples. It was his first journey outside the Papal States but the first of many, for he enjoyed travel.

Consalvi was appointed Referendum of the Signature, a junior legal post, in 1785, and in January 1786 was also given a place on the Congregation del Buon Governo which provided him with the opportunity to study the socio-economic make-up of the Papal States. This rapid promotion was due to papal favour, his own reputation, and the influence of his backers, Cardinal Negroni, Cardinal York and his uncle Monsignor Carandini (created a cardinal in 1787). He received some advice from Negroni when he entered the curia, which he followed with one exception: 'It is not necessary to ask for anything, never put your heart into advancement, but clear away any obstacles to it by the punctilious discharge of your duties and by a good reputation.' At first it was not clear whether his career in the curia would be administrative or legal; the distinction between the two was in any case somewhat blurred in eighteenth-century Rome.

The eighteenth-century curia was made up of two systems of government superimposed on top of each other. The ancient structure of the government of the Church, comprising tribunals and offices, still survived but it had been partly overlaid in the sixteenth century by a more coherent Renaissance administrative structure of congregations of cardinals, to each of which specific aspects of the papal government were delegated. These congregations had begun to emerge in the early years of the sixteenth century, but were not converted into a new, ordered, system of government till the brief reign of that energetic organizer Pope Sixtus V. His Bull *Immensa* dated 22 January 1587 apportioned all the business of the Church, including the administration of the Papal States, among fifteen congregations, most of them newly founded by himself. Sixtus V's framework survived till 1908 when Pius X's Bull *Sapientia Concilio* reorganized the curia. But many of the Counter-Reformation congregations survive to the present day.

The principal tribunals of the Church were the Rota and the Signatura. The Rota was the supreme ecclesiastic court for civil affairs and dated back to the fourteenth century. It enjoyed a European-wide reputation and its legal decisions carried great authority. It was the ecclesiastical court of appeal for civil and criminal cases and had ten judges called auditors, the senior of whom was known as the prefect. It heard appeals, referred to Rome from all over Europe, against the judgments in episcopal courts of law. The *Signatura Justitiae* (Signature of Justice) was also a court of cassation, but dealt with cases in which the auditors of the Rota themselves were concerned, hearing objections against their decisions with a view to the sentences being annulled or revised. Its judges were all cardinals, whereas the auditors of the Rota were prelates.

The ancient offices of the Church comprised the chancery, Dataria, Camera and the Palatine Secretariats. The chancery was responsible for the dispatch of the most solemn papal letters, known as Bulls, which were written (originally in Lombard script) on thick parchment and sealed with lead. The chancellor was a prelate, not a cardinal. The Dataria dealt with the nominations to benefices, special dispensations, and suchlike religious matters. It was run by the Pro-Datarius, a cardinal. The Camera was the pope's treasury, both as head of the Church and as the sovereign of the Papal States. The chief of the Palatine Secretariats was that of the Cardinal Secretary of State, the pope's prime minister, in effect, responsible for all internal and foreign affairs. He was a political figure and exercised control through a network of delegates within the Papal States and nuncios abroad. Unlike many of the other positions at the top of the curia, it was an appointment not for life, but for the reign of a particular pope. The Secretary of Briefs was responsible for sending out and signing letters in a less solemn form than Bulls called *brevi manu* or 'briefs'. These were written on thin parchment and sealed with wax stamped with the 'fisherman's ring', a depiction of St Peter in a little boat casting a net. The Pro-Datarius, the Secretary of State, the Secretary of Briefs, and a fourth called the Secretary of Memorials (who was responsible for passing special requests to the pope from supplicants for favours) were known as the Palatine Cardinals because they had the right by virtue of their offices to live in the papal palaces, the Quirinal, Lateran and Vatican. There were also four Palatine Prelates who had the right of residence, the Major Domo, the Superintendent of the Household, the Master of the Chamber (responsible for arranging audiences) and the Auditor (the pope's private secretary).

This, very briefly, was the august organization of which

Consalvi became a member at the age of twenty-five and over which he was one day to exercise absolute control. At the time of his entrance into the curia the pope was Pius VI (Braschi), a vain and worldly nobleman from Cesena in the Legations, who spent his days hunting and collecting antique gems. Stendhal, with a somewhat acid pen, described him as 'a man common enough in prosperity' but who when driven into exile in old age showed a passive courage in the face of disaster which increased his moral stature and won general admiration. But in the earlier years of his reign he 'displayed all the pretensions. He liked to be told he was the most handsome man in his states. As he grew older and lost his looks he aspired instead to pretensions to scholarship.'[13]

Pius VI was a characteristic product of the late eighteenth-century Enlightenment and tried to improve his backward and impoverished state according to the ideals of the day. In Rome, he erected three more obelisks, and was largely responsible for making the Vatican museum the most magnificent in the world and the first to provide proper facilities for scholars and the visiting public. He began a vast new scheme, financed by a joint-stock company, to drain the Pontine Marshes between Cisterna and Terracina, by digging a canal, the Linea Pia, and building a new road from Velletri to Terracina; he himself visited the works annually in great state to survey the slow progress. He also carried out new works to the harbour at Ancona and prepared various schemes for the financial, administrative and political reform of his states, though most of these did not come to fruition. Like the schemes of many of his predecessors over the previous two centuries this practical failure was due in no small degree to nepotism which he revived by making one of his nephews a duke and the other a cardinal. The draining of the Pontine Marshes failed, partly, because instead of dividing the reclaimed land among enterprising farmers who would have developed it for agriculture, he gave it all to his nephew, the Duke of Braschi, who neglected it. Large sums of money were also diverted into the erection of the beautiful Palazzo Braschi,*

*The chief model for Vulliamy's Dorchester House in Park Lane, demolished in 1927.

designed by Cosimo Morelli, for Cardinal Braschi and his brother the Duke of Braschi.

As he was handsome himself, Pius VI liked, so Stendhal tells us, his court to be good-looking too. It was in these circumstances that Consalvi, who even in old age remained remarkably handsome and must have been especially so when young, came to the pope's attention. So also did another handsome young prelate, Annibale Della Genga (eventually Pope Leo XII). He and Consalvi were rivals from the start. The seeds of this reciprocal hostility were sown in the early 1780s when they were both fledgling monsignori. Stendhal retails the gossip with a northern relish for the machiavellian machinations of a Renaissance court. He was telling the story at several removes and thirty or forty years later, so what he says cannot be fully accurate, but there may be a grain of truth in it. When Pius VI on account of his fading looks took to writing a historical treatise on the German Church, he looked around for a young prelate who could do most of the work for him and who could be sworn to the utmost secrecy. He chose Della Genga who, as a result, visited the pope four times a week to write under his dictation. If there was a scrap of paper on the floor outside the door to the pope's apartment, he was to knock and the pope would let him in. Cardinal Carandini and his faction at court were agog to discover what the pope was working on and who was helping him. He asked his nephew, Consalvi, to watch the pope's apartment. On the third occasion Consalvi recognized the pope's visitor as Monsignor Della Genga and said to him, 'We come here for the same purpose. I beg you, my dear Della Genga, not to betray me.' By dint of clever allusions he managed to wheedle out of Della Genga the information that he was assisting the pope with the compilation of a religious history of Germany, that they had finished the chapter on the bishops and were now working on the nobles.

A month passed before Cardinal Carandini, to whom the pope was speaking familiarly of his health, replied, 'Your Holiness will make yourself ill with these studies of Germany.' The pope asked how he knew, to which the cardinal replied airily that Della Genga had a mistress whom he had told all about his work and she in turn had told everybody else. This was done deliberately to alienate the pope from Della Genga, as the cardinals did not wish there to be a papal favourite among the prelates. That night a spy saw poor Della Genga looking in vain for a piece of paper on the floor and knocking with no result. Thirteen or fourteen months passed during which the pope ignored his erstwhile research assistant, whose health was affected by the unexplained hostility and neglect. One day, however, moved by Della Genga's sad expression, the pope summoned him and said, 'My child, tell me the truth.' Della Genga told him about his discussion with Consalvi. Pius, realizing that Della Genga had not knowingly betrayed his confidence, but had been trapped by a clever ruse, renewed his employment as historical research assistant. Further, to show that he did not care a fig about Della Genga's mistress, Madame Pfiffer (the wife of an officer in the Swiss Guard), he said at dinner one day, 'I can't eat all these partridges, take some of them to Madame Pfiffer.' Consalvi is supposed to have been made ill by this special favour shown to his rival and this was the origin of the dislike for Della Genga that lasted for most of his life.[14]

Consalvi's own career continued to flourish. In 1786 he was appointed secretary of the commission in charge of the Ospizio di S. Michele a Ripa. There had existed for a long time a congregation of three cardinals responsible for its administration, but they were inefficient and when two of them died Pius VI took the opportunity to abolish the congregation as part of his piecemeal reform of the papal government. Cardinal Negroni, the third cardinal, was left as the head of a new administration of prelates with Monsignor Vai as secretary. When the latter died, Consalvi, on Negroni's recommendation, was appointed to succeed him and so become responsible for the day-to-day running of the hospice, the largest charitable organization in Rome, a shelter for the destitute with five separate divisions: one for old men, one for old women, one for young women, one for children, and one for male 'down and outs'.* In a new departure,

*'Debauchés'

Consalvi established the manufacture of woollen blankets at the Ospizio with the purpose of usefully employing the more able inmates, and as a means of raising money towards the cost of running the establishment. A report on Consalvi's administration from January 1787 to December 1789 shows that during his time there the capital endowment increased, the use of the hospice increased and the number of debts decreased.[15]

Cardinal. Negroni died in 1789 and the pope completed his plan for reforming the administration of the hospice by reducing the status of the president from a cardinal to a prelate. Consalvi took it as more or less certain that he would be promoted to the new position of prelate-president, a job which carried a salary of 1,200 scudi a year, as well as free accommodation. To his surprise and distress, the pope passed him over and gave the job instead to Monsignor Gonoli, the retiring governor of Loreto, as a reward for his service there. The pope, it turned out, was not displeased with Consalvi. On the contrary, he was so impressed by the ability he had shown at the Ospizio that he had marked him out for more exalted employment. On Good Friday 1790, as he passed in procession from Tenebrae* in the Sistine Chapel to his dinner, the pope stopped and gave Consalvi an audience, saying that he was pleased with him for not complaining about being passed over and that he had removed him from the Ospizio because he wanted him '*al tavolino e non in bottega*'.[16] He was to be made Votant of the Signature, a legal promotion guaranteeing him a career in the judicature rather than practical administration.

In the same year, on 17 December, he was admitted to the Sovereign Military Order of Malta as a prelate of the Priory of Rome, having proved his sixteen quarterings of nobility.[17] This together with his legal promotion provided a welcome boost to his spirits after the gloom and depression of the previous year. The outbreak of the French Revolution would always make him think in retrospect of 1789 as the year of disasters. The death of Cardinal Negroni had been upsetting, the loss of an old friend, as

*Matins and Lauds with the famous setting of the Lamentations of Jeremiah by Allegri.

well as a powerful protector who had always given him good advice. A number of other members of his circle had died suddenly in the same year, including Charlotte, the thirty-six-year-old Duchess of Albany, the niece of Cardinal York and illegitimate daughter of Bonnie Prince Charlie and Clementina Walkinshaw, who succumbed to cancer of the liver. Most shocking of all had been the murder of Consalvi's own secretary, 'a young man aged twenty of angelic manners, intelligence and integrity', who returning from S. Michele a Ripa with his wife one day was accosted by four drunken soldiers who started to insult her. The husband asked them to desist whereupon they stabbed him with their bayonets and he 'expired in a sea of blood'.[18]

Two years after his promotion to Votant of the Signature, Consalvi heard that Monsignor Origo, one of the auditors of the Rota, had died. Twenty-three prelates immediately applied for the post. Consalvi was very anxious to get it, and this was the only occasion in his life when he did not follow Cardinal Negroni's advice but actively lobbied for a position. He turned down the Nunciature of Cologne* so as to leave the way clear to the Rota. He wanted the job because of the long vacations which would enable him to travel. So far, he had only been able to satisfy his itch for travel with journeys to the kingdom of Naples and the grand duchy of Tuscany but, if he was appointed to the Rota, he would have nearly half the year free; the court only sat from December to June, leaving five months off in the summer and autumn. He asked the secretary of state, Cardinal Boncompagni, to speak to Pius VI on his behalf and also asked for an audience with the pope in order to press the point. These manœuvres were successful and Consalvi got his appointment to the Rota in June 1792. Thirty-five years old, he thought that he had reached the summit of his ambition, and intended to remain at the Rota for life. In the event he was to be there for only eight years, and during the last two of those he did not perform his duties because of the French occupation of Rome.

*It went to Della Genga instead.

During these years of his rise in the curia, Consalvi was leading a busy and worldly social life in Rome; hunting, going to the opera, taking part in the masked balls during the Carnival, and spending much of his free time in the Roman princely palaces. His charm and accomplishments made him a favourite of the great families; the Odescalchi, the Ruspoli, the Patrizi, the Chigi and the Giustiniani were all his close friends, especially the two beautiful Giustiniani sisters, Isabella and Catherina. His personal accounts for these years, with their record of payments for double boxes in the three Roman theatres for the Carnival season, payments for clothes, horses, and not least a four-in-hand carriage bought from Prince Doria Pamphili, outline an existence not at all clerical and no different from any other young nobleman. Also prominent in his accounts are the signs of his enthusiasm for music; payments for the purchase of musical instruments and sheet music, or payments to contemporary musicians and composers. He formed a large library of printed and manuscript musical scores and grammars of music. His instruments included, as well as his violin, a magnificent German piano made by Wagner of Dresden.[19] One name in particular jumps from the pages, that of Domenico Cimarosa, who in Consalvi's eyes was the greatest living artist in Italy, the Raphael of music. The two of them could not have been more different. It was a case of the attraction of opposites. Consalvi was tall, slim, distinguished-looking, a man of education and culture; Cimarosa, fat and hideous, the son of Neapolitan peasants, eight years older than Consalvi. After studying at the celebrated Conservatory of Santa Maria di Loreto from 1761 to 1772, Cimarosa divided his time between Rome and Naples till 1787 when he went to St Petersburg at the invitation of Catherine the Great. Five years later he returned via Vienna where he composed the best known of his sixty-six operas, *Il Matrimonio Segreto*, which is generally considered to be the high point of work by native Italian composers in the eighteenth century. He returned to Rome the following year, 1793, and was greeted as a long-lost friend by Consalvi. They spent a lot of time together; Consalvi, who admired Cimarosa enormously, commissioned several new works from him, the payments for which appear in his accounts. One or two of Cimarosa's manuscript scores are also still preserved among Consalvi's private papers, including a rondo, '*Ah tu Sai*', a duetto, '*Voi piu non siete degno del Pittor Parigino*', and various liturgical settings.[20] Their relationship was not just the patronage of an aristocrat for a talented artist, but a deep and genuine friendship. Cimarosa was closer to Consalvi than anybody else, apart from his brother Andrea, and Consalvi later described him as '*mio amicissimo*'.

The pleasant round of his social and musical life and the even tenor of his days as an auditor of the Rota received an extra burden when Consalvi was appointed secretary to a special congregation of five cardinals set up to examine the complaints of the citizens of Bologna against a scheme of administrative and financial reform evolved for their benefit by Pius VI, his treasurer, Fabrizio Ruffo, and the secretary of state, Cardinal Boncompagni. The reforms had followed a thorough investigation begun in 1780 into the commerce, system of landholdings, customs duties, taxation and other financial arrangements in the province of Bologna. On the recommendation of Ruffo and Boncompagni, Pius VI had instituted free trade in Bologna on 28 November 1791, and the following year a detailed economic plan for the province was promulgated, aimed at bringing about a more equitable system of taxation and landholding and the elimination of outdated feudal dues and privileges which were strangling the economic life of the province. Though well-intentioned and urgently necessary, this sensible plan ran into opposition from the citizens of Bologna who did not accept that it was 'favourable to the interests of the people and not onerous to the nobility'. As a result the implementation of the plan was suspended and Pius VI set up the new congregation to hear the various complaints. These problems were not resolved before the French invasion of the Legations and the incorporation of Bologna into the Cisalpine Republic, and in the event Pius VI's enlightened plan of reform was to be implemented by the French. Consalvi took a keen interest in the Bologna affair and kept copies of all the relevant papers, which served as a model for his own plans of reform when he became secretary of state.[21] In the short term however, the unfavourable reaction of Bologna, the largest and richest city in the Papal States, put a brake on any more sweeping reforms. Having misfired so badly there, the experiment could hardly serve as a trial run for the reform of more backward areas.

The loss of his guardian, Cardinal Negroni, seems to have brought Consalvi even closer into the orbit of Cardinal York. While at Frascati with him in August 1794, Consalvi witnessed Cardinal York's meeting with HRH Prince Augustus, Duke of Sussex, a younger son of George III. He wrote a description of the royal encounters on three successive days, to Sir John Coxe Hippisley, the British minister in Italy. The two first met while both were taking the air in the garden of the Bracciano. The prince stopped his carriage, removed his hat and bowed to the cardinal who returned his greeting. The second time, the cardinal stopped and spoke to the prince saying that 'he was very pleased to have the occasion to make known his feelings which were free from all prejudice'. On the third occasion they met on foot at the Villa Conti and spoke to each other in English for an hour about Britain and the Stuart family.[22]

Cardinal York, as a mark of his feelings for Consalvi, attempted to make him the vicar of St Peter's. The Cardinal-Duke was the archpriest in the basilica (the equivalent of the dean of an Anglican cathedral), but was not able to attend routine services himself as he was mainly resident at Frascati, his episcopal see, and therefore needed somebody to take his place in choir at St Peter's, if not every day then at least on feast days. The post carried with it a magnificent benefice of 1,000 scudi a year (his own salary renounced by Cardinal York in favour of his vicar).

Though the post was technically in the cardinal's gift, the pope thought the job was incompatible with that of being an auditor of the Rota, and wanted it to go not to Consalvi but to somebody else, though he never said so outright. Pius VI asked the Vatican archivist to check the precedents, and received the answer he wanted, namely that there was no previous occasion on which an auditor of the Rota had also acted as vicar of St Peter's. This was not in fact the case, and Cardinal York drafted a strong reply to the pope listing examples of auditors of the Rota who had been vicars of St Peter's in the past, and adding for good measure that, as he had already appointed Consalvi, he hoped that the pope would not quash the appointment. Consalvi was horrified when he read this undiplomatic letter and prevailed on Cardinal York not to send it. After much argument he agreed not to, but asked how he should protect his prerogative as archpriest. This provided an excellent opportunity for Consalvi to deploy his diplomatic skill. He advised Cardinal York to let him write to the pope saying that he had had to withdraw because of pressure of work and before the cardinal made another appointment, as was *his* prerogative, he wondered whether in the light of His Holiness's great love of St Peter's, the pope would like to suggest a candidate to the cardinal for his consideration; if so, Consalvi would be happy to pass on the name. The pope replied, 'Oh no, certainly not, we do not have anybody in mind. Our maxim is never to usurp the rights of others, and to leave to everybody complete liberty of action.' Thus, thanks to Consalvi, the cardinal's prerogative was protected, while leaving the place open for the pope's nominee, and no touchy Stuart sensibilities were bruised in the process. After several discussions and much pretended indifference, Pius VI finally suggested Monsignor Brancadoro as vicar of St Peter's, 'though of course it was entirely up to the Cardinal-Duke to make the decision'. Cardinal York appointed Brancadoro, and the pope replied: 'The Cardinal-Duke has made a good choice.' He had never said outright that he wanted Brancadoro to be vicar of St Peter's. Consalvi was much struck by this and took it as an object lesson in how to get one's own way as gracefully and diplomatically as possible.[23]

The Cardinal-Duke was in the process of rewriting his will and named Consalvi as his executor, together with Canon Cesarini, rector of the college at Frascati. In compensation for the disappointment over the vicariate, he also offered Consalvi a legacy of 6,000 scudi. Consalvi accepted the executorship, but turned down the financial offer; he advised the cardinal to use the money to augment the bequests to his *familia* (household and employees) who had served him with such zeal and attachment over the years. The cardinal was somewhat offended and refused to discuss the subject any further, but he did not erase the legacy from his will, though Consalvi was never to receive it, partly because of his own wish not to, but partly because the fortune of the Cardinal-Duke was to be lost totally in the cataclysm that was shortly to engulf the papacy in a tidal wave of war and revolution, and to reduce the last male representative of the royal house of Stuart to a pensioner of King George III of England.

II
Revolution

THE events of 1789 and 1790 shattered the Catholic Church in France, but it was to be six or seven years before the outward ripples rocked the Papal States, and nine before they toppled papal Rome. Long before a French army occupied the Castel S. Angelo, however, there was a nagging sense of impending doom; and the papal curia, threatened by the dynamic and destructive forces across the Alps, had the air of a rabbit mesmerized by a stoat, waiting defenceless for the sharp teeth to plunge into its throat.

To the Romans, the overthrow of the Church in France seemed an almost incomprehensible disaster. France contained more Catholics than any other state. The Church there was rich, powerful and thriving. It was the headquarters of many of the historic religious orders: Cîteaux, Cluny, Grande Chartreuse, Premontré, La Trappe. French theologians and ecclesiastical historians were known and respected throughout Europe. But this ancient and magnificent edifice was largely demolished within two years, beginning with the confiscation of Church land in November 1789, the abolition of religious vows and most of the monastic orders in February 1790 and the publication of the Civil Constitution of the Clergy on 12 July 1790. The latter drastically reduced the number of bishoprics in France and imposed a civil oath on all priests. After several months of procrastination Pope Pius VI condemned it on 10 March 1791, and in April of the same year declared the oath to be sacrilegious; any priest who took it being threatened with suspension. This created a schism in France between those clergy who supported the Constitution and those who remained loyal to the pope. When papal Avignon was annexed by France in September 1791, relations between the Holy See and the French government were to all intents and purposes severed.

The hostility between the Revolution and Rome was confirmed when, after the French had declared war on Austria in 1792, Pius VI sent as an envoy to the emperor the Abbé Maury, an *émigré* French priest notorious for his reactionary opposition in the National Assembly. This had the unfortunate effect of seeming to ally the Church with the political powers warring against France. There was a fierce reaction in Paris. Every priest was now suspect as a traitor: 223 clergy, including an archbishop and two bishops, were murdered in the September Massacres; 30,000 French priests fled abroad, 7,000 of them to England and many to Rome which, as it filled up with *émigrés* and Austrian agents, was becoming a focus of opposition to the Revolution. In France the Church was driven underground. Clerical dress was banned. Church buildings were closed, looted and demolished. Religious feasts were replaced with feasts of 'Humanity', and the calendar changed to omit Sundays. In retaliation, French shops in Rome were looted by the mob, and the French Hospital invaded. Hugon de Basseville, a young Frenchman who was tactless enough to drive down the Corso waving the tricolour and shouting revolutionary slogans, was dragged from his carriage and murdered by the Roman populace.[1]

It was against this unsettling backdrop, and the filtration of revolutionary and democractic ideas over the mountains and into northern Italy that the pope decided to reorganize his paltry armed forces to protect his states from the spread of anarchy. His main object was to combat the bands of French agitators who were prowling round the principalities of Italy urging revolt against their lawful sovereigns. Pius called to Rome General Caprara, a papal subject who had served under the Austrians and thus was the only person with the military experience necessary to execute the papal plan. The pope did not want the general under orders to a prelate, but answerable directly to himself through the secretary of state. He therefore abolished the post of Prelate-President of Arms, which had hitherto been in charge of the papal forces, and created a new congregation of military affairs made up of the General-Commandant (Caprara) and four or five other secular army officers, with one prelate as assessor (secretary), to organize the proceedings. This reform established an important precedent because, for the first time, it admitted laymen to positions of responsibility in the administration of the Roman government.

Consalvi was appointed prelate-assessor to the new congregation. Despite misgivings about the grave responsibilities which had been delegated to him, he set to work with his customary vigour, and proved successful in organizing the new institution from scratch. With the aid of a great deal of patience, hard work, firmness and energy, he set about demolishing the ancient uses, abuses and powerful vested interests of the old military regime. In the event, the reformed armed forces proved unexpectedly efficient in policing the Papal States and preventing outbreaks of local unrest. The papacy was a neutral and peace-seeking body, and its army was chiefly an internal police force for the purpose of maintaining tranquillity and public order: its small size alone would have made it useless for any other purpose. Because of the success of Consalvi, Caprara and the army in preventing internal revolts, the French had to forgo the satisfaction of dethroning the pope by stealth, as had happened in the adjoining state of Modena, where the duke had been driven out by a carefully fomented revolt. Consalvi noted grimly that the Directory was forced to lower its mask and proceed directly against the papacy with armed force.[2]

On 10 May 1796, General Bonaparte, having crossed the Alps, won a great victory at Lodi. Six days later he entered Austrian Milan in triumph. He was welcomed as a liberator: 'People of Italy, the French army comes to break your chains.' By December 1796, the Cisalpine Republic was established throughout Northern Italy. The invasion of papal territory took place on the pretext of an anti-French missive from the secretary of state to Vienna, which was intercepted. The papal troops who guarded Romagna were routed by the Cisalpine army and pursued as far as Foligno. In order to stop 'the torrent of destruction' and to save the centre of Catholicism, the pope made 'the great sacrifice of Tolentino' on 19 February 1797. By this treaty, dictated by Bonaparte to the pope's nephew, the Duke of Braschi, and Cardinal Mattei, Pius VI agreed to renounce his right to Avignon, Bologna and the Legations; to pay thirty million livres to France (partly in silver and jewellery); to give the French Republic a hundred works of art (to be selected by French commissioners); to close his ports to warships fighting against France; to send envoys to Paris to disavow the murder of Basseville and to compensate his family; and to free all imprisoned Jacobins. For his part, Bonaparte agreed only to evacuate the remaining papal territory, and to do no harm to religion in the Cisalpine Republic, which included Pius VI's own birthplace at Cesena. No previous pope had been forced to make such concessions, although Bonaparte thought the terms mild: he was being urged by the Directory to march on Rome to avenge the murder of Basseville and to depose 'the last pope'. Pius, on his side was persuaded that the manifest injustice of the French aggression would annul the effect of the treaty when order was re-established in Europe. The immediate consequences, however, were distressing. The aspect which the Romans found most offensive was the loss of the works of art: 'these doctrinaire cannibals running around, catalogues at the ready,' in museums, churches, galleries and libraries, picking out the most famous art treasures in the world: the Apollo Belvedere, the Laocoön, the Dying Gaul, Raphael's 'Transfiguration' and Domenichino's 'Last Communion of St Jerome'.[3]

For Consalvi, struggling at the military congregation, the most important problem was the further impoverishment of the state caused by the financial indemnity exacted by the French and the loss of the richest area of the Papal States to the Cisalpine Republic. Severe economies were necessary and the number of troops had to be reduced, to cut down the payroll. In an ill-judged measure, General Colli, who had succeeded Caprara as General-Commandant, went further and downgraded all the officers by one rank. Thus the majors all became captains, and the captains, lieutenants, their salaries being docked accordingly. Not surprisingly, this caused great resentment and destroyed any feeling of *esprit de corps* that might yet have persisted in the papal army following its defeat by Bonaparte, while Consalvi's job at the military congregation was made peculiarly unrewarding as a result.

As was to happen on several other occasions in his life, the gloom induced by public events was exacerbated by a number of personal misfortunes occurring at the same time and further depressing his spirits. In April 1796 his mother died of an apoplexy. She had spent her last years contentedly in the Tor di Specchi, a community of respectable women who lived together and followed a 'rational, regular, religious life'. They were similar to nuns, but did not take vows, and maintained their personal freedom and independance. 'A most respectable and comfortable asylum for unprotected, unmarried women and widows of small fortune' is how it seemed to a Scottish visitor a few years later.[4] It was in these tranquil surroundings that Consalvi's mother died, a good woman who loved him. She was buried in the family vault at S. Marcello, Consalvi paying for the funeral and for a thousand masses for the repose of her soul.[5] Then in October 1797, while out hunting with the Duke of Braschi near the Porta S. Giovanni, he had an accident and broke his right arm, causing much pain which persisted for a long time and made it difficult for him to write. Indeed, his illegibly cramped handwriting later in life is likely to have been a result of this accident.

The Napoleonic guarantees in the Treaty of Tolentino were rapidly proved worthless. Almost immediately, the French army occupied papal Pesaro, and in May 1798 the Cisalpine Republic, desperate for funds, followed the French example and nationalized the property of the Church in Italy, dissolved the monasteries, banned religious processions and tried to impose democratic election of the clergy. This rendered null the efforts to

reconcile the Catholic Church with the new Republic. Conservative popular opinion in Italy had, in any case, already been
affronted by Bonaparte's looting of the shrine of Our Lady at
Loreto from where the miraculous statue had been removed and
sent to Paris to be displayed in the Bibliothèque Nationale as a
monument of superstition. In Rome, Napoleon's brother
Joseph, installed as French minister following the Treaty of
Tolentino, had taken up residence in the Palazzo Corsini on the
Trastevere bank of the Tiber. Staying with him in December 1797
was a French general called Duphot, twenty-eight years old and
engaged to Joseph's sister-in-law, Desirée. Egged on by Duphot,
a party of five hundred Roman Jacobins or 'patriot rebels',
occupied the garden of the palazzo on 28 December and started
to shout *Liberté*, *Vive la République Française*, *À bas le Pape*.
Duphot did not hesitate to join them and at their head attacked a
nearby police post manned by papal dragoons, part of the forces
of order controlled by the military congregation. Duphot and the
Jacobins charged the dragoons outside the Porta Settimiana;
overwhelmed, the dragoons opened fire and Duphot was shot
dead.

'Providence had it that in all that multitude, only Duphot was
hit and killed,' Consalvi sadly recorded.[6] It was a disaster and
threw the papal government into consternation. The unrest
spread throughout the city with tumults and spasmodic gunfire
in different areas. Consalvi and the military congregation sat up
all night trying to control affairs. Detachments of soldiery with
cannon were mounted in all the key places, and a strong posse of
guards sent to protect the house of the French ambassador. The
secretary of state was now Cardinal Joseph Doria, and Consalvi
called on him three times during the night to report conditions
and to receive further orders. He himself spent the night at the
barracks in the Piazza Colonna as did General Santini, the new
commander who had replaced Colli. Consalvi was always able to
do without sleep when the occasion demanded and to keep
working like a machine made of iron rather than flesh and blood.

By dawn it was clear that Consalvi's measures to preserve the
peace had been successful, and calm returned to the city with

daylight. That morning, however, Joseph Bonaparte demanded his passport and left Rome in a great display of righteous indignation: 'No prayer or offer of reparation from the Holy See could move him.' That this attitude was assumed for effect is proved by a letter which Joseph wrote to Napoleon in 1801: 'You know as well as I, the details of this deplorable event. Nobody at Rome gave the order to fire or kill. The General (Duphot) was to blame. Let us not mince words, he was culpable.'[7]

As soon as the news reached the Directory in Paris, they sent 15,000 men against Rome, under the command of General Berthier. He refused to receive the four deputies sent from the pope to meet him at Narni, but declared that he would give them audience at the gates of Rome. On 9 February 1798, the French army camped on Monte Mario, the steep hill two miles from Rome overlooking the Vatican. Their lights at night could be seen from all over the city. The following morning a French officer and trumpeter appeared at the Porta Angelica, near St Peter's. They found it open, with no preparations for resistance. The pope did not have the force to resist the French, and in any case did not wish to imperil the population by a useless defence. The officer and trumpeter proceeded to the Castel S. Angelo which was only a short distance inside. There they asked to see the commandant and told him that in three hours a thousand men would enter the city to take possession of the fortress; they would expect to find it evacuated by papal troops. The commandant, after telling the secretary of state, went back with the French officer to Monte Mario to learn the intentions of General Berthier, who announced that the French army had come not to destroy the Holy See, but only to exact reparation for the death of General Duphot.

The Romans had no reason to disbelieve him; they did not consider the French their enemies, and had put up no military resistance. Berthier asked for hostages and for certain individuals to be handed over whom the government in Paris considered to be responsible for the 'outrage'. The commandant returned and explained these terms to Cardinal Doria, who told him to let them enter the castle and to retire the Roman troops to their barracks. These orders were sent to Consalvi at the military congregation to execute. He viewed them with consternation: apart from anything else, the time allowed for the evacuation was too short. He was obliged to go to the Castel S. Angelo in person to speed up the chaotic proceedings, and with a great effort, he did manage to evacuate the castle in the time specified, without any public disorder, though with great sadness in his heart. As he said himself: 'By these means I helped the French in their plan to proclaim to the people that they were against the papal government.' Though he also realized that if it had not been Duphot, there would have been some other pretext for the French occupation of Rome.[8]

The following day, 11 February, 10,000 French soldiers occupied all the high points, including the Quirinal, S. Pietro in Montorio, Trinita dei Monti, and the two most populous areas of the city, the Piazza Colonna and Trastavere. That evening, the French announced to the secretary of state the intentions of the Directory. They would keep the papal government, but reform it. They wanted a huge indemnity, the first portion within forty-eight hours, and they suggested that the pope exact it from the richest families. As hostages they wanted cardinals, prelates and the pope's nephew, the Duke of Braschi.

Consalvi went as usual that morning to the Vatican to judge the processes at the Rota, for it was sitting that day. On his way out of the courtroom, he was summoned to the secretary of state. He knew what it was about, for he had already been warned by a Roman partisan of the French, who had advised him to flee to Naples before it was too late. The name of Consalvi, as assessor of the military congregation, was at the top of the list of 'culprits' who were to be handed over to the Directory. The French assumed that he was the head of the papal troops, and he was thus the indispensable victim to lend colour to their pretext for occupying Rome. His arrest was to be expiation for the death of Duphot, which the Directory blamed directly on the military congregation. The secretary of state advised Consalvi to leave immediately for Terracina before the French could arrest him. With the courage which would later enable him to defy

Napoleon, he refused, believing that it was part of the French plan to make him run away so that they could proclaim his guilt and use it as an excuse for dethroning the pope. Consalvi told the secretary of state that he would prefer to remain at his post at the military congregation in order to maintain order in Rome and prevent the French stirring up a popular revolt against the pope. It appeared that the French general, while he was investigating Consalvi's responsibility for Duphot's death, would allow him to remain under house-arrest rather than imprisoning him in the Castel S. Angelo.

The following day, Consalvi was visited by the French commissioners who searched his rooms and interrogated him. When he asked what was happening they replied that they did not know, they were only acting on orders. On 13 February, a French adjutant appeared at Consalvi's house and took him away dressed in clerical black, not as a layman. They collected *en route* General Santini, the papal commandant, and both Consalvi and he were imprisoned in the Castel S. Angelo. Two days later, on 15 February, the anniversary of the pope's accession, the papal government was abolished and the Roman Republic established. Shortly afterwards, the pope, weak with age, was ordered into exile. When he asked to be allowed to die in Rome, Berthier told him: 'One can die anywhere.' He was taken off by the French to Siena, then to the Certosa at Florence and finally to Valence where he was to be imprisoned in the citadel.

Soon after the pope's removal from Rome, Berthier was replaced by the more ruthless Massena and the French, having so far behaved well, started looting the city. Cart-loads of silver were taken from the sacristy of St Peter's, works of art were stolen, including the Raphael tapestries from the Vatican; even the great bell of the Capitol, which for centuries had tolled the death of the popes, was melted down. The cardinals and prelates were imprisoned or exiled.[9]

Consalvi remained in the Castel S. Angelo for several weeks without being further interrogated. The French commandant of the castle was a civilized man and Consalvi, who could speak French, got on well with him. They played piquet in Consalvi's room every evening. It was presumably the commandant who provided him with writing paper, printed with '*Liberté*' and '*Égalité*' at the top, to write to the French authorities proclaiming his innocence. The letter survives and is worth quoting at length because it has never been published and sums up the affair succinctly:

> The day following the entry into Rome of the French army, I received the order to remain at my house on my word of honour. I conformed to this with a very great tranquillity of soul, sure of my innocence and the justice that the French would render. Three days later I was transferred to the Castle . . . It was only after forty days in prison that I learnt the official cause . . . I learnt that I was held responsible by the French Republic for the death of General Duphot, that I without doubt, as a member of the military congregation, had given the order on the day of the 28 December which cut the life of the general.
>
> I declare on my honour that this is false. I am innocent of any part in that sad affair.
>
> It is true that I was one of the members of the military congregation, but it was also of the greatest notoriety in Rome that this congregation was not able to rule by itself and that it was simply the executor of the orders of the secretary of state.
>
> In consequence, whether such an order never existed, or if it came from the secretary of state, it cannot be blamed on the military congregation. As an executant it cannot be reproached because it was not able to disobey the Government. That is clear.
>
> But I declare the truth is that the secretary of state did not give the military congregation that order. Without entering into other detail, I confine myself to joining here the attestation made by the two commanders of cavalry and infantry of Rome. One reads expressly that the military congregation never gave the supposed order. But for those who still regard me so, I will add that I never was the

president of the military congregation. All the orders which were given were done in writing ... and were about nothing but discipline. I will say, however, that the president himself was not at all culpable and never gave that order. The proof is easy. The orders, given in writing, exist and so can be verified. [The French were in possession of the archives of the papal government.]

I wish to add, further, on my own account, that I did not contribute in any manner to the death of General Duphot; it was on the contrary due to my care that his sabre and belt were brought to Major Azara the following day. In the vicissitudes following the Peace of Tolentino, it is difficult not to have made enemies. I may have been misrepresented by an ill-disposed person ... For the rest, ask the public about my character and my constant conduct ...

The military congregation was a surcharge on my ordinary occupation as Auditor of the Rota. I must always obey my Sovereign. I have exercised that employment with great delicacy, without bribes, without force, without injustice or harshness ...

I have spoken the language of truth and innocence. You must allow* for a man who does not write in his native tongue ...

I do not demand vengeance against my accusers ... I demand my liberty ... I have been arrested and detained in this castle for forty days like a criminal. My honour exists ...

E. Consalvi at the Castel S. Angelo
30 Ventos A6 [1798] of the French Republic.[10]

The only upshot of this was that suddenly one day, while Consalvi was eating his dinner, a French officer appeared and conveyed him to the former convent of the Convertites in the Corso where a cardinal and some other prelates were imprisoned, including many officials of the curia and the former governors of the provinces of the Papal States.[11] They learnt that

*'*donner le style*'.

they were all to be sent to Civitavecchia, where eight cardinals and other prelates had already been taken, preparatory to being transported to the Island of Cayenne. Consalvi was aghast at what amounted to a sentence of death. They were taken at night to Civitavecchia under an escort of French cavalry, Consalvi with only a small sum of money that his brother Andrea and impoverished aristocratic friends had managed to scrape together to lend to him. He arrived at Civitavecchia the following day and was shut up with the other cardinals and prelates in an old convent. There they discovered to their immense relief that Cayenne was an exaggeration. They were to be deported from the Roman Republic, on pain of death if they returned, but they could choose their own place of exile. 'We received the news like condemned men hearing that their sentence has been commuted.'[12]

Consalvi decided to join the pope in the Certosa at Florence, although the French had ordered the Tuscan government not to allow the prelates and cardinals to come near the pope and his plan was beset with obstacles. Nevertheless, he persevered and managed to secure a place on a ship to Livorno. Just as he was about to embark, a courier arrived and announced that the others could go, but not Consalvi; he was to return to Rome immediately. He imagined that the French authorities had changed their mind and thought up some new punishment for him. This intervention was, however, due not to the malevolence of his enemies, but to the good offices of the Marchese Patrizi and Prince Ruspoli who, thinking that he was going to be transported to Cayenne to die of yellow fever, had pulled every string at their disposal and gone in person to the French general to plead for Consalvi's release. They had unwittingly done him an ill service, for instead of being allowed to go free to a place of his own choice, he was returned to the Castel S. Angelo. His secretaries, Niccolo Brunati and Giovanni Luelli, who had accompanied him to Civitavecchia, went back with him to the fortress as well. The only bright spot was that the French commander of the castle was genuinely pleased to see him: he had missed the games of piquet. When he heard Consalvi's story and how he had been plucked back on the very brink of freedom, the kindhearted French officer shared his sadness.

Consalvi had good reason to be apprehensive. His return had put him at the mercy of the Jacobin consuls in Rome who were determined to avenge what they saw as his guilt in the Duphot affair. His friends and his brother were horrified when they realized that all their efforts had merely helped to transfer him into the clutches of his enemies. Andrea, when the French invaded Rome, had been in Venice, but had returned immediately when he heard that Ercole had been arrested. He now made great efforts to get him released. The commandant allowed Andrea and friends such as Prince Chigi, Prince Ruspoli and the Prince di Teano to visit Consalvi at the Castel S. Angelo, and 'Citizen Ruspoli' signed a testimony to the French authorities for him, vouching for his good conduct on 25 March 1798.[13] It was his friends who told him what the consuls were planning for his punishment. He was to be paraded through Rome tied to a donkey and flogged. Already the windows in the streets along which he would pass had been let at large sums to would-be spectators, 'Jacobins and the wives of the Consuls' as Consalvi sharply noted.

Before this barbaric sentence could be carried out, Massena was replaced as governor of Rome by the more accommodating Gouvin Saint-Cyr. Andrea and the princes were able to get him to refuse to sanction the sentence. Instead, he approved an order for Consalvi's exile to Naples.[14]

'I was deported towards Naples, in accordance with the democratic spirit of the times, in a mixed company of eighteen galley slaves . . .' This unusual party left Rome towards the end of April 1798. There were heart-rending farewells between Consalvi and his brother, his friends and his servants Brunati and Luelli, all of whom had been so loyal and helpful during his imprisonment. He was allowed to use his own carriage, possibly the one he had bought from Prince Doria Pamphili, and was followed by another carriage containing two lawyers, an army officer and a monk. The galley slaves brought up the rear in a cart. Near Lake Albano, Consalvi's carriage had an accident, and he and his valet had to squash into the other carriage with the four honest men. At Albano they all had dinner together, including the galley slaves, in an inn. There, by a stroke of luck, Consalvi came across his friend the Baron Gavotti, who had a little house at Terracina. He offered to lend it to Consalvi while he was waiting at the frontier for the necessary passport to enter the kingdom of Naples.

They arrived at Terracina the following day. Consalvi spoke to the commandant in French and explained his position, and the series of adventures that had brought him to this pass. He asked not to be imprisoned with the galley slaves, but to be allowed to stay at the Casino Gavotti under guard instead. The commandant, an honest old soldier called François-Xavier Leduc, acceded to his request. In thanking him, Consalvi asked for one further favour. Would the commandant use the galley slaves to test the frontier? He did so and they were refused access by the Neapolitan guards, confirming Consalvi's doubts. The commandant kept his word and allowed Consalvi to stay at the Casino Gavotti: he would have dispensed with guards, but Consalvi asked for them, otherwise the Jacobins might have accused him of using the opportunity to receive priests and counter-revolutionaries.

Consalvi found the air at Terracina bad for his health and, without much hope, set about the tedious business of trying to get a passport for Naples. He realized that this would only be possible if he found someone with free access to the Queen (a sister of Marie-Antoinette), who with her husband's minister, General Acton, controlled affairs in the Two Sicilies. With one of the extraordinary strokes of luck that accompanied Consalvi throughout his career, it turned out that Cardinal York was in exile in Naples, and he firmly demanded a passport for Consalvi. Acton, being of English stock, was not a little flattered to be able to assist the *de jure* King of England and the passport duly materialized. So, after only twenty-two days at Terracina, Consalvi departed for Naples on 16 May. Leduc issued him with a certificate of good conduct: 'The said Monsieur Consalvi spent twenty-two days in my command here and I can vouch for his good conduct.'[15]

In Naples, Consalvi was received with great favour by General Acton, King Ferdinand and especially the Queen. He always got on well with grand ladies of a certain age, who were bowled over by his charm and good looks. The climate was wonderful, the atmosphere relaxed and it was pleasant to see so many old friends again, especially the Cardinal-Duke. He was happy there, but could not stay since he felt it his duty to join the pope, and not to have a holiday while his sovereign languished in prison. In trying to leave, he encountered an unexpected problem. The Neapolitan court had conceived the idea of nominating the next pope and getting him to reside at Naples and to this end, they were trying to concentrate all the cardinals and prelates there and forbidding them to leave. Consalvi used as an excuse for departure his uncle, Cardinal Carandini, who had taken refuge in Venice. He painted a moving picture of his old relation languishing in solitude. On this pretext, he was allowed to leave Naples after a pleasant stay of two months and he departed in August 1798, first to Terracina and then by boat to Livorno. His heart missed a beat or two as he passed Terracina, but Leduc had got a pass for him: 'The commandant of Terracina is authorized to allow the Citizen Consalvi ex-Roman Prelate to depart by sea by the first boat for Livorno or other state of Tuscany. Signed the General en Chef du Corps d'Armée de Rome.'[16]

He arrived safely in Livorno after a calm voyage on 25 or 26 August and left immediately for Florence. He walked the last three miles from the city centre to the Certosa on the hill to the south. Consalvi passed through the gatehouse and down the threadbare cloisters to the little cell where the pope sat in solitude eating a frugal meal. The poor old man was feeble and half paralysed. What a difference between this and the days of his prosperity when he had been surrounded by sumptuous and beautiful things, lapis lazuli inkstands and antique gems in precious settings designed by Valadier.*

Consalvi threw himself at the foot of his sovereign and

*Stolen by the French and still in the Louvre.

benefactor. The air charged with emotion, he told the pope all he could remember of his adventures and the condition of Rome under the French occupation. He asked to remain in the pope's service, but was told that this was impossible.

On his return to Florence he told nobody of his visit to the Certosa. He then went south to Siena where the Patrizi had retreated from Rome and stayed for some time with these old friends before setting out again to join his uncle at Venice. Before leaving Tuscany, he returned once more to the Certosa to ask for the pope's last blessing. Pius received Consalvi with great affection and gave him a message for the much doted-on nephew, the Duke of Braschi, who was also in exile in Venice. The blessing is best described in Consalvi's own words: 'He placed his hands on my head, and, like the most venerable of the ancient patriarchs, he raised his eyes to heaven, prayed out loud, and blessed me in an attitude so resigned, so august, so holy and so tender that until the last day of my life I will treasure that memory engraved on my heart in indelible characters.'[17]

Consalvi left the Certosa with tears in his eyes, but encouraged by the pope's serenity and peace of mind. Spending less than twenty-four hours in Florence, he continued on his way to Venice, arriving towards the end of September 1798.

In Rome, meanwhile, the French had dismantled the entire administration, not only of the Papal States, but the Catholic Church throughout the world. The papal arms had been removed from all buildings, the republican calendar introduced, and place names changed. The Piazza di Spagna was now the Piazza of Liberty; the Piazza Venezia, the Piazza of Equality and the Castel S. Angelo, the Castle of Genius. The exile of the pope and curia, however, had undermined the finances of the city which were largely based on tourist revenue. To compound the situation, the French in the summer and autumn of 1798 had moved against the practice of religion, suppressing feasts and clerical dress, abolishing monastic vows and closing convents. Article 267 of the new constitution of the Roman Republic compelled every official to take an oath 'to hate monarchy and anarchy, and to be faithful to the republic and the constitution'.

In September 1798, Pius VI declared the Constitution to be 'absolutely illegal', and this helped to stir up the Roman people against the French and encouraged the Neapolitans to invade the Papal States. They were driven back and the French in turn conquered Naples and set up a republic there, after Nelson and the British fleet had evacuated the royal family to Sicily. The French occupation of Naples was short-lived and it was not long before fierce guerrilla bands of crusading peasants, the Sanfedisti, swept them from southern Italy and reconquered Rome with the help of a British naval contingent.*

In the north of Italy the counter-revolution was Austrian-led. The Imperial troops occupied Venice in 1797 and by the summer of 1799 had taken control of much of northern Italy, including the papal Legations. This was the dramatically changing political situation when Pius VI died in captivity at Valence on 29 August 1799, after a reign of twenty-six years, the longest pontificate up to that date.[18]

On his arrival in Venice, where he stayed with his uncle, Cardinal Carandini, Consalvi was told that the French in Rome had confiscated all his property as an *émigré*. He protested to the consuls, whereupon they issued two further decrees: one, that they restored his property because he was not an *émigré*, two, that they confiscated it again because he was an enemy of the Roman Republic. By the time the news of the pope's death reached Venice, many of the cardinals had gathered there, including Cardinal York, who had arrived as a penniless refugee from Naples. This provided Consalvi with the chance to do his old benefactor a good turn. Through Sir John Coxe Hippisley, the British agent in north Italy, he was able to bring the cardinal's plight to the notice of the English government. Andrew Stuart, an official in the Foreign Office, wrote to Henry Dundas on 30 October to report the destitution of Cardinal York caused by the 'rapacity of those who deserve to be considered not only as the Enemies of England, but the Enemies of the Human Race'. After

---

*The Union Jack flew briefly from the Capitol for the only time in history in 1799.

careful consideration, George III agreed to provide the Cardinal-Duke with an annual pension.[19]

Cardinal Albani had been made responsible by the late pope for summoning the conclave. He asked the protection of the Emperor Francis II who made available the Benedictine monastery of S. Giorgio on the island opposite the Piazza S. Marco and the Doge's Palace. He also agreed to pay the expenses of the conclave, providing 24,000 scudi for the purpose. The secretary of the Sacred College, Monsignor Piero Negroni (nephew of Consalvi's guardian), was still in Rome, so the cardinals decided to give his office as secretary of the conclave to one of the prelates already in Venice. Their choice fell on Consalvi because of his legal experience as auditor of the Rota, though Cardinal York's influence, as sub-dean of the Sacred College, may also have been a determining factor. Consalvi's first task was to write to the absent cardinals convoking the conclave, and to write formally to the Catholic sovereigns announcing the death of Pius VI. This was not an easy task.

The circumstances were without precedent and, being away from the papal archives, Consalvi had no model to go on. Though he had made a special study of Latin literature at school, he was now very rusty and the Latin he was used to in the legal documents of the Rota was far from elegant. A standard letter to the sovereigns was not appropriate in the circumstances, with Louis XVIII in exile, the King of Naples occupying Rome, and the emperor the Legations. It was necessary to write individual letters to the different rulers couched in terms which reflected their current relations with the Holy See. Consalvi enlisted the aid of an ex-Jesuit resident in Venice and gave him the easiest letters to do, those to the absent cardinals. The results were so mediocre that he decided to do the royal letters himself. It took him two whole days and a night to finish the job.[20]

He then devoted his attention to arranging accommodation for the cardinals at S. Giorgio. This occupied him for most of October and November. The conclave opened on the feast of St Andrew, Sunday, 30 November 1799, with a mass of the Holy Ghost in Palladio's beautiful classical church. The cardinals then went in procession to the conclave in the adjoining monastic enclosure. Of the forty-six extant cardinals, eleven were too old and infirm to attend, and Herzen, the Austrian cardinal, did not arrive till after the opening ceremony, which delayed proceedings as the others did not want to begin without him when they were the emperor's guests. The conclave lasted for three and a half months and for most of that time there was deadlock between those who wanted to please Vienna and those who wanted to take an independent line. At first, it looked as if Cardinal Bellisomi, the Bishop of Cesena, would be elected. He was a popular character with a mild disposition and a reputation for personal holiness. At the first session he received eighteen votes. Though a good start, this fell short of the two-thirds majority required; it was serious enough to plunge Cardinal Herzen into an anxious state, because he had arrived with specific instructions from the government in Vienna: Austria wished to keep the Legations, and wanted a pope who would allow them to do so. They assumed that Cardinal Mattei, the Archbishop of Ravenna, who had signed the Treaty of Tolentino with the French, would have to go along with his own actions, so Vienna supported his candidacy. Herzen asked Albani, the dean, to help promote Mattei. This made it impossible to elect Bellisomi as pope.

The cardinals were in a difficult position. They did not want to alienate the goodwill of the emperor, who occupied a large portion of the Papal States and had moreover provided the location and funds for the conclave. On the other hand, they did not wish to be dictated to by a secular sovereign in their choice of candidate. Albani dithered, then agreed to delay proceedings for eleven or twelve days while Herzen sent a messenger to Vienna to consult the emperor.

Consalvi, as secretary of the conclave and with his strong historical sense of the rights of the papacy, was scandalized by Albani's behaviour. It was without precedent for a conclave to consult a lay ruler, when he had not pronounced his exclusion*

*The principal Catholic monarchs had the right to object to a candidate for a papal election, but this involved a formal notice of exclusion which could only be used once.

and when the preferred candidate enjoyed the goodwill of all the cardinals. Consalvi thought Albani feeble and trivial in his handling of extremely serious matters. Herzen used the delay to form a faction of voters opposed to Bellisomi's election. As the voting proceeded, the number of Mattei's votes rose – ten, eleven, twelve – while Bellisomi's stuck. Consalvi, on his own initiative, decided to break the deadlock because he considered the protracted delay to be dangerous for the papacy in the unsettled international circumstances. Together with Monsignor Despuig, the Spanish envoy, he devised a plan which involved the promotion of a third candidate who would be acceptable to both sides. They went first to Bellisomi's supporters and got them to agree to vote for another candidate for the good of the Church. Their first choice fell on Cardinal Gerdil, but the Mattei party would not support him. Days passed in inaction while other candidates were canvassed. All had drawbacks; they were too old, or too unpopular. The secret of success lay in choosing a cardinal from the Bellisomi party who would be acceptable to the Mattei contingent. Consalvi suggested that Cardinal Antonelli, in the Mattei faction, should select one of Bellisomi's supporters. He finally chose Cardinal Chiaramonti, Bishop of Imola. Chiaramonti was a Benedictine monk with all the necessary religious and personal qualities. By papal standards he was young, only fifty-seven years old, and had a not entirely reactionary reputation. Under the Cisalpine Republic he had printed 'Liberty' and 'Equality' on his writing paper, called himself Citizen-Cardinal Chiaramonti and had delivered a famous sermon in support of the Cisalpine Republic at Christmas 1797. Like Pius VI, he was a native of Cesena, which appealed to Cardinal Braschi; the latter helped to organize the Bellisomi faction in support of Chiaramonti, while Cardinal Antonelli, stimulated by the difficulties and wishing to demonstrate that with his skills nothing was impossible, welcomed the chance to negotiate. He went to Herzen to explain the position. Herzen did not know Chiaramonti, who had spent his life in his diocese at Imola, not in the curia at Rome, and made an excuse to visit him to judge for himself. As luck would have it, he was enchanted by the bishop's unworldly character, his sense of humour, his scholarly mind, his humility. He found him in his room dressed not as a cardinal, but a monk in a plain black Benedictine habit. Herzen agreed to support Chiaramonti, feeling that he had done his best for Vienna at the conclave, and it was time to break the deadlock. So Chiaramonti became pope by premeditated assent of the whole conclave and not by chance. He was elected unanimously on 14 March 1800. Albani, the dean, announced '*Habemus Pontificem*' and the bells rang out. The new pope took the name of Pius VII. Vienna was disappointed and refused permission for the coronation to take place in S. Marco. The pope was therefore enthroned at S. Giorgio and the overspill congregation sat outside in gondolas or filled the rooftops of the piazza opposite, watching the ceremony through telescopes.[21]

III

First Ministry

A S SOON as the conclave and coronation were completed, the cardinals started to speculate which of them the new pope would choose to be his secretary of state, the most important post in the curia. The Austrian party thought that, having acceded to the election of a simple and unworldly monk as pope, they would be able to impose on him a prime minister of their own choice who could be relied on to toe the imperial line. Cardinal Herzen hoped by this means still to be able to control events, and he went to see Pius VII at S. Giorgio to recommend Cardinal Flangini as secretary of state. Pius did not want Flangini and told Herzen that as he had no state, he did not need a secretary of state. Herzen then suggested that at least His Holiness would require somebody to deal with foreign governments. The pope replied that he was served in this capacity by the very able secretary of the conclave, Monsignor Consalvi.

Consalvi had returned to his own lodgings for a few days' rest after the election of the pope and had not seen Pius since. He was surprised to receive a sudden summons to S. Giorgio where the pope greeted him warmly and explained his predicament about Herzen's proposal that he should take Cardinal Flangini as secretary of state; that in order to counter this he had announced that Consalvi would continue to serve him, as pro-secretary of state. Consalvi remonstrated: he was happy as an auditor of the Rota; he did not want to take on a job of such great responsibility and felt that he was far too timid and uncertain to control affairs. But Pius VII would not take no for an answer. No other person could give him such a good excuse for evading the machinations of Austria.[1]

On 18 March 1800, Consalvi found himself appointed pro-secretary of state to the pope at the age of forty-three. Pius VII was chiefly interested in the spiritual aspect of his office and less so in the day-to-day government of his secular realm. As the years passed, he would come to delegate more and more of the latter to the secretary of state, so that Consalvi was to find himself in due course virtually the ruler of central Italy with almost unlimited freedom of action. The combination of the two men made an ideal working partnership for the papacy as it was constituted in the early nineteenth century. Pius VII was saintly, mild-mannered, unworldly, given to hesitancy and changes of mind. Consalvi on the other hand was highly intelligent, deter-mined, far-sighted and a master of diplomacy. From the start he won the new pope's complete trust. Both were conservatives, but not blind conservatives. The pope was always open to modern ideas, and with his quiet Benedictine independence, proved a courageous leader in times of political upheaval. Neither wished to return to the unreformed *ancien régime*. They wanted to change and improve the papal government according to the tenets of the Enlightenment, while restoring the essence of the old. Theirs was to be the middle way, neither revolutionary nor reactionary. Moreover, they both had a scholarly grasp of history and this gave them a much wider perspective and understanding of world affairs than the later eighteenth century popes.

At the outset, in Venice, however, they had no proper machinery of government. The curia was dispersed and the papacy was bankrupt, while the Papal States were occupied by foreign troops. The pope and Consalvi worked on their own at S. Giorgio with the clerical assistance of the few *monsignori* who had assembled at Venice for the conclave. Financially they were dependent on the remainder of the money that the emperor had provided for the expenses of the conclave, some of which

Consalvi had been able to save by his economical management of the arrangements, and also on money from the Roman banker, Torlonia. But this situation was soon to be reversed with dramatic speed and suddenness.

Herzen, not yet willing to concede defeat, suggested that the pope should go to Vienna to visit the emperor. Pius, shrewdly guessing that this might have a detrimental effect on his prospective relations with other powers, refused to go in person, saying that his pastoral and sovereign duties required his presence in Rome as soon as possible. The pope and Consalvi did, however, send a private messenger to Austria, Pasquale Ojatti, who spent May and June 1800 in Vienna.[2] Herzen retired baffled from the contest, and the Marchese Ghisleri, a Bolognese employed in the chancellery in Vienna, red-headed, young and impatient, but well-intentioned, arrived as a special ambassador to announce that the emperor was happy to restore the portion of the papal states lying between Pesaro and Rome provided that the pope would renounce any claim to the Legations, which Austria had decided to keep. He was in fact asking for a confirmation of the Treaty of Tolentino in Austria's favour. Ghisleri discussed this proposal first with Consalvi, who was astonished by so blatant a demand. He replied that he would report the terms to the pope, but thought it most unlikely that His Holiness would concur in any such proposal. The pope gave an absolute negative which Consalvi repeated to Ghisleri. He refused to accept it and went in person to the pope where he got the same answer from his own mouth. Pius asked why Ghisleri's master was not content with his own clothes: if he took those of others he could hardly complain if somebody else snatched his in turn, a reference to French aggression past and future. Consalvi wrote a formal letter to the Baron von Thugut, the chancellor in Vienna, to claim the Legations for the pope, backed up by an autograph letter from Pius VII to the emperor himself.

Having made this statement of papal rights, Pius announced his intention of leaving Venice for Rome. The Austrians, faced with a surprising display of firmness on the part of the monkish new pope and his inexperienced secretary of state, could hardly refuse, but in order to avoid popular demonstrations of loyalty to the papacy in the Legations, it was decided to send the papal party by sea as far as Pesaro. The sea journey was to prove uncomfortable because of the mismanagement of the arrangements by the Austrians. The only boat available was an old frigate, the *Bellona*, which had no provisions on board and an unskilled crew. This, together with poor weather, led to a journey that should have taken no more than twenty-four hours lasting for twelve days. The pope took with him Cardinals Braschi, Doria, Borgia and Pignatelli, as well as Consalvi, the Marchese Ghisleri and one or two prelates. Arriving at Pesaro, they travelled down the coast via Fano and Sinigaglia to Ancona in a triumphal procession, with the pope blessing cheering crowds all the way. At Ancona news reached them of Napoleon's great victory at Marengo of 14 June, and the destruction of Austrian power in Italy. They were also told of Napoleon's speech in Milan Cathedral, in which he had promised to restore and protect religion. Buoyed up with the news that the Austrian fetters had been dramatically loosened, the papal party continued on its way, through Loreto, Macerata and Tolentino to Foligno, the journey beginning to resemble a continuous popular ovation. The Marchese Ghisleri made formal restitution of the Austrian-occupied area of the Papal States to the pope at Foligno, and news also arrived that the King of Naples had rendered up Rome a few days earlier.

On 3 July 1800 the papal procession finally entered Rome. A Neapolitan guard of honour was drawn up ten miles to the north of the city, and escorted the pope for the last stage of the journey. Pius, accompanied by Cardinals Doria and Braschi, rode in the first carriage, while Consalvi occupied the second. Long before they reached the walls, the road was lined on either side by huge crowds, and at the entry to the city a triumphal arch had been erected to welcome the pope. After Pius VII himself, the main object of attention was his new secretary of state. As he surveyed the noisy scene of cheering people, the Neapolitan guards saluting, the roar of cannon from the Castel S. Angelo and the ringing of church bells, Consalvi recalled his departure from this same city two years earlier amidst a party of galley slaves, and quoted to himself a line from Horace:

> *Tu quamcumque Deus tibi fortunaverit horam*
> *Grata sume manu.**3

On entering the city, the papal cavalcade went straight to St Peter's where, dismounting, they went inside to give thanks at the tomb of the Apostle.

Seven days later, Consalvi moved into the Quirinal. At Pius VII's first consistory on 11 August, he was made Cardinal Deacon of the Church of St Mary of the Martyrs (the Pantheon) and was formally appointed secretary of state. On 20 October, he was made a member of the various Roman congregations, including the Propaganda Fidei, the Supreme Inquisition, the Concilio and the Consistory, as well as Apostolic Visitor of the Ospizio di S. Michele which renewed his association with that institution. As secretary of state he was entitled to the first life appointment that came up.† This turned out to be the Prefecture of the Signature which he obtained on the death of Cardinal Antonelli on 1 July 1805.

From this impressive power-base, Consalvi began the difficult job of reconstructing and reforming the papal government. Resolutely refusing all bribes and presents, including a commandery of the Order of Malta, he worked for seventeen or eighteen hours a day, restricting himself to only four hours' sleep. From July to October, he kept the provisional government set up by the Neapolitans, and confirmed the best men in their jobs, while a new congregation of prelates, cardinals and some laymen drew up a programme for the restoration of papal government. The aim was to keep the old foundations, but to reform the super-structure along the lines already adopted by other enlightened despotisms in Italy, such as Tuscany and Naples. Consalvi had

---

*'Whatever hour of good fortune God may have given you,
  Seize it with grateful hand'.
†It was intended as a long-term insurance policy because the post of secretary of state was only for the life of the reigning pope, not for that of the incumbent.4

daily audiences with the pope in which he explained how the work was getting on.

The new constitution was published on 30 October 1800 in the papal Bull *Post Diuturnas*, the text of which had been written by the distinguished Latinist, Monsignor Stai.[5] Immediately, the proposals ran into the opposition of various vested interests and assorted reactionaries. The reforms had two main objects, one was the introduction of free commerce and the abolition of parasitical privileges, the other was the inclusion of the lay nobility in the papal government, hitherto composed entirely of clerics. Pius VI and his Treasurer-General, Fabrizio Ruffo, had tinkered with the idea of introducing free trade, but had given up after the trial scheme at Bologna had run aground on a shoal of objections. Consalvi now faced up squarely to the problem; he had little option as the depleted finances of the government made it impossible to pay for subsidies on the old scale. The richest provinces of the Church were in other hands, and the coffers were empty. Nevertheless, it took courage to decree an innovation so antipathetic to the Romans and so similar to the action of the French revolutionaries. At first free trade caused increases in the prices of grain, fish and other food-stuffs, but the long term results were beneficial.[6] The introduction of free commerce was accompanied by the withdrawal of bad money. Pius VI had hastened the debasement of the papal currency in the late eighteenth century by the introduction of inflationary paper money, and this had been further exacerbated by the bankruptcy of the Roman consular government during the French occupation. Consalvi was able to bring the situation under control within a few months and bad money disappeared entirely. For his economic programme, he was able to draw on the experience of three old hands who formed the new economic congregation: his uncle, Cardinal Carandini, a considerable financial and legal expert who had been one of the minds behind Pius VI's abortive reforms, together with Pius VI's secretary of state, Cardinal Doria, and his treasurer, Cardinal Ruffo. Consalvi had made a careful study of Fabrizio Ruffo's trial plans for Bologna in the 1790s and developed his ideas from them.

The introduction of free trade earned him the undying enmity of the late pope's nephew, Cardinal Braschi, who as Cardinal Camerlengo had controlled export and import duties and the trade in grain at Rome. He lost out financially under the new system, and in order to compensate him for this loss, Consalvi appointed him secretary of briefs, but Braschi was not mollified. He set himself up as the leader of the reactionary opposition to Consalvi's reforms and opposed them with all his power. 'But,' in Consalvi's words, 'the government, immovable as a rock, sustained its programme so useful to the state, and the cardinal defeated at last resigned his charge.'[7] Gone was the millstone of nepotism with which Pius VI had again weighed down the papal government after it had been extirpated by previous reforming popes.

The way was now open for the rest of Consalvi's programme. As well as instituting free trade, sweeping away the old muddle of local customs, and restoring the money, he renewed the efforts to stimulate the turgid economic life of the Papal States by practical encouragement. He set up two new congregations to this end, the economic congregation and a congregation for the encouragement of inventions useful to agriculture and manufacture, though neither of these was able to achieve much in the short time that was to be available.

The other prong of Consalvi's attack was the involvement of the laity in the government of the Papal States. The Roman nobles had proved themselves loyal to the papacy in the face of the French Revolution and the Roman Republic, and Consalvi wanted to reward them by admitting them to public employment. Pius VI's military congregation had created a useful precedent, and there were many areas where it was more appropriate to have lay officials than prelates in charge. From now on, all the theatres and public spectacles in the Papal States were to be controlled by secular functionaries. Likewise, the ministry of roads and the treasury would be staffed with lay officials of appropriate abilities. In all these cases, as a sop to the clerical opposition, a prelate was kept as the titular head of the department, but all the staff were laity. This was a remarkable breakthrough.

Consalvi's longest-lasting innovation of this sort was the creation of the Noble Guard. Before the revolution, the papal bodyguard had been composed of mercenaries of 'low and vile extraction' under clerical control. Consalvi had not forgotten the murder of his secretary by drunken soldiers and was determined to eliminate this undesirable class from Roman society. The old military organization had been conveniently destroyed by the French. In its place Consalvi decided to set up an entirely new guard composed of young noblemen. This cleverly solved two problems. It gave well-born young Romans an honourable way of offering their services to the state, fired as they were by the military spirit of the age. They were provided with a uniform of scarlet and gold, and polished silver helmets with plumes of white ostrich feathers, on the model of the French army. A guard composed of nobles was also an economy measure, as they did not require salaries. The state merely paid for the upkeep of their horses and left the men to provide for themselves and their uniforms out of their own patrimony. In addition to these advantages, the Noble Guard was a way of attaching the loyalty of the great Roman families to the Holy See. Consalvi's opponents threw up their hands in horror and claimed that the state would go to perdition if the control of affairs was taken out of the hands of the clergy; Consalvi, tongue in cheek, replied that his reforms were very good for general morality. If it were not for the long hours on duty, the young men who formed the Noble Guard would have 'spent their time very differently.'[8]

In Rome, Consalvi with the whole-hearted support of Pius VII inaugurated an ambitious scheme of architectural improvements, not all of which were completed, or even begun, because of shortage of money and the difficulties of the times. An idea for creating a public promenade and park along the Tiber from the Porta del Popolo to the Ponte Milvio was not executed. Nor were schemes for street lighting at night or for establishing two or three healthier cemeteries outside the walled city. But the houses were numbered, and street names erected for the first time. The excavation of the Forum and the repair of ancient monuments was also begun under the direction of Carlo Fea who was

appointed by Consalvi in 1803. The arches of Septimus Severus
and Constantine, hitherto half-buried, were cleared of earth
down to the Roman pavement, and the Colosseum, which was in
severe danger of collapse, was saved. One by one, the arches of
the outer perimeter had been falling down, following the plun-
dering of sections of masonry in earlier centuries. Consalvi
commissioned a four-page report from the architects Giulio
Camporese and Rafael Stern, who predicted 'orribili conse-
quenze' if action were not taken immediately. They recom-
mended building a huge sloping brick buttress, like a book-end,
to prop up the arcade, and counter the thrust of the outer
masonry, and this ambitious project was carried out.[9]

As part of the same programme to ensure that Rome remained
the artistic capital of Europe and a centre of tourism, the latter
being the city's chief source of income, new laws against the
export of works of art were introduced and strictly enforced.
From now on there was an absolute interdict on the removal of
antique sculpture from Rome. Any classical statues dug up in the
course of the new excavations were the property of the pope. In
addition 2,000 scudi a year were allocated for the purchase of
works of art. It was hoped by these means to make good the
depredations of the French after the Treaty of Tolentino. In
order to house the new acquisitions, a vast gallery was added to
the Vatican museum by converting one of Bramante's corridors.
This was the Museo Chiaramonti, a room over three hundred
feet long leading from the Raphael Loggia, then the museum
entrance, to the Museo Pio Clementino in the Belvedere. The
arrangement of the sculpture, with the busts on tiered shelves
above the statues and sarcophagi, was entrusted to Antonio
Canova (1757–1822) who, throughout the reign of Pius VII, was
to be closely involved in the official artistic policies of the
government. In 1802 he was appointed Inspector General of
Antiquities and Fine Arts in the States of the Church, President
of the Academy of St Luke, and Curator of the Vatican and
Capitol museums.

Consalvi and the pope were anxious not just to protect and
display ancient art, but also to encourage modern art, notably the

school of neo-classical sculpture which Canova and his pupils had established in Rome. In order to replace the Apollo Belvedere and the Laocoön in their specially designed niches in the Vatican, modern statues by Canova of Perseus Triumphant, and a pair of pugilists, Creugante and Damossene, were bought in 1801 and installed on the empty pedestals.[10]

As well as the involvement of Canova in the official artistic policy of the state, Consalvi also commissioned directly from him, and paid for out of his own pocket, a marble bust in memory of Cimarosa for the Pantheon. Cimarosa's premature death was a great sadness to him. The composer had got into serious trouble in Naples for welcoming the French in 1799 and writing a republican hymn for them. On the restoration of the Bourbons he was imprisoned and in danger of being condemned to death as a traitor, but was saved by Consalvi who used his influence to secure his freedom. Cimarosa had then set out to return to St Petersburg, but got no further than Venice where he died on 11 January 1801. Since it was universally reported that he had been poisoned, Consalvi ordered a private investigation which proved the cause of death to have been a 'bilious colic'. Consalvi was greatly upset by the death of his friend and musical hero. Cimarosa had recently completed his third and last requiem mass which he had dedicated to Consalvi and this gave the idea for a splendid commemorative requiem in Rome, which Consalvi paid for out of his own private income. It took place in the richly decorated seventeenth-century baroque church of S. Carlo ai Catinari, with a large black-draped catafalque surrounded by tall unbleached candles in the centre of the marble floor under the gilded dome. The third requiem was sung on this occasion for the first time.[11] Consalvi in fact had something of a flair for ceremonial funerals. When the late Pius VI's body was brought back to Rome from Valence Consalvi organized his funeral in St Peter's as his own tribute to his early benefactor. He claimed the occasion was the most splendid and moving ever held in Rome.

The late eighteenth century saw the emergence in many European countries of a foreign minister responsible for external affairs in addition to the chief minister. But this was not the case in the Papal States where the secretary of state remained in charge of all foreign affairs, as well as the internal government of the country. A division between the two functions was not to take place in Rome till the 1830s. In Consalvi's time, he was personally responsible for all the relations with foreign powers and it is in his conduct of policy towards the other European countries that he excelled and upon which rests his lasting reputation as one of the most brilliant diplomats of his day. While his internal administration and plans for reform were hampered by financial constraints and reactionary clerical opposition, in his conduct of foreign policy he achieved nearly all that he set out to, thanks to his conciliatory nature, charm and boundless tact. Never sacrificing anything which he thought essential, he readily gave way on lesser issues. It was a rare clarity of mind and greatness of vision which enabled him to identify the essentials, and to concentrate his efforts on the targets that really mattered.

In his first ministry, following the initial problem over the Legations, he was able to restore good relations with Vienna and the other Catholic German courts. The cordiality of the friendship which he established with the Austrian diplomat Count Lebzeltern, a protégé of Metternich's who was for many years the Austrian minister in Rome, was to stand the papacy in good stead on several future occasions. Spain Consalvi saw as the model of frank and friendly loyalty to the Holy See. Indeed, he found Spanish enthusiasm positively embarrassing, for the King of Spain kept bombarding him with rich benefices and other monetary gifts. Though he attempted to turn these down, he was appointed against his will a canon of Seville Cathedral and eventually received a very large cheque to cover the arrears of his income from the chapter there, via Drummond's Bank in London, though he never cashed it.[12]

Relations with Naples, by contrast, he found a strain. Joseph Acton, the Neapolitan minister, was far too devious, and Consalvi considered it one of the crosses of his job 'to have to treat with a man like him'.[13] Though Naples had been willing to restore Rome and the surrounding states in 1800 as a buffer between themselves and the Austrians, and then the French in the north, Ferdinand IV and General Acton had attempted to retain the detached papal enclaves of Benevento and Ponte Corvo within the kingdom of Naples itself, and it was only as a result of French pressure at the Treaty of Florence that the Neapolitans handed these back to the pope. That Consalvi was able to rely on French support in this business is one manifestation of the greatest single achievement of his first ministry, the Concordat with France which reconciled the Catholic Church with the revolution, and established good relations for four or five years between Napoleon and the pope.

At first, after Pius VII returned to Rome in 1800, there had not been much cause for optimism. Following the defeat of the Austrians at Marengo, the French had retaken the Legations and negotiated an unfavourable treaty, the Act of Foligno, with a Monsignor Caleppi who had not been empowered by Rome to act as an emissary. Pius VII and Consalvi were mortified when they heard what Caleppi had done. When the *Général-en-Chef* of the Italian army, Napoleon's brother-in-law, Joachim Murat, was sent to Rome to ratify it, Consalvi explained to him that Caleppi had had no authority to negotiate the Act of Foligno in the first place. Fortunately Murat and Consalvi had taken an immediate liking to each other and had got on very well. The upshot was that Murat said to Consalvi: 'Oh well, since the treaty is so painful to the Holy Father and to you, let us throw it on the fire and not speak about it any further.'[14]

Shortly afterwards, a letter arrived from Cardinal Martiana, Bishop of Vercelli, announcing that Bonaparte, while passing through at the head of his army, had charged him to notify the Holy Father of his wish to re-establish religion in France and asked for Monsignor Spina, whom he had once met at Valence, to meet him at Turin. Spina was sent immediately with the power to negotiate, but when he arrived in Turin he found that Napoleon had already returned to Paris. Spina followed him there and in November 1800 diffidently started a complex process of nego- tiation with Napoleon's representative, a tough ex-guerrilla

priest from the Vendée, Etienne Bernier. Spina, a slow, sus-
picious lawyer, sent all his drafts back to Rome for expert perusal
by a congregation of the most learned cardinals.[15] Meanwhile,
when Spina arrived in Paris, Napoleon sent his own plenipotentiary, François Cacault, to Rome to renew French relations with
the Holy See. Cacault was a good choice for he had spent a lot of
his youth in Rome and knew the place well. When he asked how
he should treat the pope, Napoleon replied: 'As though he had
200,000 men.'[16]

Napoleon had lost his Catholic faith while a student at the
military academy of Brienne, and considered Christ to be merely
a man, but he continued to believe in God in an eighteenth-
century deist manner. Thanks to the influence of his pious
mother, he also retained a marked sentimental attachment to
Catholicism and was easily moved by the sound of church bells
or the sight of candles burning in dim chapels. At the more
practical level, he admired established religion for its ability to
cement order in society, and his experience both in north Italy
and in France had convinced him of the advantage to his
government of restoring Catholicism. Napoleon liked to do
things properly and this, combined with the French tradition of
centralization, uniformity and authority, made it almost certain
that he would do a deal with the pope.

Pius VII, for his part, was the type of saintly, other-worldly
cleric whom Napoleon respected. While Bishop of Imola, he had
shown his readiness to come to terms with the new republican
movement, and he was able to draw a line between the eternal
religious aspect of the papacy and its transient temporal character. He was also determined to avoid any mention of the Treaty
of Tolentino, the Legations, or the material harm done to the
papacy by the French. When Napoleon made it a prerequisite of
any negotiations that the French state should retain all nationalized Church property and that the clergy would be paid salaries
by the government, the pope agreed. Consalvi's practical realism
complemented the pope's high-minded spirituality, and he
appreciate Pius's determination to put religion before all other
considerations and to achieve a *modus vivendi* with the new

regime. Both were determined to hold out for the rights of the Church, including sole direction of seminary education of the clergy, the freedom of religion from any police control, and the right of the pope to correspond with the local clergy free from any state interference. In particular they were determined that Napoleon should declare Catholicism to be the official religion of France.

Draft after draft was received from Spina and was amended in Rome. Napoleon began to lose patience and finally sent his own version direct to Cacault with the ultimatum that if it was not accepted by the pope within five days, negotiations would be broken off and the French minister withdrawn. Consalvi was seriously perturbed by this. The French army under Murat was at Florence and everything seemed set for a repeat of the invasion of 1798. On the other hand, the pope was not prepared to accept Napoleon's draft as it stood. 'We are prepared to go to the gates of Hell – but no further,' he remarked.

Consalvi discussed the situation with Cacault. Finally they decided that Cacault would leave after five days in accordance with his instructions, but his departure would take place in Consalvi's carriage and the secretary of state would leave with him and then go on to Paris. The First Consul would surely appreciate the pope's gesture in sending his prime minister to resolve the impasse and bring the negotiations to a satisfactory conclusion. Consalvi took his brother Andrea with him as his secretary, and they left Rome with Cacault on 6 June. They broke their journey at Florence, where Cacault was dropped off, and Consalvi had a word with Murat to make sure that the French army did not march on Rome in his absence. He then continued north, arriving in Paris on 20 June. He was amazed by the appearance of the churches in France, ruined, shut up, or re-dedicated to Liberty, Equality and Fraternity. It provided a strong reminder of the purpose of his visit.[17]

As soon as he reached his lodgings at the Hôtel de Rome, Consalvi sent word to Bernier to inform Napoleon that he had arrived, and to ask when he should present himself and what should he wear. The reply came back immediately: at two p.m.

that day and 'as cardinal as possible'. Cardinals usually only wore their full dress of scarlet on state occasions in the papal household, so Consalvi compromised and wore court dress of black with red buttons and piping, red skull cap and red stockings. At the appointed time, the master of ceremonies arrived with a carriage to collect him from his lodgings and to convey him to the Tuileries where he was left alone in the Salon des Ambassadeurs, a comparatively small room. After a short time, he was collected and taken through a side door to the Grand Staircase, where a brilliant spectacle awaited him. The whole French court was assembled *en parade*, the senate, tribunate, *corps legislatif*, palace dignitaries, the chief ministers and generals of the army. The consuls held a court every fifteen days and Napoleon had chosen the occasion to display to Consalvi, on his first visit, the magnificence of French power.

Hiding his surprise, the cardinal was conducted through a long enfilade of rooms crowded with people, all agog at the sight of a cardinal in full clerical dress, to an ante-room where he was met by the foreign minister, Talleyrand, who introduced himself and took Consalvi into the saloon, a vast room, full of people arranged symmetrically around an isolated group of three figures in the centre whom Consalvi rightly took to be the consuls. Talleyrand led him to them and presented him to Napoleon. The First Consul greeted him 'neither with politeness nor lack of it', and plunged straight into a discussion of the business in hand before Consalvi could utter a word. 'I know the reason for your journey to Paris. I wish discussions to begin immediately. I give you five days and I wish you to know that if at the end of the fifth day the negotiations are not completed, you will go back to Rome.'[18]

Consalvi, not showing that he was somewhat taken aback, replied suavely that the pope's sending him was proof enough of a serious intention to bring the negotiations for a concordat to a swift conclusion, and he would be only too happy to complete the business in the time specified. Napoleon realized that he was dealing with a different calibre of person from the plodding, pedantic Spina, and took a liking to Consalvi's more open, sensible and flexible character. He treated him to a thirty-minute discussion, half in Italian and half in French, on the concordat, the Holy See and religion, 'without anger or hard words'. Consalvi replied quietly and frankly to all his points. Abruptly, Napoleon announced that there was no time to lose, graciously inclined his head and stepped back to his place with the other consuls. Consalvi bowed and was conducted out once more by Talleyrand, that 'old viper that had shed its skin,'[19] the ex-Bishop of Autun, no less.

Talleyrand had been responsible for several of the previously unacceptable clauses in the draft concordat, because he wished to marry an actress called Madame Grand (described by Napoleon as 'a stupid old tart') and wanted to protect the position of ex-clergy like himself. Now, foreseeing defeat, he departed from Paris to take the waters at Bourbon l'Archâmbault. Soon after Consalvi had got back to his lodgings from the Tuileries, the Abbé Bernier arrived and they started work. They spent their days discussing the sticking points and making drafts; during the evenings and far into the night, their little staff corrected and made fair copies of the resulting documents. In punning reference to his own name, Consalvi described the negotiations as 'a labour of Hercules'. He had two further meetings with the First Consul, saw Josephine at Malmaison, dined at the Ministry of Foreign Affairs and visited the Spanish and Austrian ambassadors. The latter, Count Cobenzl, became a good friend and used his influence several times to ease the negotiations through difficult patches. Consalvi also made friends with a number of figures in Napoleon's entourage, and this in due course may have saved his life.

Before Consalvi arrived in Paris, the Holy See had already accepted the confiscation of Church property as irreversible, as well as Napoleon's wish to reduce the number of French bishoprics by half and even his insistence on a clean sweep of all existing bishops and a fresh start with new appointments. Consalvi, realizing that this last was abhorrent to the pope, tried unavailingly to get Napoleon to retract it. He pointed out that asking the pope to remove all the existing bishops would be contrary to the Gallican tradition of French ecclesiastical independence. It would in practice be a new power for the papacy. Hitherto, the pope had exercised the right to invest all bishops, but not to depose them. Ironically, it was Napoleon's insistence on this piece of administrative convenience which was later to open the way for the growth of centralized papal control over the local churches and the ultramontane revival.

Consalvi concentrated his main efforts on eliminating those clauses that subjected the Church and the practice of religion to the State, and to police control. On the evening of the fifth day, Bernier took the ninth and, it was hoped, final draft to Napoleon who wanted to announce the Concordat on Bastille Day, 14 July. It was to be signed on the 13th at the house of Napoleon's brother, Joseph.

Opening the *Moniteur* on the morning of 13 July, Consalvi read: 'Cardinal Consalvi has succeeded in the negotiations, with which he was entrusted by the Holy See.' It was a pre-emptive move by the First Consul to prevent any last-minute changes of mind. At four o'clock, Consalvi went to Joseph Bonaparte's house where he was received politely and allowed, in his quality as a cardinal, to sign first. Taking up his pen and dipping it into the inkpot, he was a little surprised to be offered a new copy of the Concordat to sign. Glancing over it, he found that the provisions were not those which he and Bernier had agreed. The paragraphs which the pope had specifically refused to accept had been surreptitiously re-inserted in the hope that Consalvi would sign without bothering to read the text again. This rather crude subterfuge revealed an unappealing aspect of Napoleon's character – he was, as Talleyrand remarked in other circumstances, a compulsive cheat at cards. Consalvi expressed surprise and refused to sign. Joseph professed astonishment: here he was, seated at a table to sign a document which all had agreed after a year of negotiation, only to be faced with extraordinary behaviour on the part of the cardinal. In fact, he knew nothing of the trick which had been played. Turning on Bernier, Consalvi asked him sharply what had happened to the text which they had prepared. Confused and embarrassed, Bernier explained that the

First Consul himself had ordered the changes to be made. Consalvi replied that he would not, and could not, sign an act contrary to the pope's specific instructions. Joseph intervened and asked him to consider the disastrous effect of a breakdown in negotiations when the successful conclusion of the treaty had already been announced in the morning papers and the signature was to be proclaimed at a state dinner at the Tuileries the following day. Napoleon would be angry if he were thwarted and it appeared to the public that he had inserted in the papers false news on so serious a subject. Surely there was some compromise?

So Consalvi, having got up to leave, sat down again, and they talked and talked – all night and till midday the following day – a session of nineteen hours. By subtly modifying the words it was possible to agree on all except the first paragraph which required religion to be 'in conformity with police regulations'. Consalvi would not accept this subjugation of the Church to the State. Negotiations broke down three hours before the ceremonial dinner at five o'clock.

Tired out and depressed by his failure, Consalvi went to the Tuileries at the appointed time with a sinking heart. As soon as he entered the room, he could see from Napoleon's face that he was furious. In front of the assembled company of ministers and ambassadors the First Consul shouted: 'Ah well, Monsieur le Cardinal, you want a schism. So be it. I have no need of Rome . . . I have no need of the pope. If Henry VIII, who did not have a twentieth part of my power, could change the religion of his own country,* the more so can I. In changing the religion of France I will change that of all Europe, everywhere that my power and influence extends . . .'[20] The angry tirade went on and on, culminating in the barked question: 'When are you leaving?' Consalvi replied quietly, 'After dinner, General.' This short, firm answer took the wind out of Napoleon's sails and he paused in astonishment, thus giving Consalvi the chance to get in a word, and to explain that he could not go against the pope's express

*Napoleon had read John Barrow's *History of England* which contained a detailed study of the Henrician reformation.

instructions. Cobenzl joined in and urged a further session of negotiations. Finally, in the drawing-room after dinner, Napoleon gave way. 'Ah well, to prove that it is not my wish to cause a rupture, the commission can meet one last time to arrange things.'

Consalvi lay awake all night thinking of the dreadful consequences if negotiations failed; he foresaw that a break between France and Rome, like that with England three hundred years before, would be irreversible. Discussions began again at midday at Joseph Bonaparte's house. The session lasted fifteen hours. The vital issue, as Consalvi saw it, was that there should be free and public exercise of religion and it was necessary to state this expressly in the Concordat. He had also wanted to declare that Catholicism was the state religion in France. The compromise form of words finally devised by Consalvi was that the Catholic faith was 'the religion of the great majority of the French people' and the religion professed by the consuls. This was accepted. The other stumbling-block was the question of police control. Again Consalvi was able to devise an ingenious form of words that satisfied both sides, namely that 'the Catholic religion, apostolic and Roman, shall be freely exercised in France. Its practice shall be public in conformity with any police regulations which the government shall judge necessary for public order.' This satisfied Napoleon by keeping in the reference to the police. But Consalvi's full stop and qualifying words limited the context of any police regulations to public worship, such as outdoor processions, implying that the Church itself was not subject to police control. It ruled out state interference in the organization of seminaries, for instance, or communications with Rome. This was an important concession on the part of the French government, and a brilliant stroke on Consalvi's part. Napoleon being satisfied, the Concordat was finally signed on 15 July 1801 in the Tuileries.[21] Consalvi, having won his great victory, stayed on in Paris for three or four days further and had a farewell audience with Napoleon on the eve of his departure. The First Consul ignored him entirely, as he stood in the line of diplomats, and spoke to his neighbour Cobenzl instead. Napoleon was not a good loser.

Consalvi returned to Rome as quickly as possible via Lyons, Milan, Parma and Florence. He rested for a short time in the latter, and visited Cacault and Murat to tell them the good news. He arrived back in Rome twelve days after leaving Paris on 6 August. The whole expedition had taken two months precisely, and left him feeling so tired that he could hardly stand up. The pope was delighted with the Concordat, and it was ratified, despite the quibbles of some of the ultras, by a consistory of cardinals on 15 August. An extraordinary courier took the Bull of confirmation back to Paris within the remarkably short time of twenty-three days after Consalvi's departure.

Then, to the surprise of Rome, there was complete silence until Easter the following year, when the Concordat was published in France, but with an appendix of 'Organic Articles' which reiterated all the traditional Gallican claims which Consalvi had been at pains to eliminate. He thought that Napoleon had deliberately tricked him, but this was not the case. The First Consul had not discussed the Concordat with his council of state until after it had been ratified. They were horrified and thought it not sufficiently Gallican, so the Organic Articles were drawn up and appended to the text of the Concordat. Even so it only just scraped through the National Assembly by seven votes. The articles which caused the most annoyance in Rome were those which subjected all papal Bulls to a government *placet*, and laid down that all seminary students should be taught the Gallican Articles of 1682.

In April 1802, Napoleon reopened the churches of France, and the bells which had been silent for a decade rang out once more. No single act of Napoleon's career was more popular than his restoration of religion, and despite Rome's misgivings over the appointment of 'constitutionals' (those clergy who had taken the oath to the 1790 Civil Constitution), Napoleon made an excellent choice of bishops. Thirty-two of them had never been bishops before, and of those who were re-appointed, twelve were 'constitutionals'. Napoleon's maternal uncle, Fesch, was appointed Archbishop of Lyons and Primate of France. Con-salvi, in a characteristically tactful gesture, chose the French artist and pupil of David, Jean-Baptiste Wicar, who resided at the French Academy in Rome, to paint a large commemorative picture showing the secretary of state presenting the Concordat to the pope.

The French Concordat formed the model for the subsequent Italian Concordat which was more favourable to the Church. Napoleon was aware of the religious differences between France and Italy, and was helpful in arranging the Concordat with the Cisalpine Republic, which was signed in September 1803. It stated that the Catholic Church was the state religion in Italy, and it confirmed the Church in possession of its remaining property and endowments, as well as making state provision for the clergy and seminaries.[22] The concordat system, defining church–state relations, was subsequently extended by Consalvi to cover the whole of Catholic Europe, and it had an important effect in centralizing the authority of the Church, greatly increasing the power of the pope.

In place of the feudal jumble of the *ancien régime*, with dozens of local churches and lay patrons, a single centralized system emerged throughout Europe in the aftermath of the Revolution. Henceforth, the parish clergy were all dependent on their bishops, and the bishops dependent on Rome; the pope now being able to depose them as well as to invest them. Thus Consalvi laid the foundations for the 'ultramontane autocracy' of the nineteenth and twentieth centuries. Though this was partly a side effect of his policies, he believed firmly in the benefits of centralization and in the traditional claims of the papacy, so such an outcome cannot be described as accidental.

Aside from the affairs of state, he had his own private business to oversee, especially the supervision of his scattered family property. Here, too, life was not without its dramas. His personal finances had been buffeted by the French occupation of Rome, his subsequent exile and the republican confiscation of his property. On his return to Rome, he had set about putting his business affairs in order. This task was made additionally complicated by the death in 1804 of his agent at Toscanella, Alberto Parisani, who had been in the Consalvi household since the age of five. With charitable forbearance, Consalvi recorded in his memoirs how Parisani had been the object of his entire confidence and that his death was a great blow.[23] The truth, as it emerges from his accounts and private papers, was slightly different. Parisani had been submitting fraudulent accounts for years and embezzling the estate revenue for his own benefit. Alberto Parisani had had the administration of the estate at Toscanella since 1767, when Consalvi inherited from his grandfather, till Parisani's own death in 1804, a period of thirty-seven years. Niccolo Brunati, the comptroller in Consalvi's household in Rome, was charged to receive the financial accounts for the different holdings and to register them in his central account book. Parisani came to Rome once a year for this purpose and was paid his expenses. In 1804, it emerged that he had failed to keep proper accounts since 1779. On his deathbed, he confessed that he had fraudulently adjusted all the figures and pocketed the difference. He owed Consalvi at least 8,500 scudi. Bills which he had recorded as being paid were, in fact, still outstanding as he had himself taken the monies provided for the purpose and, as a result, the estate was in debt. The accounts were in such a mess that Consalvi had to dispatch agents to Toscanella to try to sort them out. Parisani's heirs, his brothers, were now responsible for the debt, and they tried to prove with false accounts that the estate was in credit. Consalvi's accountant in Rome sifted through all the material and built up a damning case against them. As more papers were investigated, the picture grew blacker. Apparently the errors in the accounts amounted to 12,500 scudi, while fake receipts added up to 6,000 more. The whole Parisani family, it seemed, had been involved in a policy of systematic fraud over a period of twenty-six years. Consalvi decided to show mercy. He told the heirs that he would not take them to court, but would settle for a payment of 8,500 scudi. This offer was gratefully accepted, and in the event he continued to employ Alberto Parisani's brother, Francesco, as his agent at Toscanella.[24]

The revelation of this biblical tale of the dishonest steward coincided with important developments in international affairs which required Consalvi's full attention. On 4 May 1804, the French Tribunate declared Napoleon Emperor of the French with hereditary title. The news arrived out of the blue in Rome and proved a matter for serious concern. It was one thing to treat with Napoleon as the representative of a republican government, quite another to recognize him as an hereditary monarch on the throne of Louis XVIII, whom the Holy See had notified of the pope's election in 1800 and officially still regarded as the legitimate King of France. Soon afterwards, even more astonishing news arrived from Cardinal Caprara, the papal nuncio in Paris, who had been dispatched there following the ratification of the Concordat. Napoleon had asked Caprara to sound out the pope, to discover whether he would crown him in person. There had been no papal coronation of a European monarch since that of the Emperor Charles V at Bologna in 1530. The pope did not wish to but Consalvi thought otherwise. He appreciated the potential benefit to the Church and advised Pius that he must go. There was no alternative; everything now depended on Napoleon. It would help to strengthen religion, while a refusal would be an affront to the most powerful man in Europe and the restorer of the Catholic Church in France. Several of the cardinals had misgivings, but only two felt that Napoleon, as the heir to the Revolution, was positively satanic. There was also the possibility of an insult to Vienna to consider; but the Catholic powers had already recognized Napoleon. Only England never did, and Russia had not at this stage. The Tsar was consequently shocked by the papal support for Napoleon's imperial pretensions. The Swedish minister at St Petersburg reported the general view there: 'The crimes of Alexander VI are less revolting than this hideous apostasy on the part of his feeble successor.'[25]

Discussions took place throughout the summer between Consalvi and Cardinal Fesch, who had succeeded Cacault as the French minister in Rome.[26] Consalvi saw the coronation as an opportunity to get Napoleon to abolish the Organic Articles, and when Fesch said that Napoleon would take an oath in the ceremony to respect the 'laws of the Concordat and the liberty of cults', Consalvi asked whether this included the Organic

Articles. Fesch confirmed that it did not. Consalvi also wanted some definite action about the scandal of the constititional bishops. He requested that they should undergo a formal act of reconciliation with the Holy See; and those who refused should be removed from their dioceses. Fesch replied that all the pope had to do was raise these matters with Talleyrand on his arrival in Paris and they would be settled to his entire satisfaction. Consalvi was therefore reasonably happy that in return for crowning Napoleon as emperor all the unresolved issues left over from the Concordat would be smoothed away. Both the pope and Consalvi, at this stage, had a special personal regard for Napoleon. The pope, in particular, looked on him with feelings that mingled admiration, paternal pride and pious gratitude. He saw the Concordat as Napoleon's initiative, an act of peace which had reconciled the Church with France, and preserved the world from violent schism. To be set on the other side of the balance was the murder at that time of the duc d'Enghien, an innocent young royalist who had been abducted from foreign soil and shot in cold blood at Vincennes *pour encourager les autres*. This made the pope and Consalvi hesitate, for neither would have gone through with the coronation if they had believed Napoleon guilty of the crime. Even in 1811, when he was writing his memoirs in exile at Rheims and had far less reason to admire Napoleon than in 1804, Consalvi still had a soft spot for him. It is perhaps worth quoting his view of the emperor in full:

I admire the power of his genius, the swiftness of his intelligence and that marvellous fecundity of resources and spirit which created him for his part, but I cannot dissimulate that all these brilliant qualities came to grief because mingled with them were innumerable faults which his success developed beyond measure. Bonaparte who must be invincible in discussion would not allow one to argue with him. I am perhaps one of the few, rare in Europe, who have held my own with him, not curbed by his iron will, and I do not repent it. In his access of anger, as much feigned as real, he threatened to have me shot; he repeated the threat frequently, but I am persuaded that he would never have signed the order of execution. I have heard it said more than once by his most devoted servants and intimate confidants that the murder of the Duc d'Enghien was more a surprise, than an act of his own will. I would not be surprised if that were true for it was a useless crime leaving behind nothing but shame and remorse and Bonaparte would have wished to spare himself that.[27]

Napoleon's judgement of Consalvi was more succinct: 'a lion in sheep's clothing'.

Convinced of Napoleon's good intentions, Consalvi told Fesch that if a formal invitation arrived from Paris, the pope would answer in the affirmative. There is no doubt that Napoleon was genuinely grateful, but as usual he managed to ruffle Roman feathers. Before the formal invitation was even dispatched, Napoleon announced in the Paris newspapers that the pope had accepted, in order to make it difficult for Pius to retract, just as he had with Consalvi over the Concordat. When the invitation did finally arrive, it was so ill-worded and brusque that the pope felt for a moment like saying no, but eventually he said yes. He left Rome on 2 November 1804, arriving in Paris twenty-five days later. Consalvi was anxious that it should not look as if the whole papal curia was going to Paris, and the pope took only six rather feeble elderly cardinals with him, none of whom could speak French. The pope also took with him a selection of splendid presents for Napoleon including his own bust by Canova, who had also been encouraged by Consalvi to accept Napoleon's invitation to go to Paris to carve an heroic marble statue of the new emperor,* and a statue of Cupid and Psyche for the Louvre. Consalvi stayed behind in Rome as Papal-Vicar, the only occurrence in history of such an office, with absolute control of the papal government and unlimited powers.

The pope enjoyed his visit to Paris. He received a rapturous reception from the populace who, wherever he went, fell on their

*The result now graces the staircase of Apsley House in London.

knees to receive his blessing. In addition to the coronation and other ceremonies and religious functions, he occupied himself sightseeing, with jaunts to the Sèvres china works and the Gobelins tapestry factory. Consalvi, in Rome, was highly sensitive to any infringement of what he considered to be the papal dignity and more perturbed than the pope at various lapses in Napoleon's courtesy. He imagined that the pope was being constantly subjected to deliberate snubs at the hands of the emperor. He was shocked, for example, to hear that Napoleon had met the pope at a crossroads in the Forest of Fontainebleau, with fifty hounds, 'as if he were going hunting'. But this was the traditional way for the monarchs of France to meet important foreign visitors, as opera-lovers will know from the opening scene of Verdi's *Don Carlos*. Far from being a snub, it was a sign of Napoleon's intention to do things according to royal precedents and etiquette. Consalvi, with his courtly *ancien régime* breeding, was upset by details like Napoleon seizing the crown and crowning himself or the pope being placed third at the coronation banquet in the Tuileries and similar solecisms. He saw them as deliberate insults to the Holy See. The simple truth, however, was that Napoleon did not have good manners. To quote Talleyrand again: 'What a pity that such a great man should be so ill-bred.' More serious was the pope's lack of headway in getting any satisfaction on the subject of the Organic Articles and the constitutional clergy. Consalvi sought an outlet for his frustration over the whole business in disparaging Napoleon's presents to the pope. The chief jewel in the tiara 'given' by the emperor had been extracted from Pius VI by the Treaty of Tolentino and so belonged to the pope anyway. The Gobelins tapestries were 'very old and very mediocre', two candelabra and a service of Sèvres porcelain were '*très ordinaire*'.[28]

These irritations aside, Consalvi had a thoroughly satisfying time ruling Rome in the pope's absence, exercising his power as circumspectly as only he knew how. It was the high point of his first ministry. Even a disastrous flood on 31 January 1805, when the Tiber flooded its banks and turned half the city into a lake, saw him in his element, dressed in his cardinal's robes directing the rescue operations in the water-filled streets and piazze from a little boat. The worst problem was the final depletion of the public finances caused by the expense of the pope's visit to Paris. This had not just cleared out the state's coffers, but also the liquid resources of Torlonia and the other Roman bankers. Nevertheless, Consalvi was able to carry out one important architectural improvement. The ancient Ponte Milvio, dating from 109 BC, which conducted the main road from the north across the Tiber and towards the Porta del Popolo, had been damaged by the flood. Consalvi took advantage of this to restore the bridge and to construct a new gate tower at one end as a powerful neo-classical overture to the formal entrance to the city. This new work was to greet the pope on his return to Rome at Whitsun 1805. The triumphal archway, a blocky stone pylon of severely military character with battered walls and four different patterns of rustication, was designed by the papal architect Giuseppe Valadier. In front of it a small piazza was laid out, still named in memory of its originator the Piazzale Consalvi, and the Flaminian Way repaved as far as the Porta del Popolo.

All was ready in time for the pope's ecstatic reception by the population of Rome, an event which was hardly less enthusiastic than his first entry into the city in 1800. Consalvi met Pius VII at the restored Ponte Milvio and 'His Holiness gave his approbation to these works.' Consalvi further recorded with pride, that the pope approved of all that he had done in his absence, and that 'nobody complained about me, and I am thrilled that everybody seemed happy with my administration.'[29] This, however, was a short-lived high point, and soon forces were in motion that would lead to Consalvi's resignation as secretary of state and his second exile.

IV

Opposition: *rouges et noirs*

THE pope's magnificent gesture of conciliation in going to Paris in person to crown Napoleon did not have the results for which Consalvi had hoped; the emperor refused to repeal the Organic Articles or to do anything about the constititutional clergy. In retrospect, it can be seen as a watershed in papal-Napoleonic relations. Thereafter a steady decline set in as Consalvi started to resist Napoleon's aggressions. The reasons for the eventual rupture between the Holy See and the French Empire are complex, involving personalities as well as international events, but as Napoleon's megalomania developed and he aimed at total European dominance, he was not prepared to allow any country, however small, to take an independent political line, while Consalvi was equally determined to defend the freedom of action of the Holy See. The basic principle at issue, therefore, was that of papal neutrality. Pius VII and Consalvi refused to enter the Napoleonic System and in particular to close the papal ports to the Allies' shipping despite Napoleon's increasing demands that they should do so. The immediate cause of the break with Napoleon was the French occupation of papal Ancona, one of the chief harbours in the east Mediterranean, in October 1805, to prevent its use by the English fleet. This was a serious infringement of the rights of a neutral country and laid papal subjects open to attack by the English or Russian fleets by making it look as if the pope was taking

Napoleon's side in a European war. It was especially embarrassing to Consalvi, for only the previous year he had written at some
length to Thomas Jackson, the British minister to the King of
Sardinia, to say that there were no French troops at Ancona, and
had explained his policy of neutrality, giving it as the reason for
impounding an English corsair in the harbour there.[1] Consalvi
was not prepared to let Napoleon get away with this aggression.
It confirmed the suspicion, aroused by Napoleon's failure to
keep his side of the coronation bargain, that the emperor was
simply an unscrupulous bully who could not be trusted.

The papal government sent an immediate protest to Napoleon
about the French occupation of Ancona, asking for its instant
evacuation. Consalvi had advised the pope to write a short letter
in his own hand directly to the emperor and not to have a formal
exchange through Fesch, the French minister at Rome. It was
hoped that a confidential letter would enable the emperor to
retire, seemingly of his own volition, without any public damage
to his *amour propre*. The pope wrote:

> We will speak frankly; ever since Our return from Paris We
> have experienced nothing but bitterness and disillusion-
> ment whereas the personal knowledge which We had
> acquired of Your Majesty, and Our invariable conduct, had
> promised, by contrast, something quite different. In a word,
> We have not found in Your Majesty, that return of Our
> goodwill which We had a right to expect.[2]

From November to January there was no reply. Napoleon
only received the pope's letter in Vienna after the battle of Ulm
and his triumphal entry into the Austrian capital. There followed
the victory at Austerlitz which left him master of all Europe. This
coloured his views when he finally had the chance to reply to the
pope from Munich on 7 January 1806. He, Napoleon, was the
emperor and the pope should regard him as earlier popes had
regarded Charlemagne. He warned Pius that if he did not enter
the Napoleonic System there would be dire repercussions for the
temporal power. Consalvi read this as an attempt by Napoleon to
impose a state of vassalage on the Holy See, for he was claiming

to be the successor of Charlemagne and supposing, falsely, that the pope had been a vassal of Charlemagne. It was a direct threat to the independence of the papacy. What Napoleon was demanding would embroil the pope in constant war: Napoleon's friends must be the pope's friends, and Napoleon's enemies must be his enemies. By the same courier, Napoleon sent a letter to Fesch developing his policy of Caesarism in more detail, and concluding with the words: 'Tell Cardinal Consalvi that if he loves Religion and his country, he can take one of two courses, do what I want, or quit his ministry.'[3]

The deterioration of relations between Rome and Paris was exacerbated by Fesch's personal dislike and jealousy of Consalvi. Ever since his return to Rome after Napoleon's coronation, Fesch had conducted a campaign of vilification against the secretary of state. Earlier, while negotiating the coronation, they had seemed to get on well, and Consalvi had regarded Fesch as a friend, but these feelings were now replaced by coolness and suspicion. Consalvi realized that this attitude on the part of Fesch had been fostered to some extent by 'a great Roman financier'. This was Giovanni Torlonia, a friend of Fesch's, who made a huge fortune lending money to both sides during the Revolutionary and Napoleonic wars, and on whom both the papal government and Consalvi personally were dependent for loans. Torlonia had resented the introduction of free trade and Consalvi's economic reforms generally, and he had been mortified when Consalvi had refused his bribes, while the vanity of Torlonia's wife had been hurt when Consalvi 'had not encouraged her advances'.[4] Unable to influence Consalvi's policies by corruption, Torlonia had determined to secure his removal from the political stage, and had worked on Fesch as the most effective lever to that end.

There remained the problem of how to reply to Napoleon's hostile letters, for Consalvi thought that such an overt threat to the Holy See could not be passed over in silence. He therefore advised the pope to distribute a questionnaire to the Sacred College of Cardinals and to convene a meeting to seek their views. He also took the opportunity to tell Fesch that, as the

French minister, he was not expected to attend. The cardinals, many of whom had always been anti-French, asked the pope to send a strongly negative response to Napoleon, and if there was any hesitation still in the pope's mind, it was removed when in January 1806, the French Civil Code, with its recognition of divorce, was introduced into northern Italy. Napoleon, with his usual tact, had taken the opportunity to announce this in Milan Cathedral, following his coronation as King of Italy by Cardinal Caprara. He never seems to have realized how profound was the resulting disillusion and anger at Rome. The pope felt he had been deceived, while Consalvi, hitherto accused by the *zelanti** of being too pro-French, appreciated that rapprochement was impossible; the moment had come to resist Napoleon; he could not be trusted.[5]

In his reply to the emperor, the pope expressed his surprise at having received a sermon on principles and doctrine. He explained that he regarded Napoleon as the Emperor of the French, not of Rome; the sovereignty of the Holy See was free and independent, and intimately linked with the pope's exercise of his spiritual authority. The Holy See could not, and would not, accept the political supremacy of Napoleon. He concluded with a reiteration of his request that Ancona be evacuated. Though firm, the pope's letter to Napoleon was expressed in moderate terms. Consalvi's concurrent letter to Fesch was somewhat stiffer: he, Consalvi, took his orders from the pope, not from other sovereigns.[6]

As a result of Fesch's insinuations, Napoleon was persuaded that the pope's resistance was entirely due to Consalvi's influence. He had met both of them: the mild-mannered, hesitant pope could not possibly write such letters on his own account, but Consalvi was a different matter. On 13 February 1806, Napoleon replied to the pope: 'Most Holy Father, I know Your

---

*Zelanti – literally the zealous. The name given to those cardinals who wanted a non-political entirely religious papacy and who had emerged as a significant force in the curia in the late seventeenth century. In the aftermath of the French Revolution their anti-political stance came to mean opposing any rapprochement or compromise with the modern world.

Holiness means well, but he is surrounded by men who do not.'
He demanded that all the papal ports be closed to enemy
nationals, especially the English fleet.

Consalvi drafted a reply which is a classic statement of papal
neutrality:

> We are the Vicar of a God of peace, which means peace
> towards all, without distinction between Catholics and
> heretics, or between those living near at hand and those
> living far away, or between those from whom We hope for
> benefits and those from whom We expect evil . . . Only the
> necessity of withstanding hostile aggression or defending
> religion in danger, has given our predecessors a just reason
> for abandoning a pacific policy. If any of them by human
> weakness departed from these principles, his conduct, We
> say it frankly, can never serve as an example for Ours.

For these reasons the Holy See could not ally itself with any side
in a European war, or take unfriendly action such as closing its
ports. To do so might jeopardize Catholics in other countries. In
the present instance, both the Tsar of Russia and the King of
England ruled over lands containing 'many millions of Catholics'. Neutrality was the central prop of Consalvi's foreign policy
throughout his career. He was later to take as strong a line with
Metternich, after the Restoration, as with Napoleon in 1805 and
1806.

It availed little. The French next occupied Civitavecchia, the
principal papal port on the west coast. In May 1806, Fesch went
to see the pope to ask him to be reasonable and do what
Napoleon asked. Pius, normally so easygoing, lost his temper
and shouted at Fesch.[7] Through Talleyrand, Napoleon again
demanded that the Holy See should enter into a permanent
alliance with France. It was intolerable for Napoleon, when he
dominated the whole Italian peninsula, to have in the middle of it
a little state which was not part of his system, which did not obey
his laws, which allowed the English fleet to visit its ports.
Consalvi sent a further negative response. The pope refused to
recognize or crown Joseph Bonaparte as King of Naples. He also

Cardinal Consalvi 1819 by Sir Thomas Lawrence

Pope Pius VII 1819 by Sir Thomas Lawrence

Medal of Cardinal Consalvi 1824 by Giuseppe Girometti

Plaster Bust of Domenico
Cimarosa by Antonio Canova

Marble Bust of Cardinal
Consalvi 1824 by Bertel
Thorwaldsen

Cardinal Consalvi 1819 by
Sir Thomas Lawrence

Elizabeth, Duchess of Devonshire by Sir Joshua Reynolds

Pietradura snuff box bequeathed by Cardinal Consalvi to the Duchess
of Devonshire

Gateway at the Ponte Milvio, Rome

Palazzo della Consulta, on the Quirinal, Rome, Consalvi's official residence after the Restoration

Braccio Nuovo, Vatican

Monument to Cardinal Consalvi in the Pantheon in Rome, 1824,
by Bertel Thorwaldsen

refused to annul the marriage of Napoleon's brother Jerome to an American actress, Elizabeth Patterson. On their side the French, who had conquered Naples in February 1806, usurped the papal enclaves of Benevento and Ponte Corvo.

It was Fesch who was responsible for making public the quarrel between the French government and the Holy See. He disliked Consalvi and was temperamentally incapable of keeping a confidence. When a pastrycook was murdered by two Frenchmen in the Piazza Navona, Fesch publicly accused Consalvi of deliberately arranging the incident in order to stir up anti-French feeling among the Roman populace. Consalvi denied this ridiculous charge in an official note and demanded an apology. Before the courier reached Paris bearing the news of this demand, the papal refusal to recognize Joseph Bonaparte as King of Naples, the formal complaint at the occupation of Benevento and Ponte Corvo or Consalvi's negative reply to Talleyrand's note, Fesch was recalled from Rome to be replaced, as Napoleon had previously threatened, by a secular plenipotentiary, the regicide and ex-Jacobin, Charles Alcquier. Napoleon did not want his uncle, and a cardinal to boot, in Rome when he overthrew the temporal power. Fesch did not have the courtesy to take his leave personally of Consalvi in the customary manner, so Consalvi went to see him, but Fesch pretended not to be at home. On the morning of his departure, he sent a servant to Consalvi with his card, a deliberate snub.

With things come to this pass, Consalvi resigned as secretary of state on 17 June 1806, hoping that Napoleon would hold back if the person whom he held responsible for the papal resistance retired into private life. In the event nearly two years passed before Rome was occupied by the French army. A detachment of troops under General Miollis entered the city on 2 February 1808, but even then the Papal States were not immediately dismantled, and when the Marches and Umbria were added to the Napoleonic kingdom of Italy, the papal flag still flew in Rome. After Consalvi's resignation, the pope left the post of secretary of state vacant and appointed Cardinal Pacca as pro-secretary to help with the administration of affairs.

Pacca was far more intransigent than Consalvi; he had been against any policy of rapprochement with Napoleon from the start. In September 1808, Miollis tried to arrest the cardinal at his room in the Quirinal, but the pope appeared, his hair standing on end like an angry dog; Miollis retired and Pacca was rescued. From then on the pope was more or less a prisoner in the Quirinal, though he had a printing press and continued to issue pamphlets publicizing the French aggression against the Holy See, and the papal point of view, till Miollis closed it down. By then the sentence of excommunication against those who seized Rome had already been printed, ready for when it should be required. On 17 May 1809, Napoleon published a decree that the remainder of the Papal States were to become part of his empire and Rome was to be an imperial city. On 10 June 1809, the papal flag was lowered from the Castel S. Angelo and replaced by the French tricolour, while the pope in the Quirinal on the hill opposite, murmured '*Consummatum Est*' and signed the sentence of excommunication. Before night fell the same day, it was pasted on the walls of the great basilicas. It excommunicated everybody responsible for the occupation of the Papal States 'however high in rank'. Thus, although it did not name Napoleon explicitly, it was obviously aimed at him.

News of the excommunication reached Napoleon just before the battle of Wagram, and he immediately ordered the arrest of Cardinal Pacca. General Radet, the second-in-command to Miollis, decided on his own initiative to kidnap the pope and send him to France. On 6 July, with a band of soldiers, he broke into the Quirinal and smashed open door after gilded door along the enfilade of state rooms leading to the Hall of Audience where the pope was waiting on his throne, dressed in white robes and flanked by Cardinal Pacca and Cardinal Despuig. Radet hesitated for an instant – 'When I saw the pope, at the same moment, I saw myself once more at my first communion' – then rallied and Pius was taken to a waiting carriage. There followed a nightmare journey in hot weather over the Alps to France. Napoleon did not want Pius on French territory, so he was taken back again to Savona on the Italian side and confined there in the former bishop's palace, while Cardinal Pacca was incarcerated in the Fenestrelle in Savoy, the great fortress used for political prisoners. The papal government was dismantled, the cardinals and archives taken to France.

In his confinement at Savona, the pope lived simply in a little room, doing his own washing and mending, spending his days in prayer, meditation, reading, and taking snuff. He proved too humble to break; and to Napoleon's surprise, continued his policy of non-cooperation, refusing to invest new bishops as French sees fell vacant. For the pope, it was a return to his old life as a Benedictine monk, and he was content.

After his resignation as secretary of state, and while these momentous affairs were drawing to their inevitable conclusion, Consalvi occupied himself in his role as Prefect of the Signature, dealing with the routine business of that court of law, and at the Ospizio di S. Michele a Ripa, of which he was now the protector. He continued to be dogged by personal tragedy. His old friend and benefactor, Cardinal York, well advanced in years, died on 15 July 1807. Consalvi was left as joint executor of his will. The bequest of 6,000 scudi had not been revoked, but he still turned it down, taking only a small annuity of 150 scudi in memory of his early protector and patron. A much worse blow was the death of his beloved brother Andrea. It was the greatest sadness of his life and tears came into his eyes whenever he recalled his brother's loss for years afterwards. They had always been the closest of friends. Andrea was modest, disinterested, well-meaning, courteous and cultivated; in Consalvi's own words, 'my only consolation and happiness'. He had sat beside his brother's sickbed continuously throughout the sixty days of Andrea's last illness, and was holding his hand when he died. Consalvi made a solemn promise that just as they were united in life, so it would be in death, they would be buried in the same tomb. He kept his word, and cardinal and marchese lie together in a marble sarcophagus at S. Marcello in the Corso. The death of his brother, even more than the ruin of his country, extinguished Consalvi's zest for life; his existence was nothing but a succession of sadness and disasters, or so it seemed then and for a number of years to come.

For five months after the removal of the pope, Consalvi and six or seven other cardinals remained in Rome, leading a twilight existence. The French liked and respected him personally, and he them. The general-in-chief of the army, Miollis, was the brother of an *émigré* priest, now a bishop, whom Consalvi had befriended when he was in exile in Rome in the 1790s, but, as a cardinal, he did not feel that he could fraternize with the French, and refused all social invitations from them. Murat, who had succeeded Joseph as King of Naples, was another old friend and was mortified when Consalvi refused to greet him on a visit to Rome. Consalvi took his stand on principle further. The French government had passed an edict that any man under sixty must join the National Guard or make a financial contribution. As the only cardinal under sixty, Consalvi alone among the members of the Sacred College met the qualifications. Though he could easily afford the levy, he refused to contribute to an occupying force. The French had with kindly intentions asked him to stay on at the Ospizio di S. Michele a Ripa, and this put him in a quandary. As an economy measure he had left the post of deputy empty and run the place single-handed. The Ospizio housed 700 or 800 individuals; he did not want to plunge them into anarchy. After careful consideration, however, he called the heads of all the different sections of the hospice and entrusted each of them with the running of their own department. He then sent his resignation to the French commandant of Rome on 20 June: 'The pope having been deprived of his temporal government, a cardinal cannot continue to serve another regime.'[8]

The French authorities were beginning to be worried by his behaviour and the steady example of non-cooperation which he was setting. On 21 November, a letter arrived from Paris ordering him in the name of the emperor to proceed there at once. He replied that he could not leave Rome without the pope's permission. Miollis tried to get him to modify the tone of his letter; at least to feign ill-health as an excuse for not going. He refused. On 8 December, a second letter arrived from Paris peremptorily ordering him to leave within twenty-four hours. Again, he replied that he could not without the pope's permission. The twenty-four hours expired, and on 10 December he was woken by a troop of French soldiers. The officer in charge commanded him to leave at once under military escort. Cardinal di Pietro, the Latin patriarch of Jerusalem, and a strong opponent of Napoleon, was escorted out of Rome at the same time; he and Consalvi travelled together. The French army left them a few miles north of Rome, but at least they had the satisfaction of not having left the city voluntarily. Their self-respect was intact; and Consalvi could continue his policy of courteous non-cooperation in Paris. The two cardinals did not hasten on their way. They took two days to reach Terni and, travelling via Cesena, Turin, and Lyons, did not arrive in Paris till 20 February 1810, to join the other cardinals already resident there.*

Consalvi took a little apartment in the Rue de Lille and lived quietly there, refusing to play any part in French social life. This was more of a deprivation for him than for many of the other cardinals, for he had been to Paris before, for the Concordat, and was known to the imperial family, the leading figures in the government, as well as several of the foreign ministers resident in the city. All these people were pleased to see him, but he consistently refused their invitations. The pope, before he was taken from Rome, had given orders that the cardinals must not accept invitations to dinners or receptions from the French but even without that instruction, he would not have felt it decent, as a member of the papal government, to accept hospitality from those who had imprisoned his sovereign and conquered his country. In this he was in a minority. Only Cardinals Pignatelli, Saluzzo and di Pietro shared his feelings on the point and held themselves aloof. All the other cardinals decided that the pope's instructions had only been intended to apply in Rome; now that they were in Paris, they enjoyed themselves dining out and going to parties. It may have been this weakness which was the cause of Consalvi's low opinion of his colleagues in the Sacred College,

*Torlonia lent him the money for the journey and for his expenses in Paris. Altogether, his exile cost him 2,153.44 scudi. The expenses of the journey to Paris came to 825.16 scudi, his carriage and subsistence in France 561.06½ scudi, and the return journey to Italy, 767.21½ scudi.[9]

and contributed to the barely concealed contempt with which he treated them during his second ministry. With his natural courtesy, Consalvi did not decline invitations brusquely, but replied firmly and consistently that his health obliged him to dine at home.

The French government had offered all the cardinals on their arrival in Paris a pension of 30,000 francs to compensate for the loss of their benefices and other incomes in Rome. The majority had accepted with alacrity. Consalvi, Pignatelli, Saluzzo and di Pietro discussed the problem among themselves, and agreed that their personal convictions and the pope's instructions forbade them to accept the pension. Pignatelli and Saluzzo went to the Ministry of Cults to decline in person. Consalvi put his refusal in writing, stressing the point which he had already made in Rome that deference to the wishes of the pope, as well as his own sentiments, prevented him from accepting any largesse from the French government. Consalvi and his three confederates became the nucleus of a peaceful resistance movement among the cardinals in exile; and as the months passed, several others joined them. Irritated though Napoleon was by this, he could not help but admire Consalvi's scruples, his steadfastness and his courage. He had formed a good impression of him when they had first met over the negotiations for the Concordat. Subsequently, during the struggle between French militarism and papal neutrality, Napoleon had become increasingly angry with the papal secretary of state, and thought he must have lost his head. This was partly a result of the slanted reports of Consalvi's behaviour which Cardinal Fesch had sent back. Now, emperor and cardinal were to meet again.

Six days after his arrival in Paris, Consalvi, with four other recently arrived cardinals, was received in audience by Napoleon. They were arranged in a semi-circle according to seniority, and Napoleon had a word with each of them in turn. Consalvi, the youngest, came last. Before he could be presented, Napoleon said, 'Oh, Cardinal Consalvi, you have grown thin. I hardly recognized you.' Consalvi replied, 'Sire, the years accumulate. It is ten years since I had the honour to greet Your

Majesty.' 'It is true,' said Napoleon. 'It is nearly ten years since you came for the Concordat. We signed that in this same room. All is gone up in smoke. Rome wishes everything to be lost. If you had continued in your post, things would not have gone so far.' 'Sire, if I had remained in that post I would have done my duty.' Napoleon did not answer directly, but continued in a monologue to the clerical semi-circle in general, elaborating on the grief that had followed the pope's refusal to enter his system. Returning to Consalvi, he repeated, 'No, if you had remained in your post, things would not have come to this pass.' Consalvi replied, 'Your Majesty knows well that I would have done my duty.' Napoleon said again, this time to Cardinal di Pietro at the other end of the line, 'If Cardinal Consalvi had remained secretary of state, things would not have gone so far.' Consalvi could not let that pass. He left his place and went up to the emperor and repeated: 'Sire, I have already affirmed to Your Majesty that if I had remained in that post I would assuredly have done my duty.' The emperor said, 'Oh, I repeat, your duty would not have allowed you to sacrifice the spiritual to the temporal.'[10]

Consalvi was perhaps the only man in Europe who dared to disagree with Napoleon to his face. It is on such exchanges that a number of, perhaps apocryphal, stories of his witty retorts to the emperor have been based. Napoleon is supposed to have said to him deprecatingly on one occasion, 'Is it not true, Cardinal Consalvi, that all the Italians are thieves and liars?' Consalvi is credited with the reply in Italian, 'Oh no, sire, not all, just the greater part.' (*'la buona parte'*, i.e. Bonaparte.) Or on another occasion: 'Do you not realize that, if I wished, I could destroy the Church?' 'Your Majesty, even we clerics have not managed that in nearly 2,000 years.'

Consalvi's policy of non-cooperation came to a head over Napoleon's marriage to Marie-Louise of Austria, and split the cardinals down the middle between the collaborators and the resistance, nicknamed respectively 'Les Rouges' and 'Les Noirs'. In 1810, Napoleon was at the height of his power and was determined to found a dynasty. Josephine had not borne him a son, so she was to be divorced and a new marriage made with a great royal house. He asked the Emperor of Austria for the hand of his daughter, the Archduchess Marie-Louise. Metternich agreed. The French Civil Code allowed divorce and the senate annulled Napoleon's marriage to Josephine by civil act. The pope could not accept this. In the eyes of the Church, Napoleon's marriage to Josephine was indissoluble, and there were no irregularities that would give grounds for an annulment. The pope knew well that Josephine and Napoleon had been married in church by Cardinal Fesch the day before the coronation, because it had been done at his own specific request when he had learnt that they had only been married previously in a civil ceremony. Consalvi was certain therefore that according to ecclesiastical law the proposed marriage to Marie-Louise was illegal. In his eyes it was a clear-cut issue and he had no doubts as to where his duty lay.

Of the other cardinals, Caprara was dying and not in a fit position to decide anything, while Fesch did not count as he was merely Napoleon's mouthpiece. Twelve of the stouter-hearted supported Consalvi. The rest were prepared to collaborate. Consalvi told Fesch that the Church could not recognize the emperor's marriage to Marie-Louise, and Fesch reported this to Napoleon. At the next audience, Napoleon was icy towards Consalvi and merely gave him a ferocious glare, while talking pleasantly to Cardinal Doria, to make it clear that it was Consalvi with whom he was angry. The wedding was due to take place at the beginning of April, and Consalvi and his colleagues were determined not to attend, whatever the consequences. Their duty was to uphold the rights of the pope and not to sanction an illegal marriage by their presence. Cardinal Mattei was deputed to explain courteously to Fesch that the thirteen could not attend the wedding. Fesch broke the news to Napoleon and suggested inviting only those cardinals who could be relied upon to turn up on the day. Napoleon would not accept this: they must all be invited; they must all attend. He did not believe that the protesters would dare to stay away if it came to the crunch. When the invitations arrived, it became clear that there were to be four separate functions, only two of which were marriage ceremonies; the other two were formalities of court etiquette. The dissident faction decided that they would attend the latter in the hope that it might soften the blow to Napoleon's feelings, and make clear that there was no ill-will involved, simply a matter of principle. The first ceremony was the presentation of Marie-Louise at St Cloud. The second was the civil marriage at St Cloud. The third was the religious ceremony at the Tuileries, and the last a reception at the Tuileries for the *grand corps d'Etat*. If the dissident cardinals attended the first and fourth it would give the emperor the opportunity to pass over their absence from the two marriage services as if it were an accident. Consalvi did not believe that it was in Napoleon's interest to make a great fuss in public.

At the St Cloud reception on Saturday, 31 March, Fouché, the minister of police, who was an old acquaintance from Concordat days, led Consalvi into a corner and spent half an hour trying by every species of flattery and cajolement to dissuade him from his proposed course of action. 'You mark well,' he said, 'you made the concordat; you were the prime minister; you are well known and above all so well-esteemed that it will be awful if you are seen to be among the absent. The emperor will be more furious with you than all the rest.' Consalvi thanked him for his well-intentioned advice, but remained firm. When the cardinals were presented to Napoleon and Marie-Louise, the emperor was specially affable in the hope of softening them. 'Ah, here are the cardinals,' he said cheerfully, as he presented them to Marie-Louise, and of Consalvi, 'He is the one who made the Concordat.'[11]

The civil marriage took place at St Cloud on Sunday. The thirteen cardinals stayed away, and three others pretended to be ill, reducing the sacred college to a minority attendance of ten.*

---

*Absent from St Cloud: Consalvi, Mattei, Pignatelli, della Somaglia, Litta, Ruffo-Scilla, Saluzzo, di Pietro, Gabbrielli, Scotti, Brancadoro, Galeffi, Opizzoni. 'Ill': Bayonne, Despuig, Dugnani. Dying: Caprara. Attended: Doria, Spina, Caselli, Fabrice, Ruffo, Zondadari, Vicenti, Erskine, Roverella, Maury. At the Tuileries, Bayonne attended, but Erskine stayed away.

The religious service in the Tuileries on Monday was conducted with immense pomp and Cardinal Fesch, as grand almoner, performed the marriage service. Seats were provided for all the cardinals. When the emperor entered the chapel, he looked at the cardinals' places and noticed their absence even though the gap had been made less conspicuous by the hurried removal of the empty chairs at the last moment. The emperor went purple with rage, and the look that flashed across his face frightened those who saw it.

The reception at the Tuileries took place two days later. All the cardinals turned up in full dress of scarlet robes as requested on the invitation. They spent two hours in the ante-rooms before the doors of the throne room were thrown open and the '*defilé*' began. The senate, council of state and legislative corps went first. When the master of ceremonies called the cardinals, Consalvi saw the emperor send an official down from the throne. He came to the ante-chamber and announced that Napoleon would not receive those cardinals who had boycotted the wedding service. They were all turned out of the palace, to find that their carriages had gone and they had to walk home in their cumbersome robes and trains.

The emperor fumed and raged about the offending cardinals, and in his memoirs Consalvi later recorded Napoleon's own comments. He particularly blamed Opizzoni and Consalvi. The others, he believed, were narrow-minded theologians and could be partly excused on that count, but he would never forgive Opizzoni and Consalvi. He had made the former Archbishop of Bologna, and it was intolerable that he should be so ungrateful. As for Consalvi, he was the worst of the lot. He was not a theologian, he was a man of the world: his only motives must be pride and hatred. He had boycotted the wedding as an act of revenge against Napoleon whom he held responsible for his downfall as prime minister. The cardinal was a profound diplomat, the emperor would say that for him. He knew how to hit where it hurt. His protest was the most calculated and most serious that could possibly have been made. It was a blow against the emperor's dynasty, it was intended to taint his heirs with illegitimacy. As he came out of the chapel, Napoleon had given orders for three of the cardinals to be shot, Consalvi, Opizzoni and di Pietro. Subsequently, he narrowed the order down to Consalvi only. Consalvi owed the non-execution of this sentence to the intervention of Fouché, who dissuaded the emperor from so drastic a course of action, but the culprits were left in suspense for a couple of days, awaiting their fate.

The following Wednesday at eight o'clock, they each received a short note ordering them to present themselves at the Ministry of Cults in an hour's time. When they arrived, they found Fouché there. He said to Consalvi, 'Ah well, Monsieur le Cardinal, I predicted that the consequences would be awful. It gives me great pain to see you among the number of the victims.' The cardinals were then given a long lecture on the heinousness of their conduct by the Minister of Cults. They had committed a crime against the state. They were guilty of *lèse-majesté*. They had put in doubt the legitimacy of the succession to the throne. Then the sentence was read. All their goods were confiscated. They were deprived of their insignia as cardinals. The fate of their persons was to be decided by the emperor.

Most of the cardinals did not have a good enough grasp of French to understand what was being said and Consalvi therefore replied on behalf of them all. There had been no conspiracy. Secret plots and rebellion were inconsistent with their dignity as cardinals. They had told Fesch of their intended action beforehand, so their conduct could hardly be described as underhand. Their duty as cardinals forced them to uphold the rights of the Holy See.

The minister was favourably impressed by this speech and advised them to write to the emperor explaining their motives. Consalvi wrote a letter and it was signed by all thirteen cardinals. The emperor, however, left for St Quentin before it could be delivered. They were ordered to comply with the previous order and were deprived of their cardinals' robes, reverting to simple clerical black. This was the origin of their nickname of 'les Noirs', as opposed to 'les Rouges' who were still able to wear red robes. Having lost their property, they were dependent on the bounty of friends. Two months and several days passed during which they waited for the execution of the third part of the sentence, while rumours and counter-rumours went the rounds. On 11 June 1810, they were summoned once more to the Minister of Cults, admitted two by two into his presence, and notified of banishment to different places in France. Consalvi was exiled to Rheims. They were offered a sum of money for their expenses. Consalvi refused and lived on alms and the remnant of his banker's draft from Torlonia in Rome. He occupied his time at Rheims writing his memoirs, going over the past and planning the programme of reforms he intended to implement, should there ever be a papal restoration in the future.

As a result of the pope's policy of peaceful resistance and his refusal to invest new bishops appointed by Napoleon, twenty-seven French sees were lying vacant by 1811 and the problem was becoming urgent. Whenever it was suggested to the pope that something should be done, he gave the same reply. He could not run the Church without the advice of his chosen councillors, the imprisoned and exiled cardinals. As soon as he was restored to Rome, and surrounded by the Sacred College, he would deal with the vacant bishoprics. Finally, the Austrian Chancellor, Metternich, intervened and suggested to Napoleon that Lebzel-tern should be sent as an envoy to negotiate. Napoleon agreed. Lebzeltern got on well with the pope and they had a long and friendly discussion at Savona. The pope was prepared to forgo the temporal power if he were allowed to return to Rome with the cardinals and was left free to administer the religious aspect of his sovereignty, assisted by Consalvi and Pacca. Napoleon would not accept that the pope should return to Rome. He next sent a deputation of 'red cardinals', but Pius gave them a frigid reception and they returned empty-handed to Paris. Napoleon's patience snapped. As he could get nowhere with the pope, from now on he would do without him. The vacant sees would be filled with 'vicars capitular', beginning with Maury in Paris.

Instructions were sent to Savona that Pius was to be kept out of the public view and more closely confined. His papers, pen, writing desk and servants were all taken away, and access to him forbidden. Napoleon hoped that stricter seclusion would break the pope's spirit, but he had not made allowance for the prisoner's self-reliance. The pope's health did, however, begin to deteriorate under the stress of his confinement. In Paris, Napoleon summoned a great council of bishops, but it refused to operate without the pope. A further deputation was sent to Savona in September 1811, comprised of four bishops and four cardinals, and this time Pius was talked into allowing the metropolitans to invest new bishops if he failed to do so himself within six months. This capitulation by the pope was due to spiritual considerations, bishops being necessary for confirmations and ordinations. Napoleon, much to the delegates' surprise, refused to accept the pope's compromise, and by his intransigence he ruined the chance of a settlement that would have meant much to him, breaking off negotiations on 7 February 1812, and ordering the delegates back to Paris through the winter snow of the Alps. It was the greatest mistake of his whole ecclesiastical policy. He now regarded the Concordat as abrogated throughout his empire; just at the moment that he needed the loyalty of the strongly Catholic Poles to guarantee his supply lines for the Russian campaign.

Afraid that during his absence in Eastern Europe the British fleet might try to rescue the pope, Napoleon gave orders for him to be transferred secretly to Fontainebleau. Dressed in black like a simple priest, his white slippers dyed with ink, Pius was moved from Savona under cover of night. For ten days after he had left, the pretence was kept up that he was still there and meals were served in his empty room at regular intervals. Despite poor health, he was rushed over the Mont Cenis and across France. At Fontainebleau, he was given the rooms he had occupied at the time of Napoleon's coronation. There he waited for the return of the emperor.

It was a different Napoleon who returned from Moscow. He had suffered his first major defeat and the Grand Army had been destroyed. He now needed to patch up his quarrel with the pope, and wrote to Pius courteously in his own hand for the first time in six years, asking to see him. They spent several days in discussions at Fontainebleau. The details are not known, but Napoleon wanted the papacy established in Paris and two thirds of the cardinals nominated by 'the Catholic sovereigns', that is, himself. The pope refused, but agreed to a new concordat, ending the differences between them, providing that the 'black cardinals' were set at liberty. The agreement was announced on 6 February 1813 and *Te Deums* were sung in Paris. The 'red cardinals' were given the cross of the Legion of Honour; the 'black cardinals' were given their freedom and allowed to join the pope at Fontainebleau. Even Pacca was released from the Fenestrelle, and he and Consalvi arrived together at Fontainebleau on 18 February, to find that the pope had given way over the investiture of bishops and virtually yielded the temporal power.

Napoleon, having promised to keep the details secret, published the text of the pope's agreement in the newspapers. Consalvi was horrified and advised Pius to retract the whole thing immediately, on the grounds that it had been extracted by force. He suggested that he and Pacca had better attend one of the emperor's receptions at the Tuileries in order to prepare him for the shock of hearing of the pope's retraction.[13]

When the emperor received the pope's letter, he shouted, 'So much for papal infallibility.' But there was little that he could do now, for time had run out. The French had been defeated in Spain by Wellington, Napoleon's father-in-law, the Emperor of Austria, had joined England, Russia and Prussia and started to mobilize his army, and the end was in sight. However, Napoleon gave orders for the 'black cardinals' to be exiled once more and Consalvi was taken under armed escort to Béziers while Napoleon hurried away to the east with a vast new army of 400,000 men, mainly raw recruits. Taking his stand at Leipzig, he was overwhelmed and his army smashed at the Battle of the Nations. When he recrossed the Rhine, it was with a mere 40,000 men and, in December 1813, France itself was invaded.

Murat in Naples abandoned Napoleon, signed a secret treaty with Metternich and marched on Rome, driving out General Miollis and the French army of occupation. Napoleon proposed at this point that the pope should be restored to Rome; at least it would help to keep Murat at bay. Consalvi, who was already in touch with Metternich, advised Pius not to deal with Napoleon, but to wait for the Allies and so Pius sent Napoleon his standard negative reply; he could not negotiate till he was restored to liberty and surrounded by the Sacred College. On 30 March, Paris surrendered to the Russians; they were met by Talleyrand, who had changed sides once more. A few days later, Napoleon abdicated and the Allies announced the restoration of the Bourbons. The pope, who had been sent south from Fontainebleau, found himself freed by the sudden rush of events, and travelled on to Parma, within the Austrian lines, while Consalvi hurried after him. They met at Cesena, the pope's birth-place, and there Consalvi was restored as secretary of state on 17 May 1814.

In the midst of the celebrations Consalvi learnt that his old enemy, Monsignor Della Genga, the Nuncio Extraordinary in Paris, was mishandling negotiations over the future of the Papal States, and decided to go there himself to treat with the Allies in person. He took his leave of the pope, who continued southwards with Cardinals Pacca and Mattei to Rome, arriving on 24 May to an ecstatic reception of triumphal arches, Latin messages of welcome, genuflecting crowds, and all the trappings of glorious counter-revolution. Consalvi sped north, armed with a papal denunciation of the Treaty of Tolentino together with detailed instructions, which he had drafted himself. He was to demand the full restoration of the Papal States; Della Genga's mission was cancelled; the nuncio was to take his orders from the secretary of state.[14]

Neither the pope nor Consalvi were ever to see Napoleon again, but by a strange twist of fate, Consalvi and the ex-emperor had encountered each other briefly at Fréjus in the south of France as their journeys crossed, one heading from Béziers to Italy and freedom; the other to Elba and exile. They had not spoken, but Napoleon turned to the person who was with him in the carriage and pointed to Consalvi saying, 'There, that man, who would never become a priest, is a better priest than them all.'[15]

V

The Congress of Vienna

CONSALVI'S contemporary renown as one of the greatest statesmen of Europe was derived above all from his brilliant performance in 1814 and 1815 in Paris, London and Vienna. Castlereagh's admiring verdict was that 'he was the master of us all in diplomacy'. In a single year of constant travel, meetings and complicated negotiations, he single-handedly secured the restoration of the Papal States and temporal power, as well as extending the concordat system between the papacy and other European governments, and laying the foundations for Catholic emancipation in the United Kingdom. It is an amazing achievement, the more so when it is remembered how few cards he held and how poorly the papacy had fared at successive peace treaties over the previous hundred years. He was merely a supplicant to the great powers and possessed few bargaining counters, apart from the legitimacy of his claims, the respect in which his master Pius VII was held, and his own skill and personality. Of the four victorious allied powers, only Austria was Catholic. Russia was Orthodox and Prussia and Britain, of course, were Protestant, the latter in particular having a long history of anti-papal prejudice. By his conduct, however, the pope had won universal admiration which cut across all religious differences. He alone among the continental European sovereigns had the distinction of having continuously resisted 'the tyrant', and of having entered Napoleon's political system at no stage. His kidnapping and imprisonment and his steadfastness in exile had won him the affection and respect of the world.

Banking on this generalized goodwill, Consalvi set about the most difficult task of his career. He faced huge problems. Metternich had already done a secret deal with Murat, promising him the papal enclaves and the Marches in return for Neapolitan support against Napoleon. Metternich wanted to keep the Legations either for Austria, or for the Arch-Duchess Marie-Louise. The Treaty of Paris confirmed Louis XVIII in possession of Avignon and the Vatican art treasures in the Louvre, because the Allies did not want to do anything which would humiliate the French and make the restored Bourbon monarchy unpopular. Tsar Alexander of Russia wished to reconstitute Poland under the Russian umbrella, and to compensate Prussia with Saxony, and Austria with a new empire in Italy for giving up their shares.

England, on the other hand, favoured the restoration of the Papal States since she preferred the European continent to be divided into small units rather than hegemonic powers, and Consalvi set to work to turn this goodwill into positive help. He was reinforced in his course of action by his love for England and the English, which had originated in his youth with the friendship of Cardinal York. On their side, the English felt to some extent obliged to the pope as their constant ally: the ruin of the Papal States had resulted directly from the refusal of the Holy See to close its ports to British ships. Lord William Bentinck, the British minister to Naples, expressed English opinion when he wrote on 1 April 1814, stressing the need 'to restore without delay the Sovereign Pontiff to his throne. The cruel sufferings of this venerable personage, combined with his extraordinary virtues and firmness, have excited, as we have seen, the greatest enthusiasm . . . the conduct of the ruler of France in this respect has, more than any other aspect of his life, excited universal detestation.'[1] The English foreign secretary, Viscount Castlereagh, agreed: 'The sentiment and the will of my government is to put the pope at liberty . . . and to restore to him all his States; and in this all England has Catholic sentiments.'[2]

On his arrival in Paris in May 1814, Consalvi began by

circulating formal notes to the ministers of the allied powers. The Treaty of Paris had already been agreed and was signed on 30 May. It confirmed France in possession of Avignon, as Consalvi had feared. He issued a solemn protest: since the treaty had been made without reference to the Holy See, it could not prejudice its rights in any way. The Holy Father wanted the restoration of all his lands, not in a spirit of domination or self-interest, but because he considered them necessary to the welfare of the Church and the needs of the Faithful. The Holy See did not recognize as valid the Treaty of Tolentino which had relieved Pius VI of his richest states. It was the result of an unprovoked and illegitimate act of aggression against a weak and innocent country which had solemnly proclaimed its neutrality. Tolentino was an infringement of all human rights. A treaty which was the consequence of such an aggression was essentially null and void. Consalvi quoted Grotius and Wattel to support his argument. The restoration of the temporal sovereignty of the Roman pontiff in 1800 had not been the work of the government which had destroyed it; Pius VI had died in French captivity. There was no political treaty between his successor, Pope Pius VII, and the French. The Concordat had not dealt with temporal matters but was purely a religious document. Seizing on the terms of the Treaty of Paris, Consalvi pointed out that its wording implied that the Allies did not themselves recognize Tolentino, because they had seen it necessary to confirm the French in possession of Avignon.[3]

Consalvi decided to follow the allied sovereigns and statesmen to London, and to continue his campaign for the restoration of the Papal States there. He obtained a passport, dated 6 June 1814, from Sir Charles Stuart (later Lord Stuart de Rothesay), the new British ambassador in Paris.[4] A question arose as to what he should wear on formal occasions in England, where Roman ecclesiastical dress was forbidden by law. He decided, nevertheless, after careful deliberation, to appear as a full-dress cardinal in order to create a 'coup d'éclat' when addressing the Prince Regent and the other sovereigns and statesmen. The only contretemps on the journey was a surly customs officer at Dover who, to

Consalvi's dismay, confiscated on some arcane technicality the little portrait of his brother Andrea which he carried everywhere. However, this was later returned to him as a result of the direct intervention of the prime minister, Lord Liverpool.[5] Consalvi officially informed the foreign secretary, Viscount Castlereagh, of his arrival in London, and the reasons for his presence there. They had a brief but cordial encounter the following morning, before a cabinet meeting, and Consalvi explained that he had brought a letter from the pope to the Prince Regent thanking him for British support during the war and recommending to his government the interests of the Holy See. He also handed to Castlereagh his own summary of the views of the papal government. Castlereagh agreed to arrange for him an audience with the Prince Regent at Carlton House.

In the interval, Consalvi composed a note which claimed the restoration of all the Papal States, with a further vigorous protest against Tolentino and circulated it to Metternich (Austria), Nesselrode (Russia), Hardenberg (Prussia) and Talleyrand (France). He had an interview with Metternich, who was polite but evasive, and cordial meetings with both the Russian and the Prussian ministers, to whom he handed letters from the pope to their respective sovereigns, Tsar Alexander and King Frederick William. He spoke candidly of the pope's financial need to have his states restored so that he could 'sustain his dignity with decency'. Without the Legations, the richest provinces of the Papal States, none of the rest was economically viable. Umbria and the Marches were mainly mountains and the area around Rome itself was largely uncultivated waste and marsh. Only the Legations contained rich, flat, agricultural land and relatively prosperous towns. He also pointed out that Clement V had paid hard cash for Avignon in 1309, while the surrounding Venaissin had belonged to the papacy since 1228. The Allies had offered no financial compensation to the Holy See for the loss of Avignon. It was his view that France herself had torn up Tolentino when she had occupied the rest of the Papal States the following year. He played his only trump card: that it would weaken the claims of other sovereigns to have their territories restored to them if they denied to the pope his richest provinces.[6]

In addition to his main object of urging the restoration to the pope of his states, Consalvi had come to London empowered to discuss terms for Catholic emancipation in Britain and Ireland. The British government wished to come to an agreement on this tiresome matter which was one of the issues outstanding from the Act of Union with Ireland in 1800. Pius sent a reminder to Consalvi in London: 'You are not only charged with a great diplomatic mission, you are at the same time the Representative of the Vicar of Jesus Christ on earth', and asked him to bear in mind the English and Irish Catholics 'who for centuries and from generation to generation have suffered in their goods, their liberty and their rights in order to remain faithful to the ancient faith of their ancestors. You are the first Cardinal, since the reign of Elizabeth, who has obtained permission to set foot on British soil. This privilege obliges us not to close our ears to the cry of the persecuted.'[7]

The keenly anticipated interview with the Prince Regent took place at 3 p.m. on 1 July. Consalvi went in his full-dress cardinal's robes and stayed for half an hour. It is possible to see him and the prince together very clearly in the mind's eye, much as they appear in Lawrence's Waterloo Gallery portraits, against the sumptuous francophile interiors embellished with blue velvet and scarlet hangings and white and gold carvings recorded in Pyne's *Royal Residences*. Consalvi particularly admired the splendid crystal chandeliers and, when he was back in Rome, he furnished his own state rooms in the Palazzo della Consulta with glass chandeliers of English manufacture. The Prince Regent was at his most affable and gracious, while Consalvi was in the seventh heaven of anglophilia. They chatted and joked in French. 'Hush, hush, Cardinal tempter,' said the Prince Regent, 'when listening to you I seem to see Henry VIII and his daughter Elizabeth following me as avenging spirits.' The Prince Regent spoke warmly of his admiration for the pope. Consalvi replied that the Holy Father had a particular attachment to England. They talked about various topics including the freedom of the press, which Consalvi thought a bad thing. 'The Prince Regent gave me an historical picture of the Press in his country; he portrayed very clearly for me its advantages and disadvantages in that altogether exceptional kingdom.' Consalvi urged the restoration of the Papal States, and the Prince Regent gave his formal promise that his government would sustain the interests of the Holy Father at the forthcoming Congress in Vienna. Consalvi was reassured by this, and touched by the Prince Regent's kindness and affability. It emerged that the objects which Cardinal York had left to the prince in his will, and which had been deposited for safe-keeping at Florence had not yet arrived in London. They comprised the cross of St Andrew set with diamonds worn by Bonnie Prince Charlie in Edinburgh in 1745, a gold ring engraved with a cross which the Scottish kings had worn at their coronation, and the George worn by Charles I on the scaffold. Consalvi promised to look into the matter and to hasten their dispatch. He kept his word, and was able to let Castlereagh have a detailed memorandum about the subject when they met in Vienna in October.

Consalvi and the Prince Regent only met once, but on the strength of this encounter considered themselves good friends ever after. Apropos Consalvi, the Prince Regent later told the Duchess of Devonshire that 'he most particularly *liked* him besides the esteem due to his character and conduct and great talents'.[8]

The Cardinal had two further interviews with Castlereagh before he left London. One lasted for three-quarters of an hour, but the more important on 4 July lasted for one and a half hours and was a detailed follow-up to his discussions at Carlton House. He asked Castlereagh to support the papal territorial claims in Italy, and Castlereagh gave general, courteous assurances. They went into the emancipation question in some depth. One sticking point was the wording of the oath of loyalty to the Crown which the British and Irish Catholics would be required to take. The first compromise suggested by the English government had been turned down by Bishop Milner, the energetic and ultramontane Vicar-General of the

Midlands District,* and by all the Irish bishops. This had caused a split between the English Catholic laity, especially the gentry, who were Cisalpine in outlook and prepared to co-operate with the English government, and the more anti-British Irish clergy. Consalvi was tactful and prudent. He found Castlereagh positive and helpful. Indeed, he was pleasantly surprised when Castlereagh suggested that Rome should send an ecclesiastic to London to discuss the emancipation problem in detail. Castlereagh wanted an acceptable oath of fidelity, a say in the nomination of Catholic bishops and a royal 'exsequatur', or right of veto, on correspondence between the Holy See and the Catholics of the United Kingdom. Consalvi only felt strongly about the latter; the two former he thought could be arranged to the satisfaction of both parties. On his side, Castlereagh asked for the papacy's support for the British campaign to abolish the slave trade, especially in securing the compliance of Spain and Portugal who were the most active slavers among European powers. He gave Consalvi a copy of Wilberforce's French pamphlet denouncing the trade: *Lettre au Prince Talleyrand au sujet de la Trait des Nègres par William Wilberforce* (London 1814). Consalvi pledged the support of the Holy See to this great humanitarian and moral cause.[9]

Apart from his official business, Consalvi thoroughly enjoyed himself during his twenty-six-day stay in London and no doubt recalled the aptness of Cimarosa's opera *L'Italiano in Londra*. Ever since his youth, he had had a penchant for travel to new places, and now he found himself in a vast sprawling city without walls, very different from anything he had seen on the Continent, and one moreover where a large-scale programme of metropolitan improvements was in progress under the direction of John Nash. He admired particularly Repton's newly landscaped St James's Park, for gardening was one of his chief interests and he had been nursing for some time a project for creating a public park in Rome where none had existed hitherto. He also pursued

*The Catholic Church in England in the eighteenth century was divided into four districts with episcopal Vicars-General: London, the West, the Midlands, and the North.

his interest in music; London, then as now, being one of the principal centres for musical performance. It seems that he visited the Italian shops selling sheet music and musical instruments around Golden Square in Soho. He also attended the performance of a grandiose special piece for piano, orchestra and chorus by Luigi Ashioli in honour of the allied commanders and acquired a copy of the score and wrote on it in his own hand the name and address of the composer, 'Luigi Ashioli, 12 Great Pulteney Street'.[10] There were plenty of parties and celebrations to attend, including a spectacular fête with music, dancing, fireworks and temporary supper tents specially designed by John Nash in the garden of Carlton House with all the lavish extravagance of which the Prince Regent was capable.[11] Another high point was a ball at Burlington House for the allied sovereigns and statesmen. Consalvi kept the invitation as a memento for the rest of his life. It is a pleasantly incongruous document for an Englishman to come across in the archives of the *Propaganda Fidei* in Rome:

> The Members of White's Request the Honour of the Cardinal Consalvi's Company at Burlington House on Monday 20 June at Nine O'Clock To a Dress Ball.[12]

Consalvi made numerous friends in London society, many of whom were to visit him in Rome in due course; and it was with feelings of regret that he crossed the Channel once more on 7 July, going first to Paris and then to Vienna where the destiny of Europe was to be decided.

He spent the remainder of July and most of August in Paris, tackling various problems of Church organization in France following the Bourbon restoration, notably the rearrangement of bishoprics and the perpetuation of the Concordat. He also sat for a portrait sketch by Ingres in one of his rare spare moments. He left for Vienna on 20 August and arrived in the Austrian capital on 2 September 1814, his groundwork laid, but the real struggle to achieve his objects only just about to begin. He had secured the goodwill of England and made useful contact with Metternich, the Tsar of Russia and the King of Prussia. Consalvi's main worry at this stage was the ambiguous response from Austria with regard to the Legations, Metternich claiming that their eventual disposal involved a consideration of European-wide issues. Consalvi told him that the future well-being of the pope depended on their restoration. In Vienna Consalvi continued the policy he had evolved in Paris and London of working on the individual representatives one by one. He often dined with Castlereagh, and attended the evening parties which the Austrians arranged for the entertainment of the delegates. He and Castlereagh had a very useful meeting of two and a half hours on 11 October, at which they clarified the position on Catholic emancipation. Consalvi gave a general exegesis on papal infallibility and the technicalities of the pope's relations with non-Catholic powers. They then went over the three chief issues: the oath, the election of bishops, the registry of papal Bulls. Consalvi thought there need be no objection to the oath, providing that one phrase were further modified. On the question of bishops he suggested a compromise whereby the British government could issue a 'certificate of loyalty' to episcopal candidates before appointments were made by Rome. He thought this would be preferable, from the papal point of view, to Catholic bishops actually being chosen by lay Protestants. Castlereagh recorded that he did 'not of course enter into discussion of the Pope's powers', but agreed to the modification of the word 'indirectly' in the oath to make the wording more acceptable to Rome, and thought that certificates of loyalty for bishops were a good idea. Consalvi mentioned 'the expediency of Great Britain having always a Minister at Rome to manage Catholic concerns as the best manner by which the pope could understand the wishes of [the] Government and act accordingly without sacrificing Principles.'* With regard to state stipends for the clergy of Ireland, Consalvi suggested they should be in the form of a 'Dotation' to the Church from the British government rather than individual pensions. 'Bonaparte when he stipulated *with him*, for he made the Concordat, to give it in the form of Dotation, but that

---

*A sensible suggestion not adopted till the First World War.

contrary to what he had promised instead of Dotations he had granted Pensions.'[13] Consalvi referred the issue of the registration of Bulls back to Rome for consideration by theological experts in the curia, where the *zelanti* did their best to destroy the whole arrangement, just as the Irish did at the other end. Dublin saw Consalvi as a 'perfidious minister [who] is the mere agent of the British Government'. Daniel O'Connell thundered, 'Consalvi the Italian either betrayed or sold our Church to the British minister at Vienna, indeed the exact amount of his price is stated to be eleven thousand guineas. Though a Cardinal, this man is not a priest. He is a secular cardinal, just fit for any bargain and sale; right glad I presume, to have so good a thing to sell as the religion of Ireland.'[14] So, though many of the chief obstacles between the Holy See and the British government had been overcome in 1814, Catholic emancipation did not arrive in the United Kingdom till 1829, after the death of George III and under the brief premiership of the Duke of Wellington.

The opening of the Congress had been fixed for 1 October, but this was postponed and various sub-committees were set up to discuss different aspects of the European settlement and to achieve compromises between the ambitions of the different powers. Meetings and negotiations continued non-stop from October to February 1815 when a drafting committee was convened to draw up the final act, and Castlereagh was replaced by Wellington as the English representative. The council of ministers of the four allied powers plus Talleyrand, now an enthusiastic supporter of the Bourbons, met at Metternich's house in the mornings. The allied sovereigns gathered at the Hofburg in the afternoons. The evenings were devoted to entertainment. Consalvi's role in all this can be traced in meticulous detail from his letters to Cardinal Pacca in Rome.[15] The long negotiations with Murat's representatives about the occupation of the Marches, and those with Austria in the attempt to regain the Legations form the main parts of his correspondence in which the complex Italian situation is presented in all its stages of development.

Consalvi had his first meeting with Metternich at Vienna on

8 September. The Austrian chancellor explained his reasons for the conquest of Lombardy – to destroy Jacobinism and the growing nationalist enthusiasm in Milan for a united kingdom of Italy. Consalvi was encouraged to hope that the restoration of the Legations could be achieved because Austria's plans envisaged the rivers Po and Ticino as natural frontiers. Consalvi and Metternich also discussed Murat and the best way of getting him to hand over the Marches to the pope.[16] On 11 September, Consalvi had an audience with the Emperor Francis I, a morose and lonely man whose chief hobby was making his own sealing wax. Francis admitted that he did not want the Legations for himself, but wished to retain Austrian freedom of action with regard to their eventual disposal. Consalvi hinted at the severe actions which the pope was ready to take against those who seized the papal territories. The emperor nervously expressed his disapproval of excommunication, and grumbled about the pope's appointment of an administrator in the diocese of Venice without informing him in advance.[17] The news of the emperor's lukewarm attitude disheartened Pacca in Rome, but Consalvi had other things to occupy his mind; chiefly the negotiations with the Duke of Campochiero, Murat's representative from Naples, about the Marches.

The great powers, meanwhile, were squabbling over the future of Poland and the dismemberment of Saxony to compensate Prussia for the loss of its territories in Poland. The excuse for stripping the King of Saxony of his realm was that he had been still an ally of Napoleon's at the end: as Talleyrand said to the tsar who was denouncing the Saxon king as Napoleon's confederate: 'It is all a matter of dates, sire.' Consalvi thought the proposed dismemberment of Saxony immoral, and wanted to have nothing to do with it. He did not wish to be officially included in the main committee of the Congress, for he did not see it in the pope's interest for his representative's name to be appended to acts of manifest injustice. His own relations with the Russian mission were good and he had a satisfactory audience with the tsar himself who was going through one of his phases of religious enthusiasm and was full of praise for the pope. The tsar expressed a strong wish to visit Rome, and offered his support for the restoration of the Legations. Consalvi reported to Pacca: 'My audience with him was short but gracious and full of goodwill.'[18]

In the middle of November, Consalvi wrote to Pacca with advice on how to deal with the King of Naples so as not to prejudice the outcome of negotiations over the Marches:

I would not advise recognizing Murat. No matter what the advantages might be, this action would put us in a difficult position with those who do not recognize him [the majority]. On the other hand, I will certainly advise assuring Murat of the Holy Father's inaction in exchange for the immediate re-acquisition of the above-mentioned territories [the Marches, Benevento and Ponte Corvo] as the Holy Father has already been following this line without any gains.

   I must also add that there is always the possibility that the Congress will not be successful in achieving what we want. Therefore, if disagreements and delays are to be expected, we may find ourselves not only without the Legations, but also without the Marches. If some sort of agreement is reached at the Congress it may turn out to be a very unstable one. Should France and Spain be forced to accept a situation that they find unsatisfactory, they are bound to cause problems in the future. Austria, England and even Prussia are extremely concerned with Russia's growing power and acquisition of Poland. Thus a war is a distinct possibility. It seems clear to me that Murat can only gain from this situation which would make it difficult for any of the Powers to declare war on him. Thus it would be foolish not to take advantage of the opportunity of regaining the three provinces in exchange for the promise of inaction, particularly since the Holy Father could continue to claim the other territories [the Legations].'[19]

Consalvi continued to be worried about his official status at the Congress. Talleyrand was pressing for him to be included not just on the principal committee of the Congress, but at the head of it. The thought of this traditional position did not please him at all. It was his policy not to take part in those formal discussions which he considered unbecoming to the Holy Father and the Church. It was one thing for him to announce that he agreed or disagreed with plans already accepted by the other principal members, and to say that the pope had sent him to deal exclusively with the affairs of the Holy See. Such an answer given only once when the issues had been resolved might not be unacceptable. But to have to give the same answer several times a day would put him in an invidious position *vis à vis* those who might want his support and who would be displeased by such an evasive reply. It might make them unhelpful when it came to a consideration of the business of the Holy See. If he were to be given the honorary precedence, he would always be the first to speak and this would make it awkward for him as a supplicant to the other powers.[20]

Consalvi found Talleyrand's constant interference in his affairs exasperating. When Talleyrand told him casually that the Committee of Eight wanted to be free to give away the Legations if the European settlement required it, not necessarily to restore them to the pope, Consalvi in his annoyance felt like going straight to Metternich and telling him some home truths, such as the fact that the Holy See regarded the marriage of the emperor's daughter Marie-Louise to Napoleon to have been irregular, indeed bigamous. If the Austrians persisted with their plans to compensate the Archduchess for Napoleon's desertion with any of the pope's territory, they could expect the most solemn pronouncements in Rome on the subject of her marital status. But prudence prevailed and Consalvi kept these thoughts to himself. In fact, his next meeting with Metternich, on 18 November, proved highly satisfactory. The Austrian chancellor had come to the conclusion of his own accord that Murat must be dropped and the Papal Estates restored, as the territorial arrangement most likely to lead to a stable settlement in Italy. Metternich told Consalvi that Austria saw herself as the interested supporter of the Holy See in its attempts to regain the Legations. The reason for this sudden change of mind was Metternich's horror at the idea of a united Italy; such a new political arrangement would lead to the loss of all Austria's territorial gains in the late war. Nationalist enthusiasm seemed to be gaining ground in the Italian peninsula and was being enthusiastically supported by Murat who saw himself as monarch of the new united kingdom. Metternich decided, therefore, that Murat must be removed, and the Bourbons restored to the throne of Naples as soon as possible. The chancellor went as far as discussing in detail with Consalvi how he intended to make war against Murat. Furthermore, he was now happy to see the Archduchess Marie-Louise compensated with Parma, and a committee of three was to be set up to deal with the settlement of Parma and Piacenza. That left the problem of what to do with Marie-Louise of Bourbon, Queen of Etruria, who had been in control of Parma as consort of the previous ruler there. But no doubt something would turn up. Consalvi just hoped that the 'something' would not be part of the Legations. He need not have worried. In the final settlement she was given Lucca,[21] a small principality which had been occupied previously by Napoleon's sister, Elisa Bacciocchi.

By December 1814, the powers had come to an agreement over most of the major issues. Russia and Austria had settled their differences over Poland. Prussia was to be content with only part of Saxony and was to receive the Rhineland as well. Flanders was to be given to Holland to make one united kingdom in the Low Countries. In view of this general settlement, Consalvi opened discussions with representatives of the various German kingdoms about the ecclesiastical restoration in Germany. The prince bishoprics and all the other ecclesiastical paraphernalia of the Holy Roman Empire had gone for ever and the diocesan map of the whole of Germany needed to be redrawn. He began with Count Wintzingerode, the plenipotentiary of the King of Württemberg about arrangements there, and they sketched out together the framework of a concordat which was later adopted. He also negotiated with the ministers of Bavaria, Prussia and Switzerland on the same subject, and these, again, formed the basis for the post-1815 concordats with those countries. As with the pioneer modern Concordat with France, Consalvi's ground-work in Germany worked entirely to the advantage of the papacy. The Holy Roman Emperor and his privileges had gone, and all the new bishoprics would be directly responsible to the pope.

By the beginning of 1815, Consalvi was optimistic about the chances of getting back the Legations and the Marches for the pope. On 25 January, he wrote to Cardinal Pacca telling him that Metternich was sending Count Neippeng to Naples to demand the restitution of the Marches to the Holy See. Consalvi empha-sized to Pacca the importance of moderation at this stage, and on no account to consider excommunicating Murat.

Meanwhile he continued to cross swords with Talleyrand. At a party at the home of the Duke of Labrador (the Spanish envoy) in February, in front of many of the other ministers, Consalvi was criticized by the French contingent, first the duc de Noailles, then Talleyrand, concerning his intransigent attitude over Avignon and his refusal to sign the Treaty of Paris which had given it to France. Talleyrand hinted that such a recognition would be necessary to gain French support for the restoration of the Legations, and he was tactless enough to mention Tolentino, a subject which was always guaranteed to make Consalvi's hackles rise. The cardinal was furious and replied, 'You are the stronger. I came here with nothing and I shall return to Rome with nothing, that is to say without the Legations, but I will not sign. *We* do not part from our principles.' As for Tolentino, he did not consider it to be in any sense a valid treaty.[22] Talleyrand was anxious to ingratiate himself with his current master Louis XVIII and was, for the moment, more Bourbon than the Bourbons. For this reason, he was happy to see Murat deposed and Ferdinand IV restored in Naples, and he pressed Consalvi to get the pope to excommunicate Murat. When Consalvi refused, Talleyrand attacked him with sarcasm, in front of several of the other representatives, at Talleyrand's own house. Consalvi's replies, which were sensible and to the point, discomfited Talleyrand and gained the approval of everybody else. He could afford to take a more acerbic line towards the French minister, as he was now certain of Metternich's support. On 25 February, he sent a top secret dispatch to Pacca in which he told him that Austria had determined to effect Murat's downfall by armed force and to restore the Marches to the pope. He advised Pacca to keep this confidence to himself.[23]

This was the situation when Napoleon escaped from Elba and returned to Paris. The episode of the Hundred Days did the papal cause nothing but good. It revealed Pius VII's immense popularity. It hardened the Allies in their attitude towards France, now making it possible to secure the restoration of the looted Roman art treasures. Above all, it sealed the fate of Murat, and made certain the restoration of both the Marches and the Legations to the pope. In the event, Murat destroyed himself, by changing sides once more, abandoning the allied cause and supporting Napoleon. He marched on Rome, and Pius VII retreated to Genoa, from where he at last excommunicated Murat at the beginning of April 1815. The Austrian army in Lombardy marched south and met Murat at Tolentino, of all places; there his forces were defeated on 2 May. Murat fled to Corsica, a defeated and broken man.* The pope left Genoa and began the return journey to Rome the following day, 3 May. In Vienna, Consalvi was happy with the turn of events, for Russia, Prussia and England all supported his claim to the Legations. Metternich, too, was convinced that the restored Papal States would be useful to Austrian interests in helping to secure a stable settlement in Italy.

On 12 June, Consalvi wrote to Rome announcing complete victory. All the papal states had been restored, apart from Avignon which he accepted as a lost cause, and a small portion on the north side of the Po which had been given to Austria to strengthen her 'natural frontiers'. Consalvi modestly attributed his success to the prestige enjoyed by Pius VII. 'Without the immense personal reputation of the Holy Father – and the view that is held about his sanctity and his character – it would have been useless (and God knows, I do not lie or flatter in saying so),

*Returning to Naples in October 1815, he was captured, court-martialled and shot by the Bourbons.

I repeat useless to have made claim and negotiated, and cajoled; or at least we should have gained very little.'[24] On the same day, Metternich sent Consalvi copies of the four articles relating to the Holy See. According to Article I, the Marches, Camerino, Benevento and Ponte Corvo, the Legations of Bologna, Ravenna and Ferrara were all to be restored to the Holy See within four weeks. Article II specified that His Holiness would allow the passage of Austrian troops from Naples. Article III laid down that the papal archives relating to the administration of the restored territories would also be handed back to the pope. Article IV stated that the convention would be ratified within thirty days. According to a secret article, Austria was to be allowed to garrison the citadel of Ferrara and the Holy See was to compensate Austria for the costs of the campaign against Murat which had reconquered the papal states, amounting to 1,700,000 francs. The Holy See had also to pay financial compensation to Talleyrand, Prince of Benevento, for the loss of his principality.

In addition to his major task in Vienna, the restoration of the papal states, Consalvi was involved in several other issues. One was the matter of diplomatic precedence. The existing table of precedence between European countries had been laid down by the pope in the Middle Ages with himself first, the emperor second, then France followed by Spain. England came seventh, after Portugal but before Sicily, while the Duke of Ferrara was last. This, no doubt, accurately reflected the power stakes in the late fifteenth century, but by the late eighteenth was badly out of date. The dukedom of Ferrara had ceased to exist (it had reverted to the Papal States in 1598), Russia and Prussia had emerged as major powers, while Portugal and Spain had slipped to second-rate status. This had led to undignified struggles over points of national prestige, even on occasions to street brawls and duels. The precedence question was always used to delay serious discussion at the beginning of every peace treaty. The Congress of Vienna tried to clear up the problem once and for all. A committee was set up to consider the matter and spent two months in discussions. It first came up with a proposal to divide the powers into three classes, but this was objected to by the

lesser republics and principalities who did not wish to be relegated so publicly to the bottom end of the table. In the end, a
common-sense method was adopted whereby precedence was
granted according to actual seniority of the ministers present: a
minister's precedence would depend on the date of his appointment. This settled the problem of diplomatic precedence for a
hundred years.[25]

The new *règlement*, laid down at the Congress of Vienna,
finally ended all papal pretensions to the status of a great political
power. The century and a half since the Treaty of Westphalia in
1648 (which Consalvi had studied as the model of behaviour for
a papal diplomat at a great European congress) had seen a steady
waning of the political prestige of the papacy. Consalvi accepted
this as a *fait accompli*. He appreciated that there was no question
of a revival of the power of the sixteenth-century papacy. He
was happy to secure the financial and political independence
necessary to enable the pope to sustain his role with decency and
to preserve a state of neutrality. He had no wish to intervene in
the wider political destinies of Europe, or to act as a mediator
between the European powers as the papal representative had
claimed to do at Munster in 1648, or at Nijmegen in 1679,
though without success on the latter occasion. A residuary
longing for this power had been apparent still in the early
eighteenth century, but the French Revolution had finished it for
good. Consalvi accepted that such a privilege on the part of the
Holy See had gone. He was a realist; he did not fight lost battles.
He did not, for instance, seek to resurrect papal claims to Parma
and Piacenza as fiefs of the papacy when a committee of three
was set up to consider the future of those principalities.

The English government was determined that the Congress of
Vienna should endorse its campaign against the slave trade. On 8
February 1815, the powers made a joint declaration condemning
the slave trade, and it was appended to the final act of the Treaty
of Vienna. This left it to individual countries to choose their own
date for terminating the trade. Once again, Consalvi reassured
Castlereagh of what he had already told him in London: that the
pope's moral force would be used to encourage the more recalci-

trant Catholic nations to co-operate, and to end their part in the trade.[26]

Consalvi's main dealings with the English and Talleyrand at the end of his stay in Vienna were concerned with the retrieval of the Roman archives and works of art from Paris. The future of the artistic loot taken by the French from Italy did not form part of the official business of the Congress. Consalvi raised the issue on his own initiative in his informal discussions with the individual ministers. He had begun to work for the return of the Roman art and archives while in Paris in May and July 1814 when he had made a formal claim for the return of the papal archives, taken by General Radet in 1810 and deposited in the Hôtel Soubise. They were, Consalvi said, essential tools of the papal administration. He also wanted the French government to pay the costs of their repatriation. He summoned Marino Marini, the Vatican archivist, from Rome to Paris to continue the detailed negotiations while he himself was occupied in Vienna. Louis XVIII had agreed in principle that the papal archives should go back to Rome and offered the sum of 60,000 francs for the purpose in December 1814, but there remained the problem of what constituted the papal archives. The French had taken to Paris not just the administrative files of the Roman government, but important collections of historical documents from the libraries at Bologna, Loreto and other places in the Papal States, the botanic and mineral collections from the natural history museum at Bologna, and the coins, cameos, prints and rarest manuscripts from the Vatican library – such treasures as the Virgils, Council decrees of the early Church, the codices and the case against Galileo. Some of these precious things had been stuffed into sacks and carted away in 1799, some in 1810. They were now distributed in different places in Paris, some in the Archives Nationales at the Hôtel Soubise, some in the Archives du Louvre, some in the royal library at the Tuileries. While the French had agreed to restore 'the archives', their interpretation of what that term comprised was narrower than the Roman government's. They wished to keep all the special treasures and everything now housed in the royal palaces, including the Louvre.

Monsignor Marino Marini, on his arrival in Paris, took up residence at the Hotel d'Hambourg in the Rue Jacob and worked through the summer and autumn of 1814 to retrieve the archives and works of art. Consalvi sent him written instructions from Vienna from time to time. On 6 October 1814, Marini issued a formal protestation: 'The Roman Government pressed strongly by all the inhabitants of the City of Rome and also the Roman provinces for the return of all the objects of art taken by the French from the Roman state, addresses itself to all their Imperial and Royal Majesties of the Sovereign Allies and His Most Christian Majesty himself [Louis XVIII] to obtain amicably this object which is of the greatest interest to the country which claims it.'[27]

Consalvi, in his letters from Vienna, as well as giving instructions, reported the results of discussions on this subject with Talleyrand. In January 1815 he wrote instructing Marini about which documents were to be sent back first. He suggested the Archivii Segreti, the archives of the Propaganda and the Concilio, the Brevi Communi and the Brevi ad Principes as the most essential to the workings of the papal government.[28] The business dragged on all through 1815 and for a considerable time afterwards. It was not until 23 February 1816 that Consalvi was able to write to Marini, still in Paris, to express His Holiness's sovereign satisfaction at the retrieval of the archives, the codices, and the medals belonging to the numismatic cabinet of the Vatican library; offering him a pension of 120 scudi a year and a set of rooms in the apostolic palace for life. Even then, much remained in Paris. As late as 1817, Consalvi was still corresponding with the duc de Richelieu about the retrieval of the Galileo papers, and the archives of Cardinal Caprara who had been the papal nuncio in Paris at the time of the negotiations for Napoleon's coronation. In the end, nearly everything was returned to the Vatican, except for the antique gems which remain in the Louvre to this day.

Encouraged by Marini's initial success with the archives, Consalvi decided to send Canova to Paris to undertake similar on-the-spot negotiations with regard to the antique sculpture and other works of art taken after Tolentino. He wrote to Marini on 12 August 1815, announcing Canova's forthcoming arrival and sending a letter of introduction to Talleyrand who had just returned to Paris from Vienna.[29] The way had been opened for this further Roman offensive by the change in the mood of the Allies towards the French during the Hundred Days. The Prussians, after Waterloo, had entered the Louvre and removed their own works of art by armed force, and though Consalvi had no troops with fixed bayonets in Paris, he was hoping that Canova's international reputation as the greatest living sculptor, together with English backing, would have the same effect.

Canova arrived in Paris on 28 August. He faced a daunting problem, for the French were determined to hold on to the Roman works of art. However, English assistance was to make his task possible. Two centuries of the Grand Tour had given the English a special affection for the collections of Rome and they were anxious to see them restored. At first Canova was not sanguine about the possibilities of success. He wrote to Consalvi on 15 September, explaining the problems. The French were claiming that it was better for the art to be displayed in a properly lit and arranged picture gallery to serve as models for artists and students than to be scattered in innumerable churches and cloisters. They were also stressing the conservation issue; it was better for the pictures not to be exposed to candle smoke and incense.[29] In October Canova wrote again with slightly more promising news: 'Your Eminence already appreciates the difficulties from my previous letter.' He went on to explain how he had stressed the determination of the court of Rome to encourage the liberal arts, and that the sculpture taken by the French had, in fact, long been on display in public museums in Rome.[30] The decisive factor in achieving a successful outcome for Canova's mission was the intervention on his behalf of William Richard Hamilton, archaeologist, diplomat and under secretary of state for foreign affairs to Castlereagh in Paris, whom Canova regarded as his saviour. Hamilton was responsible for securing the all-important support of the Duke of Wellington. By the French logic of conquest, the works of art now belonged to the

Prince Regent who waived any such rights in favour of the pope. The Duke of Wellington was eager to see the collections returned to their true owners for if the treasures of sculpture and art were left in France 'They must necessarily have the effect of keeping up the remembrance of their former conquests, and of cherishing the military spirit and vanity of the Nation', he wrote to Lord Liverpool. Wellington developed his views in a letter to Castlereagh on 23 September 1815: 'The Allies ... could not do otherwise than restore them to the countries from which, contrary to the practice of civilised warfare, they had been torn during the disastrous period of the French Revolution and the tyranny of Bonaparte ... Neither has it appeared to me to be necessary that the Allied Sovereigns should omit the opportunity to do justice and to gratify their own subjects in order to gratify the people of France.'

Wellington's view was decisive in swinging allied opinion to the papal cause. On 1 October, Castlereagh reported to Lord Liverpool: 'Canova was made happy last night by Austria, Prussia and England agreeing to support him in removing the pope's property. The joint order is issued, and he begins tomorrow.' Consalvi, now back in Rome, was thrilled by the news. He gave Canova all the credit, but it was a clever stroke of diplomacy on his part to have sent the famous artist, rather than a prelate or cardinal to negotiate in Paris. It freed the issue from any clerical taint, kept it on purely artistic ground, and it showed admirable foresight and tact. Canova started packing on 2 October 1815. Not everything was taken back to Rome. Some very large statues like the Tiber, Augustus and Melopomena were left in the Louvre. But all the most famous statues and pictures were returned. The British fleet provided transport by sea from Antwerp to Civitavecchia in the storeship, HM *Abundance* and the British also paid all the expenses of packing and transporting the Roman works of art, amounting to 200,000 francs. The pope as a token of gratitude sent the Prince Regent a cup of Rosso Antico and a little model temple.

The statues arrived back in Rome at the beginning of 1816 after an absence of nearly twenty years. Canova himself went on to

London from Paris on 29 October 1815 where he received several commissions for sculpture and, at the request of the Duchess of Devonshire, was given a set of plaster casts of the Elgin Marbles for the Vatican museum by the Prince Regent. He did not get back to Rome till 5 January 1816, when he was rewarded by being created the Marchese d'Ischia by the pope and given a pension of 3,000 scudi a year.[31]

Consalvi's personal attitude towards the works of art in Rome, and their preservation, is indicated in a letter which he wrote from Vienna to Cardinal Pacca on 18 January 1815, describing his negotiations with the Crown Prince of Bavaria (later King Ludwig I) over the Barberini Faun which the Crown Prince had bought from the Barberini family through his Roman agent, Wagner, and which he wished to remove to Munich:

> My lengthy meeting with the Royal Prince of Bavaria having just ended successfully, I feel as if a heavy weight had been lifted from my shoulders . . . I have been able to make the prince realise, without irritating him, that there could only be a negative response to something that he cares for a great deal. He has accepted that he cannot obtain permission to export the Faun . . . Bearing in mind the advantages of retaining the statue of the Faun which I believe is one of the very few, if not the only statue of great importance left in Rome, I did not entirely dismiss his proposal. I made it perfectly clear that I personally could not at this stage promise him anything; I said that I would write to Rome to establish whether it was possible to do what he asked.
>
> If you agree with me as to the advantages of retaining the statue and feel uneasy about it remaining the property of the Prince, I would suggest that Signor Canova is secretly consulted before Herr Wagner is approached. If Signor Canova is in agreement, he (together with Monsignor Sostituto who has already been involved) could be asked to negotiate with Herr Wagner . . .
>
> Having made it clear that he intends to have the option of

retracting what he was about to suggest, he said that he would be willing to renounce his property if the 8 thousand crowns (which we have offered him) could be used to buy one or more antique statues, (naturally of much less importance than the Faun) if he were to be allowed to export them. I replied to him that the law forbade the exportation of anything that is antique. I added, though, that he may consider buying some paintings, as they are not so strictly controlled, or one of Signor Canova's beautiful statues which are as good as anything antique. He did not seem too interested in buying modern art and replied that naturally he would choose much less valuable objects which would not be as well known as the Faun or one or more works of art to the satisfaction of Herr Wagner for the amount of 8 thousand crowns. These works would have to be secretly exported. Thus Signor Canova should make sure that they would not be a serious loss for the city of Rome . . .[32]

The Prince was persistent and in the end he was allowed to export the Faun to Munich on the personal intervention of his sister the Empress of Austria, in 1819. It remains in the Glyptotek, the last major classical statue to be removed from Rome. After the return of the bulk of the antique sculpture from the Louvre in 1816, Consalvi did not feel so strongly about retaining the Faun. His policy of encouraging would-be collectors to buy modern art, especially 'some beautiful statue or a composition sculpted by Canova', rather than classical antiquity, had its best expression in the collection of the sixth Duke of Devonshire who, accepting that it would be impossible to export antique statues, formed a collection entirely of the work of contemporary sculptors in Rome for his new gallery at Chatsworth where it remains.

This discussion of works of art has taken us away from the territorial settlement at Vienna which was Consalvi's chief personal concern in 1815; he left the detailed negotiations regarding the works of art to Marini and Canova in Paris, while he himself concentrated in Vienna on securing the future of the temporal power. Although the final act of the Congress of Vienna, signed on 9 July 1815, restored the great majority of the papal states, and gave him far more than he had expected at the outset, Consalvi nevertheless refused to sign the treaty, in protest against the loss of Avignon. It was a statement of principle on his part and was courteously accepted as such. A Latin note of his protest was included in the final copy of the Treaty of Vienna, similar to that which Fabius Chigi, Bishop of Nardos, had appended to the Treaty of Westphalia in 1648. In fact, Consalvi was more than content with what had been achieved. He wrote to Pacca: 'The Lord has finally crowned with a happy success the efforts of the Holy Father . . . Eight provinces and one small principality . . . return under the domain of the Holy See . . . The pontificate of Pius VII . . . will count among its glories that of having recovered these provinces at a time when everything seemed to render the thing impossible.'[33]

Consalvi left Vienna on the same day as the battle of Waterloo, and made haste to reach Rome and gather up the reins of government before the *zelanti* could make any more decisions which would adversely affect his plans for the restoration and reform of the pontifical government. He took with him many splendid diplomatic presents from his colleagues at the Congress, including a series of fifteen magnificent gold snuff boxes, carrying miniature portraits of the allied kings and emperors framed in diamonds. His first task on his return was to assist the pope in the preparation of the consistorial allocution to the cardinals on 4 September announcing the restoration of the papal states. This contained a very pointed compliment to Great Britain which was published in the English newspapers and created an excellent impression in London: 'Nor can we forego the pleasure of mentioning the Prince Regent of England who so vigorously supported us at the Congress . . . the British government was amongst the chief of our supporters, in procuring our return to the pontifical chair, and our restoration to our ancient independence in the exercise of those spiritual rights, which the hand of violence had wrested from us.'[34]

VI

Restoration

IN JUNE 1815, after an absence of five years, Consalvi returned to Rome in triumph, to be greeted by a shower of florid odes from his poetic colleagues at the Arcadia. Once the celebrations were over, he faced the huge challenge of re-ordering the affairs of the restored territories. His task in 1815 was more difficult than it had been in 1800, partly because of the scale of his success in Vienna. The Legations, which had been under French rule for twenty years, were now back in papal hands. As well as being more prosperous and populated and developed than the rest of the states, they had grown accustomed to liberal secular government and did not relish the prospect of a return to clerical autocracy. On the other hand, the *zelanti* in the curia were more entrenched and determined in their opposition to all political reform than they had been during his first ministry. Moreover, they had had a year to put the clock back while Consalvi was in Paris and Vienna. Monsignor Rivarola, the papal legate in Rome who had been in charge pending the return of the pope in 1814, had done much harm and this was to hamper Consalvi's efforts later. Rivarola suppressed all the new French laws except those relating to mortgages; and persecuted those who had supported the French, including several distinguished university professors. By an order of 5 July 1814 he took away their positions from all the more prominent of the 800 clergy who had taken the French civil oath contrary to the pope's instructions.[1] Cardinal Pacca, who acted as pro-secretary of state in Consalvi's absence, supported Rivarola and continued the policy of reaction. The Jews were sent back to the ghetto. The public torture of criminals, 'the *corda*', was revived. The Jesuits were restored on 7 August 1814, the Inquisition re-established, and a commission set up to supervise the re-acquisition of secularized church property, thus alienating powerful lay interests. It was as if the Enlightenment had never existed.

Consalvi, when he heard what was happening in his absence was seriously embarrassed; he was at the time assuring the Allies that, if the Legations were restored to the pope, he would grant a general amnesty and retain the Napoleonic civil code and the reformed secular administration. In August 1814, due to his influence, a belated amnesty was announced in Rome by Cardinal Pacca, and immediately on his return, Consalvi abolished torture and the ghetto, slowed down the restoration of the Jesuits by making their revival in each country dependent on the request of the ruler, and rendered the Inquisition innocuous by making himself head of the congregation responsible. He also abolished military conscription, which the French had introduced and which he despised as 'a blood tax, hateful to an agricultural and pastoral people'.[2] The damage to the reputation of the papal government had been done, however, and though he was not personally responsible, Consalvi reaped some of the odium for this short-lived reaction. Mrs Eaton, the British authoress of a contemporary guide to Rome, noted sarcastically: 'Thanks to the enlightened policy of Pius VII and his minister Cardinal Gonsalvo [sic], we have lived in the nineteenth century to see that upright fraternity – the Jesuits – restored, and that righteous court, the Inquisition, re-established.'[3]

The truth is that Consalvi went out of his way to be magnanimous to his former enemies, and Rome under his rule became a haven for victims of ill-fortune and scions of fallen dynasties. Most of the Bonaparte family spent the remainder of their lives there, notably Cardinal Fesch and Madame Mère who established themselves in the Palazzo Rinucci, renamed the Palazzo Bonaparte, at the corner of the Corso and Piazza Venezia.

Madame Mère wrote to Consalvi in 1818: 'I wish to thank Your Eminence for all that you have done in our favour since the exile of myself and my children.' Fesch called Consalvi 'an example to all of forgiving injuries'.[4] The *émigrés* became a distinctive part of the social mix in Restoration Rome and Mrs Eaton recorded, 'There is the most amusing collection of ex-royalty, of all sorts and kinds, – remnants of old dynasties, and scions of heir legitimates and illegitimates, all jumbled together just now in Rome. Besides the old King and Queen of Spain, there are the ex-Queen and young King of Etruria – the abdicated King of Sardinia, turned Jesuit – Louis Bonaparte, the deposed King of Holland, living like a hermit – Lucien Bonaparte, the uncrowned, living like a prince – and Pauline Borghese his sister, living like – like – but comparisons are odious.'[5]

Consalvi's first task was to discover the exact state of affairs in the Papal States before deciding what needed to be done. To this end he instituted a number of investigations through the Economic Congregation and various special commissions set up for the purpose. These produced reports on the population, finances and administration of the territories. There was in addition a census of the population of Rome, a survey of land-holding throughout the Papal States, an account of mortgages, a list of the personnel of the papal army, and an analysis of the territorial areas of the towns re-acquired in 1815, their communes, administration, annual income and expenditure.[6] He also gathered material relating to the history of the Papal States which explained the anomalies in their administration, and the reforming policies of previous papal administrations. The cities, lands and castles of the Papal States had all been acquired at different times and this partly explained the varied system of administration, law and feudal privileges which prevailed, while the medieval duchies of the Colonna, Orsini, Savelli and Frangipani had survived as private fiefs. This situation had been made worse by the policies of sixteenth- and early seventeenth-century popes who had invested portions of the states in their own families and supporters; the descendents of the D'Este, Varano, Della Rovere and Farnese had all possessed semi-independent domains. Thus some areas were *ducati* under the control of great families, while others were *vicariati* ruled directly by clerics. There had been continuous attempts through the centuries to create one uniform economic, civil and judicial administration out of this feudal jumble. Sixtus V and Clement VIII in the late sixteenth century, Innocent XI in the seventeenth century, Clement XI, Benedict XIV and Pius VI in the eighteenth century, had all in turn tried to subjugate their realm to one universal system with decreasing success; the eighteenth-century reforms in particular having been largely ineffective. Now it was Consalvi's turn.

Armed with the necessary background information the secretary of state and the revived Economic Congregation, under its new secretary Luigi Marini, drew up new plans for reforming the administration and finances of the Papal States. Consalvi also attempted to reform the chaotic legal system. Pacca and Rivarola's suppression of the Napoleonic Code extended only to the Patrimony and Umbria; French civil law survived in the Legations and Marches which returned to papal control too late to be affected by the 1814 counter-revolution. This had created a double legal system; added to which Roman canon law and civil law contradicted each other on several important issues. Consalvi's plan was to create a new integrated code of civil law, broadly similar to the Napoleonic Code, which would prevail throughout the Papal States. In the face of bitter opposition from the *zelanti*, especially their ringleader, Cardinal Riganti, himself a distinguished lawyer, Consalvi appointed Vincenzo Bartolucci, who had been the president of the Court of Appeal in Rome under the French and a Councillor of State in Paris, to head a commission to achieve this reform of the penal code. The *zelanti* hated Bartolucci as a collaborator and wanted to exile him from Rome, but Consalvi wished to make use of his experience of Napoleonic law.

After a year of work, the papal *Motu Proprio*, published on 17 July 1816, set out Consalvi's plan for the new administration, law and public finances of the Papal States.[7] There were immediate and violent recriminations from both sides; from the Legations because they thought it not liberal enough; from the *zelanti* because they thought it too Jacobin. So strong was the reaction that the new civil code was not put into effect, but shelved indefinitely though Consalvi never gave up hope of having it implemented. The Papal States were left in a legal muddle, with the Napoleonic civil code and lay courts in the Legations, and canon and common law administered by church courts in the Patrimony and Umbria.

Consalvi was so discouraged by this defeat that he thought of resigning. But, reassured by the pope's confidence in him, he continued with his other reforms. He had learnt two lessons: that there was a fundamental difference between the Legations and the more backward southern part of the states; and that the majority of *zelanti* among the cardinals were intent on obstructing his work. He saw that it was necessary to bypass his colleagues in the Sacred College if he was to achieve anything, and he therefore set about concentrating all authority in his own hands. The pope encouraged Consalvi in such a policy. Following the Restoration, Pius VII had gone into a kind of permanent spiritual retreat and was happy therefore to delegate the whole of the secular government to his secretary of state who constructed a position of absolute control by appointing himself head of many of the congregations in the curia. The foreign minister of Naples complained about Consalvi's rule:

> The present pope, dedicating himself to spiritual matters, and moreover being old and infirm, is not occupied by temporal things and delegates them all to different congregations. An expedient made useless because of Cardinal Consalvi, the Secretary of State. This man of minuscule and much-limited talent but of the greatest ambition who had gained a great ascendancy over the confidence of the Pope has gathered to himself the heads of all these congregations. He has control of the smallest matters. Everything is manipulated by him. He is trying to concentrate and rationalise everything in his own hands with the same power as a sovereign has.[8]

Consalvi was restored to his former posts on the Supreme Inquisition, the Propaganda Fidei, the Concilio and Consistory; as Prefect of the Signature and as Apostolic Visitor to the Ospizio di S. Michele a Ripa in 1815. At the Restoration he was also appointed Secretary of Briefs. In 1817 he succeeded Cardinal Luigi Gonzaga as Vatican Librarian, and in 1818 was appointed Cardinal Protector of the English College. Thus he created a system whereby nearly every aspect of the temporal power was controlled directly by himself. With a few exceptions he thought his fellow cardinals feeble and mediocre, albeit pious – their conduct in Paris had not attracted his admiration. No doubt he shared Napoleon's view that they were, in the main, a fourth-rate bunch. Stendhal wrote in 1817:

My respect and admiration for Cardinal Consalvi redoubles at the measure that I see better with what abject *canaille* he is surrounded. Ye Gods! Why does not England have such a minister?

The Pope wishes to devote himself to his salvation and thinking in conscience that Cardinal Consalvi has the most talent for government gives him the civil despotism. The religious despotism is in the hands of the ultra party, the chief of which is the virtuous Cardinal Pacca. Two or three times a month, this party in working with the pope on religious affairs expose the measures of Cardinal Consalvi as tending to increase the number of the damned among the subjects of the Church. Then the Pope with tears in his eyes has an explanation from his minister. The latter responds with the maxim 'I judge sins by the crimes which are brought to the attention of the courts and not by the reports of the confessors ... I am reviving the French measures and already I have 300 less murders a year; that is probably 600 less damned a year.' As nothing is above the modesty and disinterestedness of this great minister, the venerable pontiff usually finishes by embracing him in tears and recommending to him the souls of his subjects.[9]

Other visitors to Rome told a similar story. Lord Colchester, an Englishman, wrote in 1821:

> Consalvi is the Pope's only ostensible and efficient minister. He is supported by all the courts of Europe. But the Pope does not always implicitly adopt his advice; and upon some important matters, especially ecclesiastical, acts sometimes on the suggestions of the Camerlengo Pacca, whom he does not like – His Holiness, now for twenty years a reigning sovereign, and with many good qualities, has no knowledge of or talent for the administration of public affairs.[10]

When Consalvi returned to Rome in 1815, he found several positions of power – the governor of Rome and the finance ministers, the treasurer and the camerlengo – already occupied by Ultra prelates, and he made it part of his policy to subdue them to his control. He was helped when Cardinal Pacca's nephew, the governor of Rome, having been drawn into 'some great errors about money', fled in disgrace under an assumed name in April 1820.[11] During Consalvi's second ministry, the cardinals continued to enjoy the greatest honours, to be treated indeed as princes, but their state was entirely passive; 'A cardinal had no more influence on the government of the Pope than the King of France.'[12] Despite his natural courtesy and *savoir-faire*, the secretary of state could not altogether disguise his contempt for the ineptitude of most of his colleagues, while they resented this and constantly grumbled and sniped at his policies. If he received distinguished English travellers, such as Lord Stuart who had obtained for him his passport to London in 1814, it was said to be 'a bow to freemasonry'. His toleration of Anglican worship for visitors in hired rooms was denounced as abetting heresy. The *zelanti* cardinals feared that he was sacrificing important principles in order to secure a *modus vivendi* with the modern world, and Consalvi ignored their criticisms and pushed ahead with his policies of centralization and secularization. By concentrating the temporal power in his own hands after 1814, he created a new image of the secretary of state wielding overall centralized political responsibility. This is reflected in the papal archives which for the first time were provided with an independent category for the archives of the office of the secretary of state; before 1814, the government papers had all been grouped according to congregations or nunciatures.

Stendhal compared Consalvi's new constitution with its proud preamble and paper perfection to a 'magnificent portico leading to a cottage'. It is interesting, however, as a demonstration of what he was trying to achieve. It outlined a centralized bureaucratic system of government on Napoleonic lines, and abolished all feudal rights except the game laws. The old irregular administrative subdivisions were swept away and replaced by a new arrangement of roughly equal regional units. Under the supreme authority of the secretary of state, there were established four Legations in Romagna: Ravenna, Bologna, Ferrara and Forli, ruled by cardinal-legates. Each was assisted by an advisory committee of four laymen nominated by the cardinal-legate from ten names submitted to him. In addition, there were in the rest of the Papal States eighteen Delegations under the control of prelate-delegates (the old governors). These in turn were subdivided into forty-four districts and 720 communes. Ideally, Consalvi would have liked to have suppressed all independent local rights, to have abolished all feudal and municipal privileges, and to have created a clear-cut separation of the administration of civil justice, but because of the opposition in 1816, combined with the lack of reliable trained officials to carry out his proposals, he had to make do with half measures and compromises. 'All his plans are mutilated, the details left to fools', wrote Stendhal.[13] In addition to the local councils of laymen, he also hoped to set up a house of peers composed of members of the nobility nominated by the government, as well as cardinals, with the power to vote on taxation. This pleased nobody. The educated laity thought that the nomination of representatives did not go far enough, while the clergy considered the mere presence of laymen in the government, even if they were nominated and not elected, to be disruptive to the state and contrary to religion. So Consalvi had to backslide. In place of a modernized, equitable and efficient administrative and judicial system combining the best features of the old regime with the rational innovations of the French, he made do with piecemeal improvements as the opportunity arose, just as Pius VI's government had done before him. Immediately after the publication of the *Motu Proprio* in July 1816, he followed up with a series of public proclamations on different aspects of the reformed administration. He set up a new body of *carabinieri* and provided them with newly built barracks in the principal towns; in Rome, in the Piazza del Popolo. He confirmed the retention of the French system of mortgages. He issued ordinances on the proper storage of public archives throughout the Papal States, and a series of new regulations affecting the organization of commerce, tariffs and public finance generally.[14]

By the time of his retirement in 1823, Consalvi had made some progress, more indeed than his initial failure in 1816 has made some commentators assume. The four cardinal-legates appointed in 1816 were far from being the mindless mediocrities they have been made out to be. Cardinal Spina at Bologna was efficient and supported Consalvi; they had worked together over the Concordat. Cardinals Malvasin at Ravenna and Arezzo at Ferrara were also pro-Consalvi. Only Cardinal Sanseverino at Forli was from the ranks of the Ultras, and he was a generous and widely-liked man who was prepared to work with Consalvi, as is clear from his helpful replies to government circulars on land tenure, rights of pasture and other local issues.

Having established, in at least a skeleton form, his new centralized and rationalized administrative structure, Consalvi set to work to tackle the two most pressing problems facing the Papal States: the shaky government finances and the decay of public order. He was obliged to increase taxes to pay for the restoration programme and to try to balance the books. He had to compensate those who lost church property: altogether, between 1814 and 1816, 612 convents and 1,824 monasteries were restored and re-endowed in the Papal States. The Roman congregations, the cardinals and other ecclesiastics also needed substantial benefices to support them. There was the indemnity to be paid to Austria under the terms of the Congress of Vienna, and to add to Consalvi's problems the population of Rome was increasing and had to be provided for. A substantial number of people had no gainful occupation and were supported by a vast structure of charities and doles paid for directly by the government out of public funds. In order to raise money quickly, Consalvi set about the collection of arrears and leased the principal taxes for twelve years ahead to tax farmers for fixed sums. This was the indirect cause of much harshness, coercion and fraud, which the Neapolitan foreign minister considered worthy of an eastern despotism and which was beyond Consalvi's immediate control, the business of collecting the taxes being the responsibility of the treasurer and camerlengo. But by these means, albeit rough and ready, he achieved his ends and cleared the government's debts as well as financing his new programme. At the end of his administration, he had succeeded in balancing the books. He also carried out a partial reform of the tax system aimed at bringing about a more equitable distribution of the tax burden. Hitherto, taxes had been levied at the same rate regardless. Consalvi changed this so that the poorer areas paid less whereas the richer paid more. This added to his unpopularity in the Legations where the population had already been disappointed by the, to them, conservative nature of his political reforms. On the other side of the fence he affronted the *zelanti* by taxing the secular clergy. By 1820, the revenues of the states amounted to 9,000,000 scudi a year. The *imposta fondiaria* or land tax was the principal source of revenue, in addition to which there were customs duties, stamp duty, registration fees, and the '*gabelle*' imposed on the sale of goods. Consalvi, in the course of his two ministries, reformed all these, except for the '*gabelle*'. His attempt to abolish the latter throughout the states was thwarted and it was only in the Legations that they were replaced with a new united tax. The direct administration of the finances was the responsibility of two cardinals, the treasurer and the camerlengo, neither of whom was keen to co-operate with Consalvi's policies.[15]

He also continued with his earlier attempt to stimulate the economy by direct state intervention. At his request in 1816

Giuseppe Mancini published a detailed programme for the improvement of agriculture and commerce to be put into effect in the Papal States.[16] The Campagna with its large estates presented an abandoned landscape largely given over to rough grazing. Consalvi attempted by curtailing grazing rights to encourage the peasantry to establish new smallholdings and to revive arable farming. He introduced grants to promote the cultivation of tobacco on the Adriatic plain of the Marches, and stimulated the planting of vines and corn in the valleys of Umbria. On 18 January 1817, he sent out a dispatch, with a copy of the papal chirograph on landholding of 23 September 1806, to the legates at Forli and Ravenna, and the delegates at Pesaro, Perugia and Ancona, asking them to report on their areas. They were also told to issue local proclamations to stimulate agriculture. In 1818, for example, the Apostolic Delegate at Perugia printed an edict encouraging the peasants and tenant farmers of Umbria to take on abandoned land for the cultivation of olives and fruit. On the basis of the reports which came back to him in 1817, Consalvi drew up a memorandum for the economic congregation on the subject of grazing, accompanied by a list of all the landed proprietors in the Papal States. Like much of Consalvi's programme in his second ministry, this was a continuation of the work begun during his first ministry, but interrupted by the war and French occupation. He set up a new college in Rome to undertake the scientific study of agriculture, and he encouraged the publication of books on the cultivation of fruit and similar topics, though it is unlikely that these had any general impact on the peasantry.[17] Nor is it clear what long-term effect, if any, Consalvi's efforts had on restricting pasture and encouraging the revival of arable farming, in the complete absence of any detailed socio-economic history of the Papal States in the eighteenth and nineteenth centuries.

The economy of the Papal States was not entirely agricultural. Crafts and manufactures were relatively healthy in the Legations and valleys of Umbria, notably leatherwork, pottery, metalwork and some cloth. But the chief source of income in Rome itself was tourism. Consalvi was spectacularly successful in attracting visitors to Rome. As Stendhal remarked, while he was secretary of state Rome was a peaceful retreat from the world and tourists and pilgrims flocked from all over Europe, bringing a large influx of money with them. The economy of the city was geared to serve this tourist enterprise. More will be said in due course about Consalvi's protection of the arts, and the pomp and pageantry which he revived for the gratification of foreign visitors. He also encouraged the setting-up of small industries catering for the tourist market, notably the Roman micro-mosaic works to manufacture souvenirs, from table tops to brooches, which proved so successful that its successors flourish to this day.

Not the least of the attractions of the Papal States was their relative tranquillity and stability. The principal achievement of Consalvi's domestic rule was to make Rome a place of enlighten-ment, moderation and clemency. The outward tranquillity was the result of firm measures on the part of the secretary of state, aided by the new *carabinieri* and the revived papal army, to extirpate the endemic lawlessness, anarchy and incipient revo-lutionary turmoil which was the chief legacy of the war years, a state of affairs rendered more serious by famines in 1815 and 1816, which reduced some of the peasantry to eating grass and acorns. This misery encouraged brigandage and the *carbonari*, and culminated on the night of 24 June 1817 when an armed rabble attacked the gates of Macerata. They were scattered by a detachment of papal troops opening fire. The ringleaders were arrested and imprisoned or executed, thus impressing on the public the fact that the restored government was not soft. Consalvi followed this up with the expulsion of persistent political trouble-makers from papal territory, the imprisonment of those who would not go into exile, and a series of edicts condemning the *carbonari* and secret revolutionary sects. He was able to deal with disaffection so effectively because of the excellence of his police intelligence. He controlled the police and army directly, the chief of police and the general in charge of the army both being under the immediate orders of the secretary of state. The foreign minister of Naples reported, in a letter which was intercepted by Consalvi's intelligence system, that the inhabitants of the Papal States were on the whole so docile and peaceful that in many respects a police force was not necessary, but that its chief purpose was the gathering of intelligence. 'The police are used more for the private surveillance of *soi-disant* liberals . . . The papal states are assuredly the most tranquil part of Italy as a result.'[18]

The police were backed up by the papal army. Consalvi had restored Pius VI's organization for running the army, not as a congregation, but as a purely secular body called the military commission. The army comprised 10,750 men divided into infantry of the line, cavalry, gendarmes, customs officers and the papal guards, distributed throughout the states, but with the heaviest presence in Rome and the Legations.[19] While not large enough or powerful enough to serve as a real army or to fight in a war, the foreign minister of Naples thought it too large for its immediate purpose of manning the customs posts, guarding the finances and providing ceremonial troops for the pope, and stressed that its real purpose was the maintenance of law and order. He thought that the soldiers were sound, but that the officers were poor. Consalvi knew otherwise. He had a list of every member of the armed forces with a brief assessment drawn up for him in 1816: for example, 'Bernardo Palma, Colonel of Infantry 1796. Served a long time. Does not have a pension. Brave and honest person'; 'Captain Camillo Sensi. Excellent officer of good family from Perugia.'[20] Consalvi knew and trusted his small army. He was not let down; even during 1820 when revolution broke out in Naples, the Papal States remained calm, peaceful and uninvolved.

On the surface, Rome remained the most unmilitary of states. Stendhal paints an idyllic picture of the Eternal City in the peaceful second half of Pius VII's reign. 'Consalvi made Rome a sweet retreat from the world – from its intrigues and passions.' He described how the secretary of state used to walk backwards and forwards on foot between his apartments in the Palazzo della Consulta and his office in the Quirinal opposite, passing the new fountain he had just had erected and a few scratching hens, but with no military parade of any kind. 'He had none of the air of a *grand seigneur*, just worldly good breeding, simplicity and beautiful eyes.'[21]

Stendhal tells the story of the most extraordinary of Consalvi's measures to suppress anarchy and lawlessness, his treatment of the brigands who infested the mountains and wastes. At the wish of the pope who had wanted to show magnanimity, Consalvi entered into a treaty with the brigands and offered them one year's imprisonment in return for the financial means to start a new life. The most important clan agreed to his terms and Consalvi went out in person to round them up and receive their surrender. He returned to Terracina with three waggon loads of picturesque brigands, including their chief Masocco, a man of ferocious appearance with gold earrings, a feathered cap and large moustaches. The brigands spent a year in prison and then were let out to begin an honest life. But there was a terrible epilogue. Consalvi sent Masocco back to negotiate the surrender of another brigand clan. Their chief, Cesare, murdered Masocco, setting off a vendetta and tribal warfare. Consalvi now resorted to force. Cesare was shot dead by papal troops, and on 18 July 1819 Consalvi, following the example of Paul IV's treatment of Montefortino in 1557, ordered the complete destruction of Sonnino, a town of four or five thousand people which had harboured the murderous brigands. They were scattered and Consalvi threatened pain of death against anybody who gave them money or sanctuary; not even their parents were excepted.[22] Nothing could have been sterner than this edict of Consalvi's, but it worked, and later nineteenth-century visitors to the Papal States thought of the brigands as picturesque models for water-colour sketches rather than murderous criminals. Consalvi was not afraid of being firm if he thought it necessary. Just as he crushed the revolt at Macerata by armed force in 1817, and suppressed revolutionaries and secret societies, so, without flinching, he wiped out the brigands in 1819. He wrote to Metternich on one occason: 'No other government could be more diligent than that of the pope in suppressing the sects and in refusing to allow any changes incompatible with the institutions which characterize his polity.'[23]

In his internal policy, Consalvi was successful in establishing peace and tranquillity, and in balancing the books. But, like all his reforming predecessors in the seventeenth and eighteenth centuries, he failed in his attempt to create one unified system of government, taxation and law throughout the Papal States. At the end of his ministry there remained significant differences between north and south. The former enjoyed a system of administration, law and taxation based on the French republican reforms, whereas the latter retained the old system with its muddle of feudal and clerical privileges, antique taxes such as the 'gabelle' and unreformed common law. Consalvi's failure to weld the two parts together was not due to lack of wisdom or lack of hard work on his part. He failed because the problems were insoluble. Measures that were appropriate in the relatively prosperous liberal north would have led to anarchy and unrest in the conservative south. Even Stendhal had doubts, and wrote of Rome and the Campagna: 'The ignorance is so crass in the enlightened class and villainy so engrained in the people that such a constitution is perhaps an imprudence.'[24] In the end it was more sensible and practical to keep the two systems side by side, and so long as Consalvi was in power, both systems were subject to the direction of an efficient powerful secretariat at the centre. All the evidence suggests that after his initial despondency in 1816–17, when he told Lord Colchester that he 'ate and drank nothing but bitterness',[25] he rapidly came to terms with the limitations within which he was forced to work, and by 1820 was content with his not inconsiderable achievement. Though given to impatience, he was basically a realist and had no illusions about the slow pace of everything in Rome. He had written to Cardinal Pacca in 1814: 'All cannot be done in a day, as the proverb runs, and again – one must give time to the times ... it will therefore be necessary in my judgement to proceed slowly, very, very slowly.'[26]

The years between 1817 and the onset of a painful illness in 1823 were the happiest since his youth. He had always worked hard and for very long hours at a time. Fr. John Lingard, the Catholic priest at Hornby, Lancashire, visited Rome in May 1817 to gather material for his *History of England* in the Vatican archives, and left an eye-witness account of Consalvi's way of work. 'After spending the morning in giving audiences he will take a few poached eggs for dinner, with two or three glasses of water, then apply again to business till eleven at night, throw himself on his sofa in his bed-gown, snatch two or three hours' sleep, dress, drive eighteen miles to Castel Gandolfo to the Pope, return again, and apply once more to business by nine in the morning.'[27] Despite this exhausting routine and the demands he made on them his staff were devoted to him. Sir Thomas Lawrence, who visited Rome two years after Lingard at the request of the Prince Regent to paint portraits of Pius VII and Consalvi for the series of allied statesmen and sovereigns in the Waterloo Chamber at Windsor Castle, told the same story:

> He has surprising strength of constitution, perpetually active, and not sleeping more at a time than three hours and a half. He has been above fifteen years the first minister to the pope . . . The unequalled activity of his character makes him the severest task-master (to his staff), but his manners to them are so pleasant and his nature so benevolent and just, that they seem to love him as if indulgence were his characteristic weakness. 'Ah!' they say, 'our cardinal is a man of iron – he is not flesh and blood as we are!' and he has either said something kind or done something liberal, and they repeat it with a pride and delight in him that is like the feeling of children to a mother.[28]

All his friends and relations were dead; his carefree youth seemed separated from the present by the long years of war, revolution and exile. There were moments when he, along with the pope, seemed like survivors from another world. His only relaxations continued to be music and gardening, and both were now saturated with sad memories. Stendhal, who often went to the same evening parties in Rome, noted:

One sees few men as sensitive to music as Cardinal Consalvi. He went very often in the evening to Madame the Ambassadress of – ; there he met a charming young man who knew by heart twenty of the most beautiful airs of the immortal Cimarosa; Rossini, for it was he, sang these when he was asked by the Cardinal while His Excellency was established in a large armchair a little in the shade. After Rossini had sung for several minutes a silent tear was seen to run slowly down the cheek of the Minister. It was the most jolly airs which produced this effect; the Cardinal had loved Cimarosa tenderly.'[29]

While music always recalled Cimarosa, gardening was sacred to the memory of Consalvi's brother Andrea whose keenest interest and study had been plants and flowers. After 1816, Consalvi established a little private garden on the 'Litus Pulchrum' opposite the Isola Tiberina in a secluded area of Roman ruins and ancient basilicas, with romantic views of the Palatine and Aventine. There he arranged a collection of plants according to the Linnaean system, which was very progressive in Rome where the city botanic garden was still pre-Linnaean. Consalvi received presents of plants for his garden from the great all over Europe. In 1822, for instance, the duc d'Orleans, Louis Philippe, wrote: 'Talleyrand tells me . . . that your sole pleasure is the cultivation of flowers', and sent a gift of some 'samples of our French hot houses'.[30] As well as plants, the garden contained a marble bust of Andrea and classical tablets with Latin inscriptions from Ovid and Virgil adapted to commemorate the brother 'whom he loved with uncommon affection':

> *Ante meos oculos tamquam praesentis imago*
> *haeret et extinctum vivere fingit amor.*

> *Te, dulcis frater, te solo in litore mecum,*
> *te veniente die, te decedente vocabo.**[31]

*Before my eyes his image clings as if he were present,
  and love makes it seem that the dead man lives.

Thee, sweet brother, thee shall I call upon, alone
  on the deserted shore, both at break of day and at its close.

To this arcadian retreat, Consalvi would disappear for a few moments' relaxation from his work, to spend some time in solitude with his flowers and his memories. He never took anybody else with him, and only one other person was ever given the key to the garden, with the privilege of access when he was not there himself – the Duchess of Devonshire.

Consalvi's partiality for the English grew even more pronounced after the Restoration. He wrote to Canova in October 1815: 'England is too great to have need of increasing her glory; but [for] what she has done on this occasion the British Government, with a generosity without example, will carve in the heart of His Holiness, in mine, and in that of all the Roman people a lasting sentiment of infinite gratitude.'[32] He sincerely meant this, and openly favoured the English, much to the jealousy of other nations. Whether humble parish priests or enormously rich dukes, he went out of his way to assist them; arranging access to the museums and libraries, lending them carriages, or even his own houses at Frascati and Tivoli. John Lingard recorded: 'Nothing could exceed the kindness of His Eminence. He sent for Monsignor Baldi, and in my presence told him to order, in his name, all the officers to give me every facility.'[33] Sir Thomas Lawrence noted the same overwhelming kindness: 'His manner but too gracious . . . The expression of every wish was pressed upon me and the free utterance of every complaint.'[34]

This love of the English in general was balanced by the love of one in particular, the Duchess of Devonshire, better known as Lady Elizabeth (Betty) Foster, the daughter of the eccentric Earl-Bishop of Derry, successively the mistress, second wife, and widow of the fifth Duke of Devonshire, and famous as part of the Devonshire House *ménage à trois*. She had been, and still was, a woman of great beauty and intelligence, affectionate, sympathetic and so fascinating that in 1789 the ageing Edward Gibbon had suddenly fallen on his knees to ask her hand in marriage. Following the death of the duke, she had been forced to leave the many Cavendish houses like a 'maim'd fox' ferreted out of its 'last hold', and after Waterloo decided to go to Rome where she was well-known as the daughter of the Earl-Bishop and where a handsome allowance from her stepson would enable her to live in a state of semi-regal magnificence and play the role of great hostess and patron of the arts. 'The Duchess is adored,' Lord Gower wrote from Rome in 1817. 'She protects all the artists and employs them and pays them magnificently, and that all along the road, the inn-keepers are asking, "Do you know who is that noble lady?"'[35]

Soon after her arrival in Rome, the duchess met the secretary of state. They became instant friends, and her devotion and admiration soon verged on the ardent. The doings of 'my friend, the Cardinal' came to fill her letters home to her relations in England who, at first, were slightly cynical about her new role. She had always had a weakness for princes of the Church and Consalvi was just the sort of intelligent kind man she admired and, moreover, was so good-looking. Stendhal wrote in 1817: 'It is impossible at fifty years [actually sixty] to be a more handsome man than Cardinal Consalvi.'[36] The duchess described him to Augustus Clifford (her illegitimate son by the fifth Duke): 'In person he is tall, thin, of the most dignified yet simple manners, a dark and animated eye, a thick dark brow, a smile of inexpressible sweetness and benevolence, his conversation natural and instructive, his temper mild, forgiving yet warm and rather impatient of delay.' And to Thomas Lawrence: 'You will be struck by the dignified animation and benevolent expression of Cardinal Consalvi . . . you will agree with me that a three-quarters or nearly a full face is what will do justice to the beauty of his countenance . . . you cannot have a subject of more distinguished merit.'[37]

They were exact contemporaries, both having been born in 1757; they shared many tastes and interests including a sympathy for the Stuarts, her grandmother, the beautiful Mollie Leppell, having been a Jacobite. Both were lonely, and their friendship for each other was to be the mutual solace of their last years, only two months separating their deaths in the spring of 1824. As early as 1816, she was writing: 'Consalvi and I are such friends that when we are at the same place the crowd gives way for him to come up to me.'[38] She adored him, and he, solitary and over-burdened, found her company and sympathy heart-warming and encouraging. As the years passed they grew closer, visiting each other and writing at least once, often twice a day. Her letters to him have been destroyed, but his to her, on gold-edged paper in the distinctive cramped writing she found difficult to read, have survived, beginning '*Chère Amie*' and concluding '*Tout à vous de tout mon coeur.*'[39] They discussed with each other contemporary political events, the arts and common friends. He sought her advice on his dinner parties, whom he should invite and how to seat them: 'I wish to give a dinner to the Danish Prince Regent . . .'[40] Sometimes he explained to her local customs: 'You do not know what is a game of tombola? It is a bad game (a form of lottery).'[41] When she was away from Rome, he would report on the state of affairs and his own business: 'The Pope is well, Rome and the provinces tranquil.' 'I have received your dear letter. I had not a moment to write to you today being so over-burdened with business that you would pity me.' Sometimes in the excitement of the moment an Italian word escaped into his French sentences. Thus on hearing of the suicide of Castlereagh (by then the Marquess of Londonderry): 'I don't doubt that you will be upset by the loss of Lord Londonderry. Me, I am *inconsolato*.'[42] He would call on her at the end of the day; sometimes if he had been very busy it was so late that she had already gone to bed and could not receive him. Sometimes they got so engrossed in conversation that he forgot his other appointments. 'He stayed talking in the kindest manner till he forgot he had to go to the French ambassador's.' Her affection grew to know no bounds and she noted in her diary, 'If there is a pure and angelic mind on earth now, it is his.'[43]

With Consalvi's help, she established herself in a vast and sumptuous set of state apartments in the Palazzo Spada which she rented from Prince Piombini. 'I shall be excellently lodged thanks to Consalvi who has made a lamb of Piombini,' and her noble landlord made a new kitchen specially for her. At the Palazzo Spada she gave a series of lavish parties and receptions that established her as the chief focus of social life in Rome. Lamartine, indeed, described her as the uncrowned Queen of

Rome. Consalvi was often present at these parties and it was in the course of one of them that the opportunity arose to repay the kindness of the Prince Regent. The duchess always tried to arrange some special point of interest or a new amusement at her evening *soirées*. It came to her ears that a shady Scot, Dr Watson, had tracked down and bought a mass of rotting papers from an Abate Lupi.* He claimed they were the papers of Cardinal York and he hoped to sell them for a large profit.

> Flattered by the solicitations of Her Grace, he allowed a small packet to be made up for her next *conversazione*. One of the most intimate and constant of Her Grace's visitors was the Cardinal Consalvi who on the evening in question was there as a matter of course and, as usual, one of the earliest of the guests. The papers were on the table and as might be expected were the absorbing topic of conversation during the evening. The Cardinal examined and read them, folded them up and said nothing; but before daylight the following morning His Eminence ordered a guard of soldiers to Dr Watson's residence and gave orders that the whole of these papers should be put immediately under the seal and wardship of the state, and they were lost for ever to Dr Watson. The Abate Lupi was arrested and thrown into prison for the gross violation of his trust. The contract was annulled on the ground of incompetence of the seller, and the 300 crowns [which Watson had paid Lupi] ordered to be paid back.
>
> Watson objected strongly. The Cardinal heard the strong language of the enraged and disappointed Scot with complacency and great forbearance, and dismissed him with the assurance that he might consider himself kindly treated, as if any Roman had dared to use such language he would quickly have paid the penalty of his temerity by a long imprisonment.[44]

*The Abate Lupi was a former amanuensis of Cardinal York's, to whom the papers had been entrusted for safekeeping by Mgr. Tassoni, the papal auditor. Tassoni denied that Lupi had any authority to sell them.

Consalvi made a present of the papers to the Prince Regent as a token of thanks from the papal government for Britain's assistance in securing the restoration of the Papal States and Roman art treasures; which is why the Stuart papers are now among the royal archives at Windsor Castle.

The duchess was careful not to seem to be interfering through Consalvi in Roman politics, though she did have considerable influence and in many ways acted as an unofficial English ambassador in Rome. She reported Consalvi's views directly to London, where the prime minister Lord Liverpool was her brother-in-law, or to William A'Court, the British minister at Naples. And she passed on their views in return to Consalvi. She was scrupulous, however, not to discuss religious matters. 'It would be improper for me to interfere in any ecclesiastical affairs both as a woman and a stranger and I have made it a rule to exert any influence which the esteem and friendship of the secretary of state might give me merely to acts of friendship and protection to individuals, but to refrain from any interference in public affairs.'[45] Consalvi was always delighted to put himself out for the duchess's friends and relations when they visited Italy. For instance, he lent the Augustus Cliffords a carriage and his house at Tivoli when they were at Rome. The duchess took great pleasure in arranging for the Cardinal Secretary of State to visit Fr. O'Meagher, the Catholic priest from Dungarvon near Lismore Castle (the Cavendish estate in Ireland) when he was in Rome.

> Our good Cardinal's friendship and kindness could never have been better timed than it has been in his civility to O'Meagher who came to me all staring with delight. 'An to be sure for a poor parish priest like myself to receive a visit from his Eminence is more than I could have expected, and I have to thank your ladyship I am sure for the honour' . . . he may keep his voters steady for the Cavendish interest![46]

VII

Second Ministry:
Art and Foreign Policy

THE most successful aspects of Consalvi's government during his second ministry, as during his first, were his conduct of foreign affairs and his programme of artistic and architectural improvement in Rome. The two were to some extent intertwined, as the prestige of the papacy in secular terms depended on the splendour of Rome and its long history as the artistic capital of Europe. Consalvi's public-works programme after 1815 was aimed at maintaining this pre-eminence: with the further embellishment of the whole city, new archaeological excavations and the aggrandizement of the Vatican museum, along lines conceived originally between 1801 and 1803. This time he was able to achieve nearly all that he set out to, making the reign of Pius VII the last which saw a large-scale programme of architectural embellishment carried out in papal Rome, as well as the last phase of the city's role as a European artistic centre. The artist Thomas Lawrence was much impressed by the work he found in progress in 1819: 'There is now here a general spirit of exertion, both in judicious repairs in preserving the great monuments of antiquity, and by excavations, in discovering their foundations and parts (many of them highly wrought) that were before hidden from the eye.'[1]

As a political entity, the papacy was a curious organism in that, though an international religious power, it was not supported by a temporal empire or a great army; successive popes had therefore lavishly fostered the arts as a source of worldly prestige, though often living personally ascetic lives. Consalvi's protection of the arts and his embellishment of the city and its museums should be seen in the context of this long tradition which stretched back at least as far as the Renaissance. It should not be regarded as a peripheral matter, but rather as something close to the centre of his political policy, and a key aspect of his aim to restore the prestige of the papacy after the vicissitudes of the wars and revolution. In his time Rome became again, as it had been in the eighteenth century, a gathering place for artistic talent from all over Europe. English poets like Byron, Shelley and Keats; English painters, including Turner, Eastlake and Lawrence; and British sculptors, including Chantrey, Gibson, Wyatt and Campbell, all visited Rome for greater or lesser periods, some spending the rest of their lives there. From northern Europe, especially Denmark and Germany, there were whole schools of artists permanently resident in Rome. The northern sculptors Thorwaldsen and Sergel, and the German 'Nazarene' painters in their cloister at San Isidoro gained international reputations. From France, Wicar and other artists maintained the classical tradition at the French Academy, while writers like Stendhal and Lamartine also spent much time in Rome. Native talent included a school of somewhat dry neo-classical painters under the leadership of Pietro Camuccini and highly accomplished neo-classical sculptors under Canova who was himself generally accepted as the greatest living artist in Europe. The official embargo on the export of antique sculpture from Rome proved an unpremeditated boost for living artists, and one which the papal government actively encouraged, as has been seen, by advising rich foreign collectors, whether German princes or English dukes, to commission modern statues from Canova and his school. The papal government also increased the number of prizes, competitions and exhibitions for artists in Rome, and set up a new school of drawing. In 1816, the Academy of St Luke and the old Institute of Archaeology were amalgamated under the presidency of Canova to create a new, more powerful Academy of Arts, and the following year, the papal architect,

Valadier, was appointed Professor of Architecture at the Academy, and Inspector of a new Council of Arts. In such ways, Consalvi's policy of centralization and state direction affected the arts as much as other aspects of the papal government.

Reform of the structure of state patronage of the arts was combined with a renewal of the ambitious programme of urban improvements, begun in the first ministry. The rating system of Rome was altered so as to raise money more effectively. Hitherto, rates had been levied on the inhabitants of particular streets for the upkeep of that street only. Consalvi's new system imposed a general rate on all households for the maintenance and improvement of the whole city and not just individual streets. The guilds of workmen responsible for the upkeep of the fountains and other public works were also reorganized. This made it possible, for instance, to turn up the water pressure in all the fountains with more impressive effects.

The major work after 1815 was the creation of the new Piazza del Popolo and the adjoining public park on the Pincio, under the direction of Giuseppe Valadier. The proposal for remodelling the piazza went back to the reign of Pius VI, but like many of the more ambitious projects of that pontificate it had never got off the ground. The idea had first been aired in public in 1773 as a competition task for the Concorso Balestra, in which architects studying in Rome from all over Europe had taken part (including the Englishman Thomas Harrison of Chester). Valadier submitted a design at that stage for a great quadrangular set-piece. In 1793 the idea was revived and Valadier produced a new scheme for a wedge-shaped piazza with colonnades down the sides, but the ruin of the papal finances following the Treaty of Tolentino had made its execution impossible. During his first ministry, Consalvi had improved the Via Flaminia outside the Porta del Popolo and restored the Ponte Milvio as part of a concerted project which was intended to include a public park along the Tiber, and a reconstructed Piazza del Popolo, but he was not able to do anything about the latter at that stage.

It was left to the French, during their occupation of Rome between 1810 and 1814, to carry the project a little further. They conceived the piazza more as an open garden square than an enclosed urban space, and switched Consalvi's scheme for a public park from the bank of the Tiber to the Pincian Hill in order to take advantage of the beautiful view of Rome from the top. This was an option which had not been available to Consalvi because the hillside was occupied by the buildings and grounds of the Augustinian priory attached to the church of S. Maria del Popolo. It was no hindrance to the French, who confiscated the priory, demolished the buildings and commissioned a scheme from Louis Berthault, the French imperial gardener, to lay out a park and pyramidal national monument on the hill; but this, like previous schemes, came to nought. Indeed, the amount achieved by the French in Rome between 1810 and 1814 has been much exaggerated. Apart from clearing the Pincio, continuing the excavations already begun under Consalvi's rule in the Forum, planting some flower beds round the Colosseum and carrying out hurried decorations in the Quirinal, including the plaster 'Alexander Frieze' by Thorwaldsen, for a visit of Napoleon which never took place, the government of occupation did little in the city, though much was discussed. Nor was Consalvi's policy after the Restoration much influenced by French ideas. His programme had been planned and begun in his first ministry, and in turn was the continuation of proposals considered at least as early as the reign of Pius VI.

When he returned to Rome in 1815, Consalvi found nothing achieved in the area of the Piazza del Popolo except for the clearance of the priory buildings but this struck him as an ideal opportunity to create a much more beautiful park than the one he had originally envisaged. He, therefore, excluded the priory garden from the church lands returned to their owners at the Restoration and commissioned a new project from Valadier who, on 27 November 1815, presented the final design for the Piazza del Popolo: an oval amphitheatre combined with curving ter-raced ramps up the hillside to the Pincio. This was approved by the papal government on 7 January 1816 and was put in hand immediately. Work was executed in stages and completed in 1822, and the financing of this ambitious project was cleverly planned by Consalvi to make use of different funds. Valadier's plan was ingenious, too, as it did not involve the demolition of any major buildings, but wove the existing fabric into a brilliant new lay-out. On one side of the Porta del Popolo, a block of barracks was built for the new *carabinieri*, and the church of S. Maria del Popolo was screened by a new side elevation to match, thus creating a symmetrical frame for the monumental gateway into the city. At either end of the new piazza, ramped hemi-cycles – gradually embellished over the years with rostral columns and allegorical sculpture – gave access to the terraces of the Pincio and the bank of the Tiber respectively. On the town side the existing pair of domed and porticoed baroque churches was framed by blocks of new domestic buildings designed by Valadier, but paid for and built by Torlonia as a private specu-lation, thus not costing the state a penny. The result of this ingenuity and careful planning is an urban square comparable with Bath or Nancy in its exquisite fusion of architecture and parkland and its exploitation of levels and vistas. In place of the pyramid which the French had proposed for the top of the Pincian Hill, was substituted the Loggiata, an elegant belvedere with Corinthian columns inspired by a Roman triumphal arch, and erected between 1816 and 1820 to Valadier's design. It was intended as a place to admire the magnificent view across the river to open country and St Peter's.[2] The new garden on top was planted with avenues of ilex trees, mimosa, flowering shrubs, and further embellished with an obelisk erected in 1822. This garden was an immediate success and became the smartest resort for an evening walk or carriage drive, both for the Romans and foreign tourists. It is described in their letters and journals by many nineteenth-century visitors to the city, who all enjoyed the 'fashionable halo of sunset and pink parasols'. The American Nathaniel Hawthorne thought the Pincian garden 'one of the things that reconcile the stranger to the rule of an irresponsible dynasty of Holy Fathers'.

Elsewhere in the city, Consalvi cleared and repaved the Piazza della Rotonda in front of the Pantheon, his titular church. The 'ignoble huts' and fish market around the fountain in the centre were all swept away, and the posting of bills on the columns of the portico was strictly forbidden. This removed one of the chief grumbles of visitors to Rome who had hitherto complained that seeing the Pantheon was like finding Westminster Abbey in the middle of Covent Garden market. The Arch of Titus overlooking the Forum was restored to its original form (as depicted on antique medals) between 1819 and 1820. In Piranesi's earlier engravings, it appears engulfed in medieval buildings, in semiruinous condition. Under the direction of Rafael Stern, who had previously been responsible for the restoration of the Colosseum, the Arch was freed of accretions, and left in splendid isolation; the missing sections were replaced in travertine in order to differentiate the restoration work from the original marble masonry, a remarkably sympathetic and modern approach to preservation. All but two of the capitals and the whole of the attic are early nineteenth-century restoration. Stern died while work was in progress and the restoration of the Arch was completed by Valadier who, subsequently, falsely claimed all the credit in a book he published on the work.[3]

The restoration of the Arch of Titus was part of a general programme of repair and excavation in the Forum which, like everything else, was a continuation of the work begun in the first ministry. The driving force behind this project was Carlo Fea, who had been appointed director of the excavations by Consalvi in 1803. He was the first scholar to establish the correct topography of the Roman Forum, and the work co-ordinated by him marked a new development in archaeological attitudes to the ruins of Rome. Previous excavations down to the eighteenth century had been undertaken in the hope of discovering antique columns, statues and marble. This was still an important consideration, but Fea's chief aim was the more scientific modern archaeological one of ascertaining and recording the original lay-out and purposes of the ruins themselves.[4] Consalvi took a strong personal interest in the work, and this was something which he shared with the Duchess of Devonshire who was keen to take part in the excavations and to help pay for them. Consalvi arranged for her to excavate round the Column of Phocas,

Byron's 'nameless column with a buried base', in the middle of the Forum. She paid for galley slaves to do the work, and cleared the surrounding area down to Roman street level, discovering the inscription which gave the date of the monument as AD 608, as well as unearthing some splendid porphyry columns which went to the Capitol museum. Nor were her practical artistic enthusiasms confined to archaeology. With Consalvi's encouragement, she commissioned de luxe editions of Horace's *Fifth Satire* (1817) and the *Aeneid* (1819) which she gave to her friends and the 'Royal Libraries of Europe'. Both were illustrated with views of the sites mentioned in the text; in the Horace after drawings commissioned from Caraccioli, and in the Virgil after Thomas Lawrence. The Virgil was based on Anibal Caro's sixteenth-century translation, but the Horace was a new translation made specially for the duchess by Consalvi's own secretary.[5]

The Duchess of Devonshire was only one of the English visitors who were involved in the excavations. It was typical of Consalvi's ability to achieve a lot on the tightest of budgets that he got several 'Milors Inglesi' to pay for galley-slave labour to clear different sections of the Forum under the general direction of the Roman authorities, and with the proviso that all important statues and marble columns discovered should go to the public museums. 'Not a leg of an old statue, nor a scrap of a *basso relievo*, nor a broken-headed bust will be suffered to escape,' complained Mrs Eaton, though she noted approvingly that 'the Pope readily grants permission to all sorts of persons to excavate as much as they please, wherever they please'.[6]

The Duchess of Devonshire in her correspondence kept up a running commentary on the work of improvement in Rome. In December 1820, for instance, she told Thomas Lawrence: 'The Improvements are continued, Artists are employed, Statues found and bought. Everything looks well.'[7] And in 1823 she wrote to the same correspondent:

Improvements are going on everywhere in Rome. The Piazza del Popolo is becoming beautiful. All the shabby houses have been demolished [and] the pavement in front of the Pantheon has been levelled and not a placard is now allowed to be on the fine columns. Your picture of the King [Lawrence's full-length of George IV] is placed in a larger room against a different colour. It is the beginning of the English school here. The statue of Pius VI is placed where Canova intended it to be – an Admirable effect.[8]

The sixth Duke, her stepson, however, was the principal recipient of her enthusiasm. In 1821 she wrote to him: 'Titus's Arch is to be restored to what it was according to the medals – the pictures at the Vatican are I believe to be in the apartment above, for better light – *your** alabaster columns for the Braccio Nuovo, the statues and columns found at Veii to be in a room called Camera dei Monumenti di Veii.'[9] A year later she added:

Rome is more beautiful than ever – the new museum is far the handsomest part of the museum, and as beautiful as any thing can be – the architecture is perfect and the effect of it quite extraordinary; it is really worthy of the best time – the effect of the ceiling, being like the Temple of Peace and of Venus at Rome in three compartments, gives it a lightness and magnificence which is very striking – the Pincian Hill gives compleat shade now and the place is ready for the obelisk. It is that which lay in three pieces at the Vatican – and is of beautiful sculpture – the Piazza del Popolo is embellishing also; the road by the Arch of Constantine is planted, that by Diocletian's baths also is planted – and a well planted walk leads to the Porta San Paolo and the way up to the Pyramid is all mended and planted also – houses everywhere are painting, and the Piazza del Pantheon also is clear of its stalls and some shabby houses are thrown down, nor are there any more *avvisos* pasted on the columns of the portico, in short there is enough to tempt you here again.[10]

The sight that moved all visitors to ecstasies, however, was the Vatican museum as reinstated by Canova in 1816. 'The accumulated creation of gifted genius', 'the treasury of the fine arts', the

*The duke had wanted these for the dining-room at Chatsworth but could not get an export licence.

'temple of taste', 'the consecrated seat of the muses' runs the litany of praise falling from the lips of those who traversed the two miles of marble halls and galleries. The Museo Chiaramonti, established in 1803–07, was also decorated under Canova's direction with a series of lunette paintings in fresco depicting some of the chief incidents in Consalvi's artistic restoration of Rome. These were an important item in the state programme for developing Rome as a centre for the study and production of the fine arts. They were intended as official encouragement for young artists to revive a medium then near extinction. The idea for the scheme of frescos was Canova's and he himself financed the project, using the pension of 3,000 scudi granted to him by the pope in 1816 as a reward for retrieving the works of art from Paris. He chose the artists and directed the execution of the work. He intended the scheme to reconcile the opposed schools of strict neo-classicists under the Italian Pietro Camuccini and the more romantic German Nazarenes. Many of the artists employed on the frescos later became famous, including the neo-classicist Francesco Hayez and the Nazarene Philipp Veit. Consalvi supported Canova closely, and he was himself responsible for choosing the subjects for the fifteen paintings; they give a good impression, therefore, of what he thought was especially important in the artistic programme. The subjects are: The Restoration of the Colosseum, The Return of the Raphael Tapestries, The Laying Out of the Pincio Gardens, The Founding of the Drawing School, Architecture Honoured, The Recovery of the Works of Art from Paris, Sculpture Honoured, The Issue of Laws Forbidding the Export of Works of Art, Painting Honoured, The Restitution of the Coin Collection, The Founding of the Museo Chiaramonti, The Founding of the Vatican Picture Gallery, The Excavation of the Roman Arches, The Establishment of Departments of Greek and Egyptian Art at the Vatican Museum, and The Union of the Two Roman Academies.[11]

The return of the antique sculpture from Paris led to serious overcrowding of the Vatican museum and made necessary the construction of a completely new gallery, the Braccio Nuovo.

This was begun in 1817 to the design of Rafael Stern and completed after his death in 1820 by Pasquale Belli. It is the finest of the series of great neo-classical museums created throughout Europe in the early nineteenth century, with its columns of antique yellow marble, Egyptian granite or Cipollino alabaster (from the Forum excavations), and a floor inlaid with antique mosaics. The walls are punctuated by niches for statues, while the busts are displayed on elegant console brackets in between. The coved ceiling, with top-lighting, was perhaps partly influenced by the Grande Galerie of the Louvre which Consalvi had seen in Paris. The central domed area was designed specially with a large apse for the gigantic recumbent statue of the River Nile retrieved from Paris in 1816.[12] Elsewhere in the Vatican, older rooms were adapted for the display of more works of art. George IV's gift of plaster casts of the Elgin Marbles, for instance, was displayed in a room in the Belvedere as the beginning of a new Greek gallery. Egyptian sculpture from Hadrian's Villa was grouped together to form an Egyptian gallery. The Borgia Rooms were opened to the public as picture galleries for the display of paintings formerly in churches, such as Raphael's *Transfiguration*, taken to Paris by the French after the Treaty of Tolentino and restored to Rome in 1816. They were joined in due course by Lawrence's bravura full-length portrait of George IV, presented by the king to the pope. In the library, Marini, with the architectural assistance of Stern, established new galleries for the display of the retrieved coins and for the collection of ancient inscriptions. Study rooms for the use of visiting scholars were also provided for the first time.

A lesser known museum established by Consalvi in these years was the Protomoteca Capitolina, the earliest public national portrait gallery in Europe. It started in the Pantheon where busts were commissioned from Canova and his pupils to continue the series of monuments of great men going back to the sixteenth century. The archaeologically-minded argued that these detracted from the splendour of the Roman architecture. Consalvi agreed, and in March 1820 he gave the order for the transfer of the busts to the Capitol where they were rearranged under the direction of Stern. There they remain, including Consalvi's gift of Canova's portrait of Cimarosa and Pius VII's gift of his own bust by Canova.[13]

Rafael Stern was Consalvi's favourite architect, and the one he used to supervise the new work at the Quirinal Palace after the pope's return to Rome. It was Stern who designed the new fountain added at this date to Pius VI's obelisk in front of the Quirinal, making use of a large circular Roman granite basin hitherto used as a cattle trough and removed from the Forum to make way for the excavations. Inside the palace, between 1815 and 1817, Stern altered a series of rooms which were decorated with paintings in fresco by Francesco Manno. These were comparable to the series of frescos in the Museo Chiaramonti, but have since been destroyed without record. Consalvi's decorations were a continuation of extensive improvements to the Quirinal Palace begun by the French in anticipation of a visit by Napoleon in 1812 which never materialized. Pius VII, on his return, is supposed to have remarked of the assorted mythological females who bedecked his apartments, that with a few alterations they would make splendid Madonnas. The further programme of decorations and improvements after the Restoration, supervised by Consalvi in person, was undertaken in preparation for the reception of another emperor: Francis I of Austria. The ubiquitous Mrs Eaton recorded:

> Another part of it [the Quirinal], in expectation of the threatened visit of the Emperor of Austria, has been recently fitted up for that great personage's reception under the special direction of Cardinal G* himself.
>
> I cannot describe silk hangings and rich carpets, neither shall I stop to criticise the Secretary of State's taste as an upholsterer ... but I was edified to observe in one of the rooms, the consideration of the minister, in providing for his Imperial Majesty's recreation several suitable diversions. There was a solitaire board, and a little table to play at fox and geese.[14]

*Often called Gonsalvi or Gonsalvo by the English.

Stern, as well as designing these rooms, was also responsible for the decorations on the Capitol devised for the emperor's reception, recalling distantly the designs of Michelangelo for the reception in the same place for Charles V. Francis I was so pleased with Stern's work that he bestowed on him the cross of the Order of the Iron Crown of Lombardy.

The state visit to Rome of the Emperor of Austria, accompanied by Metternich, in the summer of 1819 was a key event in Consalvi's post-1815 foreign policy. After the defeat of Napoleon, Austria was left as the major Catholic power in Europe, and by far the strongest in the Italian peninsula; for in addition to the direct rule of Lombardy-Veneto, the Austrians controlled Tuscany where the emperor's brother was the Grand Duke. Under the terms of the Congress of Vienna, the Austrians had also been given the right to garrison the papal city of Ferrara on the south bank of the Po. The maintenance of easy relations with Metternich was therefore essential to the well-being of the temporal power and the rule of order in Italy.[15] In addition to Italian territorial considerations, the papal government was anxious to negotiate with the Austrian emperor a concordat which would restore the independence of the Catholic Church in his lands and demolish the late-eighteenth-century nationalistic 'Josephist' system which had part-secularized the Church and subjected religion to state control in accordance with the principles of the Enlightenment. Though some progress was made in reversing this state of affairs by Consalvi, he was not able to achieve all that Rome wanted, and it was not till 1855 that a concordat was signed between the Holy See and Austria favourable to the Church. In his diplomatic relations with the Emperor of Austria, Consalvi had to walk a narrow tightrope between political dependence on the one hand and papal neutrality on the other. In the event, he proved more successful in dealing with Metternich after 1815 than with Napoleon in 1804 to 1806, partly because Metternich admired him and the Austrians were in any case more prepared to accept papal claims at face value.

The state visit of the emperor in 1819 saw the high point of Austro-Roman relations. Recalling the way that the stateless

Pius VII had been summoned to Vienna after his election in 1800, the visit of the emperor in person to Rome and his reception in state marked an impressive revival of the prestige and independence of the papacy. Consalvi stage-managed the visit from beginning to end, and spared no efforts to impress Metternich and his royal master with the grandeur of the restored papal power. He arranged a series of splendid entertainments, some of them a revival of traditional festivities which had fallen into desuetude during the wars and French occupation. Thus the annual horse races in the Piazza Navona were organized with special care that year. The external illumination of St Peter's with thousands of little lanterns and the fireworks at the Castel S. Angelo on St Peter's Day, recorded by many eighteenth-century painters, including Joseph Wright of Derby, were revived and executed with particular panache. Consalvi himself gave a splendid state banquet for the imperial visitors. Thomas Lawrence who was in Rome at the time recorded his impressions in one of his letters home:

> The splendour of the papal power is of another description; and in St Peter's, and a few other churches, equally beyond all expectation or conception of it, that I had formed; and I should think the extent of the impression must be as new and powerful to every traveller. I understand that it is so to the Emperor. And I know from himself that it is so to Prince Metternich . . . After dining yesterday at a superb dress public dinner given by Cardinal Consalvi, I went with Prince Metternich to view by torch-light Canova's beautiful statue of the Venus, for which the Princess Borghese is said to have sat to him.[16]

Lawrence attended the illuminations and fireworks on St Peter's Day, as well as the papal mass in St Peter's:

> I was yesterday, St Peter's Day, a spectator of doubtless the most superb ceremony and spectacle . . . that this world can exhibit: the celebration of high mass in St Peter's. No words of mine have any power of conveying to you the magni-

ficence and grandeur of it ... Titian never conceived anything more gorgeous, and at the same time solemn in dignity.[17]

The enhancement of the pomp and pageantry surrounding the pope was another element in Consalvi's policy, intended to reinforce the international reputation and standing of his sovereign. The revival and augmentation of traditional state ceremonial was in any case a European-wide phenomenon in the early nineteenth century and could be encountered as much in George IV's England or the restored Bourbon monarchies as in papal Rome. The smooth perfection of the arrangements for the emperor's visit in 1819 was partly due to practice. Consalvi had had the chance to perform a small-scale dress rehearsal in the spring of the previous year when the Crown Prince of Bavaria (the emperor's brother-in-law) spent several months in Rome on a 'private' visit. Consalvi had concluded the negotiations for a concordat with the kingdom of Bavaria in 1817 and took the opportunity of the Crown Prince's visit in 1818 to follow that up, and to cement good relations between the Holy See and the most prominent of the new German Catholic kingdoms. Once again there is a description of the special events by a contemporary British visitor in Rome. Mrs Eaton witnessed the illuminations and fireworks on Easter Sunday: 'The old custom ... has been revived, in compliment to the Prince Royal of Bavaria, who has been here several months; and it is only one of the many pleasures his residence at Rome has yielded.' She also attended High Mass at St Peter's on Easter Sunday and, like Lawrence the following year, was greatly struck by the grandeur of it:

> The church was lined with the Guarda Nobili [sic], in their splendid uniforms of gold and scarlet and nodding plumes of white ostrich feathers, and the Swiss Guards, with their polished cuirasses and steel helmets. The great central aisle was kept clear by a double wall of armed men for the grand procession, the approach of which, after much expectation, was proclaimed by the sound of a trumpet, from the further end of the church. A long band of priests advanced, loaded

with still augmenting magnificence, as they ascended to the higher orders. Cloth of gold and silver, and crimson velvet, and mantles of spotted ermine and flowing trains, and attendant train-bearers, and mitres and crucifixes glittering with jewels, and priests and patriarchs and bishops and cardinals, dazzled our astonished eyes, and filled the length of St Peter's. Lastly came the Pope in his crimson chair of state (*sedia gestatoria*) borne on the shoulders of twenty *Palefrenieri*, arrayed in robes of white and wearing the tiara, a triple crown of the conjoined Trinity, with a canopy of cloth of silver floating over his head; and preceded by two men, carrying enormous fans composed of plumes of ostrich feathers, mounted on long gilded wands . . . he was slowly borne past . . . liberally giving his benediction with the twirl of the three fingers as he passed.[18]

Such was the restored and augmented magnificence of the papacy with which Consalvi enveloped the simple and frugal old man who was his sovereign. Some foreign observers saw this pomp as a substitute for the fully reformed system of govern-ment which Consalvi would have liked to have brought about. The Neapolitan foreign minister, for instance, criticized all the expenditure on art, festivals, fireworks and religious ceremonial as 'foolish extravagances'.

An important part of Consalvi's foreign policy during his second ministry was the extension of the concordat system initiated with France and northern Italy under Napoleon. After his preliminary discussions with several other Catholic powers at Paris and Vienna in 1814 and 1815, Consalvi followed up on his return to Rome with a whole series of new concordats. After considerable discussion with Louis XVIII and Talleyrand, in the hope of achieving a new concordat more favourable to the papacy than Napoleon's, the original 1801 French Concordat was reconfirmed in 1817. As has already been mentioned, a concordat with Bavaria was signed in the same year. A similar concordat was ratified with Naples in 1818 after lengthy nego-tiations, and one with Prussia, now in possession of the Catholic

Rhineland, in 1819. Even where no formal concordat was arranged, Consalvi was indefatigable in negotiating on issues which appertained to Rome, and he evolved a regular centralized system governing the relations between the Holy See and the local churches which exceeded anything that he was able to bring about within the Papal States themselves.

A particular concern after 1815 was the settlement of religious affairs in the newly united kingdom of the Low Countries, Catholic Flanders having been given to the Protestant King of Holland at the Congress of Vienna. Consalvi was determined that the king should not interfere in the appointment of Catholic bishops, and conducted a lengthy correspondence on the subject with Reinhold, the Dutch foreign minister, of which he sent copies to Castlereagh because of the parallel to British policy in Ireland.*[19]

Consalvi continued to correspond with Castlereagh, whom he regarded as a friend, and later with his successor as foreign minister, George Canning, on the subjects of Catholic emancipation and the abolition of the slave trade. He maintained the good relations established in 1814 with the Prince Regent and the British government and took a keen interest in events in England. He was, for example, much affected by the death of the heir to the throne, Princess Charlotte, and sent a formal letter of condolence from the pope to the Prince Regent on that occasion, an unprecedented courtesy between the Holy See and a Protestant monarch. But as the Duchess of Devonshire told the Prince Regent: 'You will easily believe how very sincerely and strongly Cardinal Consalvi is affected by the misfortune to you, my dear Sir, to whom he is so gratefully attached, he wrote to me to tell me of it this morning.'[20]

A particularly delicate diplomatic problem was caused by the intermittent sojourn in the Papal States of the Prince Regent's estranged wife, Caroline of Brunswick. It was not too difficult while she was still Princess of Wales and so did not in any case qualify for the honours due to the wife of a reigning monarch,

*In the longer term, this problem was solved by the rebellion of Belgium and its establishment as an independent kingdom.

and could be treated with friendly informality by the papal government. James Brougham wrote to his brother Henry Brougham in 1819 about the princess, while she was living at Pesaro to economize:

> The Pope and Gonsalvi [sic] are extremely civil to her, and on the best of terms. This is certainly the best country for her to be in. She is on such good terms with ye Pope and Cardinals – and there being no [British] Minister at Rome, she is not insulted there as at Vienna and other courts.[21]

The problem became more acute when the Prince Regent succeeded to the throne the following year; his wife started to sign herself 'Caroline R' and assumed regal airs despite impending divorce proceedings in the House of Lords. Consalvi did not want to upset her, nor on the other hand, did he wish to give concern to the English government. In February 1820, he wrote to William A'Court, the British minister in Naples, describing her first visit to Rome as Queen of England. She had written a letter to the pope announcing her imminent arrival, signed 'Caroline R'. Fortunately, she did not leave enough time for a reply, thus obviating for Consalvi the problem of how correctly to address her. She lodged in Rome at the Palazzo Canino. The secretary of state compromised and gave her a guard of honour of fourteen soldiers, which was appropriate to her royal status, without necessarily implying recognition of her as Queen of England.[22]

On a more serious topic, Consalvi continued negotiations with Castlereagh on the subject of the Irish bishops, in an attempt to clear away the obstacles littering the path to Catholic emancipation in the British Isles. At the Roman end, he played a large part in the restoration and reopening of the English College, the oldest English institution abroad, which had served as a seminary for training English priests since the sixteenth century. It had been reduced to ruin during the French occupation of Rome. Consalvi took pains to see it revived and in 1817 assumed the management of the college himself, ensuring that all its property was retrieved. The following year, 1818, the pope formally appointed him Cardinal-Protector of the college. Consalvi was determined that the college should now be run by English secular clergy and not by the Jesuits as it had been in the past. He understood official English prejudice against the Order and wanted to do everything possible to ease the way to emancipation by not causing gratuitous violence to English feelings. He thought it would be a political mistake to recognize the English Jesuits, and it was entirely due to Consalvi that the new rector of the English College was not a Jesuit, but a secular Catholic priest from Lancashire, Fr. Gradwell, formerly the chaplain to the Brockholes family at Claughton-on-Brock near Preston. Under Consalvi's influence a new constitution was drawn up for the college, simpler than the 1600 constitution which it replaced. His role as Cardinal-Protector was far from being a sinecure; he was in charge of the admission of all students to the college, and also had the last word on much of the day-to-day running of the college. He followed the careers of the first post-Restoration generation of students who included Nicholas Wiseman (later the first cardinal-archbishop of Westminster), and was pleased when they all did well in their exams.[23]

It was characteristic of Consalvi's special regard for England that he received the English painter, Sir Thomas Lawrence, who came to Rome in 1819 to do portraits of the secretary of state and the pope, as if he was a special ambassador from the Prince Regent. He provided Lawrence with a whole suite of rooms in the Quirinal, and arranged for him to attend all the religious services, state ceremonies and other public events as if he were a guest of honour. Lawrence, naturally, was delighted with his reception and painted in Rome the two finest of his Waterloo Chamber series of the allied statesmen and sovereigns; indeed his portraits of Pius VII and Consalvi are probably the masterpieces of his whole *œuvre*. Lawrence had been prepared for his task in Rome by a series of letters from the Duchess of Devonshire:

> You will be struck by the dignified animation and bene-
> volent expression of Cardinal Consalvi. Vicard [sic] intirely
> failed by painting him in profile. I feel assur'd that you will

agree with me that a three-quarter or nearly a full face is what will do justice to the beauty of his countenance . . . this will be one of your best portraits yet.[24]

Immediately on his arrival in Rome, Lawrence was presented by the British consul, Mr Parkes, to the secretary of state on 17 May. 'I was yesterday presented by the English Consul to Cardinal Consalvi and most graciously received and also had an audience with the pope at the Quirinal.'[25] After his first sitting for the portrait, Consalvi conducted Lawrence through all the rooms as far as the door of the hall, a mark of particular courtesy. Lawrence, for his part, made an immediate and excellent impression on the papal court.

> There is always a something, that one imagines at least, to be got over, in the intercourse of a stranger with the friends, suite, and dependants of the great who are always more distant and *great* than the personage himself; but my picture of the Cardinal has so gratified and conciliated all, that every countenance has instant cheerfulness that I meet . . . On the first day, I painted in the whole head, and very like him. He has a penetrating and pursuing eye, and I make him look directly at the spectator. Edward [Lawrence's assistant] told me that when I left it, two domestics came in very softly and quietly, looked at it for a moment, and then *ran* out and brought in, according to his phrase 'a dozen'.[26]

All the time Lawrence was in Rome he continued to be bombarded by the duchess with advice on his portraits; he also painted for her a small sketch in pencil and watercolour of Consalvi which she carried everywhere with her thereafter, in her carriage and even when she was staying in her friends' and relations' houses. Consalvi himself made one or two suggestions about the pope's portrait and it was at his suggestion that Lawrence omitted the papal tiara from Pius VII's portrait, 'with that delicacy of intent that extends to everything', as he thought that such an overt symbol of papal claims might be objectionable to Protestant feelings in a portrait destined for an English royal palace.[27] He himself was painted with his hand resting on the 1816 constitution of which he was so proud; the words '*Motu Proprio*' are just discernible on the spine.

Pleasant relations with England, the regular negotiating of concordats with the continental powers, the maintenance of warm and close relations with Austria, the careful defence of papal neutrality and independence; these were the corner-stones of Consalvi's post-1815 foreign policy. This calm progress received a severe and dangerous jolt, however, in 1820 – from Naples of all places – and there followed a coolness between the papal government and Austria. Consalvi had been irritated by Neapolitan dragging of feet over the restitution of the enclaves after 1815. Relations between the Holy See and Naples had been further strained by the king's retraction of his solemn coronation promise of a white horse which all the kings of Naples had rendered to the pope at their coronation since the accession of the Angevins. The king now claimed that it was a mark of vassalage. Consalvi countered that it was nothing of the sort; it was a symbol of investiture. He took the Duchess of Devonshire into his confidence, and she enlisted William A'Court, the British minister in Naples, on the side of the Roman government. She wrote to him:

> If I hint at the Pope's letter to Consalvi, is there not a danger as all letters are open'd at the Post here, that my information would be traced to you, as you told me the letter was a secret at Naples to all but you, you caution'd me so strongly against letting my information be traced to you. I wonder why they keep it so secret if they think it makes against the Pope – I can't help thinking that the indignation of His Holiness is upon the King's breach of promise and violation of his solemn oath on his accession, and not on the mere refusal . . . pray read over again the letter which I have sent you, an extract copy by me as Consalvi's writing is so difficult.[28]

The quarrel over the white horse was a minor irritation compared with what followed. In July 1820, a full-scale revolution broke out in Naples, led by the army which was riddled by the *carbonari*. In a bloodless coup absolutism was overthrown and constitutional government established. The king was forced by army officers to adopt the 1812 Spanish constitution, which was not particularly well suited to Naples, but was the only constitution model they knew. Vienna refused to recognize the new constitutional government in Naples, which put the papal government in a difficult position. On the one hand, Consalvi did not wish to endanger the practice of religion in Naples or provoke the invasion of papal territory by antagonizing the new Neapolitan government. Equally, he did not wish to upset Vienna, or indeed to uphold 'constitutionalism' and revolution as examples to the inhabitants of the Papal States, by formally recognizing the new government. It was a situation which could only be met by great tact, absolute impartiality and strict neutrality, and Consalvi was faced with the problem of remaining on friendly terms with Naples without recognizing the new government. In his handling of this crisis he once again showed his mettle as one of the most accomplished diplomats of his age, and succeeded both in defending papal neutrality and in preserving internal tranquillity within the states of the Church.[29] The immediate prospects were alarming however. The revolutionary fever quickly spread to the enclaves of Benevento and Ponte Corvo, leading to the overthrow of the papal government in those duchies. The papal delegate and garrison were driven out of Benevento on 11 July, and the papal governor and garrison from Ponte Corvo on 16 July, following the incursion of a detachment of Neapolitan troops. Much to Consalvi's satisfaction, however, the Neapolitan government refused to co-operate with the rebels in Ponte Corvo and Benevento. There was a real danger, nevertheless, that similar revolts would spread to the 'mainland' papal states.

Consalvi set up a border patrol of military to guard the frontier and stepped up his drive to enlist additional men for the army, beginning with an edict against the 'able-bodied unemployed'. If they did not change their idle way of life within ten days, they would be enrolled into the army. Cardinal Bernetti, the head of the papal police, and the local delegates and governors also tightened up their activities against revolutionary activity throughout the Papal States. All known *carbonari* were arrested and imprisoned, and the guards doubled at the major prisons. A republican riot in the gaol at Civitavecchia, where many of the 1,600 prisoners got out of control and started to shout political slogans, was treated with the greatest severity, though, as Consalvi later admitted, the trouble may have been as much a protest at the bad food and poor conditions as a serious political revolt. At the time, however, the government could not afford to take chances. The ringleaders were tried by court martial, set up by the papal delegate at Civitavecchia, and thirty-two of them condemned to death. Though two were reprieved on the grounds that the judgements against them had not been unanimous, thirty were shot by firing squad.[30] Such drastic measures on the part of the local governors and delegates, and the mobilizing of the papal army proved successful in preventing the spread of revolution.

At the moment, however, that the internal danger seemed to have been averted, Consalvi was faced with a more serious danger from without. His tightrope policy of strict neutrality did not meet with the approval of Vienna. Metternich wished to use Austrian military power to crush the Neapolitan revolt. This would involve Austrian soldiers from northern Italy marching through the Papal States, inviting a similar invasion by the Neapolitan army from the south. There was a danger that the Papal States would be ravaged by warfare; perhaps Rome would be occupied by one or other of the opposing sides; the pope might even be kidnapped by the Neapolitan rebels. At the international conference at Troppau in October and November 1820, Metternich was successful in establishing the principle that the Great Powers should intervene to maintain order in Naples. Consalvi, while secretly assuring Metternich that he would not oppose the speedy passage of Austrian troops through the Papal States, publicly upheld the principle of papal aloofness from the fray and refused to take the side of either Naples or Austria. He sent his most trusted deputy, Cardinal Spina, to the Congress of Laibach in January 1821 to uphold the neutrality of the pope, and otherwise to refrain from taking part in the deliberations of the allied sovereigns, while on 8 February 1821, he issued an official notification stating that if war broke out 'The Holy Father, because of his position as visible head of the Church, and an essentially peaceful sovereign, will continue to maintain, as he has maintained to the present, a perfect neutrality towards all nations.'[31] He followed this up with a declaration that regular troops, in uniform, from both sides would be allowed to enter the Papal States, but not 'malicious irregulars' who would be apprehended and deported.

This detached even-handedness was fine in theory, but in practice things were a little more difficult to control. Shortage of food for the Austrian troops caused problems, and Consalvi had to intervene and order the populace to supply them at the expense of the papal government (which would reclaim the relevant sums from Vienna in due course). He was, however, successful in refusing to allow the passage of troops through Rome itself and in preventing the Austrians from garrisoning the citadel of Ancona, an issue of the greatest sensitivity as it had been the French occupation of Ancona in 1805 which had led directly to the Napoleonic overthrow of the papal government. In order to keep himself informed of events, Consalvi established a system of beacon bonfires to flash important news to Rome from the frontier. Just in case, he also repaired the Castel S. Angelo, filled the moat with water diverted from the Vatican gardens, and mounted all the available artillery on the ramparts. In the event, these precautions were not necessary for all opposition in Naples collapsed on the arrival of the Austrian army.

As usual, the secretary of state's greatest admirer was the Duchess of Devonshire:

> The Cardinal has held a firm, temperate and dignified conduct which has secured great consideration for Rome from all parties. Naples has declared that she will not pass the frontiers. Austria has consented not to march through the capital. The Romans are so pleased with the Cardinal's

proclamation of yesterday that they now look on their Carnaval [sic] as certain . . .[32]

Benevento and Ponte Corvo returned voluntarily to the Roman fold; and papal arms spontaneously reappeared on all the public buildings. Consalvi sent back the delegates and small contingents of troops with instructions to treat the population of the two enclaves leniently, to take no reprisals, merely to announce that papal laws were now back in force, and not to proclaim either pardon or punishment for the rebels. He hoped that the rebels, who were in any case a very small proportion of the population, would flee of their own accord, thus sparing the papal government from any act of harshness. This in fact happened, and in April he granted a general amnesty to the inhabitants of Benevento and Ponte Corvo, except for the ringleaders; they were retrospectively exiled for ever.[33]

Consalvi's handling of the events of 1820 and 1821 showed his diplomatic skills to great advantage. He was successful in adhering to the essentials of his policy throughout, never departing from strict neutrality. He was able to maintain reasonably good relations with Naples, without provoking Austria too far, though Metternich was not entirely pleased with the 'strange inflexibility' of the papal secretary of state. He thought Consalvi's neutral stance was indefensible and hypocritical when in fact the papacy was entirely dependent on the Austrian army to maintain the monarchical status quo and public tranquillity in Italy. To the Austrian chancellor it seemed that Consalvi wanted to have his cake and to eat it. Metternich and Lebzeltern continued to bombard him with letters urging the Holy See to abandon its aloof stand in the face of the troubles, disorders and threats of revolution which threatened to spread throughout Italy:

> In these times, a union of royalty is necessary in the face of the causes which are undermining them . . . rulers should present a united front . . . The Court of Rome is one of the objects most agreeable to the heart of the Emperor, but . . . the Court of Rome wishes to adopt a destructive neutrality

... The Allies are not asking for the active involvement of the papacy, just for an attitude that would be helpful to their movement. The Minister of the Pope, himself has said that he supports the interests of the Allies. He sees the dangers of revolt in Italy. But there is a gap between the two sides of his sentiments in this matter.[34]

Consalvi remained steadfast in his refusal to get involved in Austrian military activity in the peninsula, but he was able to thaw any coolness in Austro-Roman relations following the invasion of Naples, for Metternich did not just want Consalvi's support for Austrian military intervention, he was also asking for the pope's spiritual assistance in the suppression of the *carbonari*, the secret political societies plotting revolution and the unification of Italy. Here, after careful consideration, Consalvi was able to oblige. Metternich first approached him asking for the pope to excommunicate the *carbonari* in 1820.[35] The Austrians wanted the spiritual support of the papacy as a prop to their military might to complete Metternich's ideal of a European union of Altar and Throne against revolution. At that stage, Consalvi was cautious. Metternich raised the subject again in March 1821, after the Austrian army had crushed the revolution in Naples. He stressed that action against the *carbonari* was essential to the 'welfare of Society and Religion'. Consalvi responded with a civil half-measure when, on 10 April 1821, he reissued Pacca's edict of 1814 against the *carbonari* in the Papal States, threatening civil penalties.[36] Metternich was not satisfied with this, and continued to ask for a spiritual denunciation. Consalvi was only prepared to advise the pope to take such a step if evidence could be brought forward of impiety on the part of the political sects. He therefore set the police to investigate them. This produced evidence that their initiation ceremonies were adapted from, and caricatured, Catholic religious rituals. This was no doubt partly to inveigle simple, superstitious peasants to join the *carbonari* by cloaking them in a pseudo-religious guise, but in the eyes of the curia it was evidence of 'the most detestable blasphemy'. This was all that Consalvi needed and on the strength of the police evidence he prepared a solemn condemnation. Before it was issued, he sent the draft to Metternich in strictest secrecy in order to ascertain his views. The chancellor replied: 'I consider it perfectly suited to the purpose for which it is intended.'[37] On 13 September 1821, the Bull *Ecclesiam a Jesu Christo* excommunicated 'a multitude of wicked men united against God and Christ with the principal aim of attacking and destroying the Church'.[38] This pleased Metternich and good relations were thereby restored between Vienna and Rome.

Consalvi, by the end of his ministry in 1823, had succeeded in restoring the papacy to the strongest position in international affairs it had enjoyed for over a century. It was admired and respected by the whole of Europe. Its relations with the Catholic powers had been restored and regulated by concordats. The principle of the political independence and neutrality of the Holy See had been upheld and exonerated. Naples was chastened and Austria was friendly. The threat of revolution had been averted and the *carbonari* suppressed. And Rome was more beautiful than ever, before or since.

VIII
Eclipse

AFTER the visit of the Emperor Francis of Austria in the summer of 1819, Pius VII, now old and frail, had suffered a sudden and frightening decline in health and taken to his bed for several weeks. It was a premonition of things to come. Consalvi exhausted himself looking after the pope. He sat up with him for several nights running, and remained immured for six weeks inside the Quirinal Palace so as to be constantly at hand. It made him fatigued, thin, pale and ill himself, full of sincere sorrow and worry for his master. But he also knew that if the pope died it would be the end of his own career, because the secretary of state always retired on the death of the reigning pontiff. The Duchess of Devonshire wrote to Lawrence about the pope: 'If he dies the prosperity of Rome is at an end, for Consalvi will no longer be the Minister.'[1] On this occasion the pope rallied, and lived for another four years, thus enabling Consalvi to bring many of his schemes to fruition. As it turned out, it was to be Consalvi himself who was to succumb first to a serious illness, though he did outlive the pope by four months.

In the spring of 1823 Consalvi, now in his sixty-sixth year, started to suffer from painful spasms in his chest and had difficulty in breathing. It was thought at first that this might be caused by his heart. Then his legs started to swell so that he could not walk. His doctors were perplexed, but prescribed a standard course of bleeding, purgatives and opiates. The cardinal continued ill into March, and the Duchess of Devonshire was distraught. In February she wrote to the sixth Duke:

> The weather continues hideous and what is worse than all, Consalvi continues ill – La Val* was there yesterday, when he told him that he had tried to go to the Pope and could not from a pain and swelling of the right leg and whilst La Val was still with him, the Pope sent to say he wished to come to see him – the Cardinal entreated him not to risk the fatigue and the *Tesoriere* returned with the Pope's answer that during twenty-two years' intimacy with the Cardinal this was 'le seul déplaisir qu'il lui avait donné.' I think it was quite touching.[2]

She was able to call on the services of Dr Forbes, the doctor of the Marquess of Londonderry. Forbes changed the treatment and ordered different medicines with marked success. After a week of the new treatment, Consalvi began to improve and, though very thin, was soon his old self again. On 15 March 1823, the duchess wrote to Thomas Lawrence: 'The Cardinal has been so ill for a month. Dr Forbes, Lord Londonderry's physician, altered the treatment and this week he has made progress towards recovery.'[3] She was so overcome that she lavished presents on the successful doctor. Henry Fox (later the fourth Lord Holland) who passed through Rome shortly afterwards recorded:

> The Duchess of Devonshire gave a very magnificent diamond ring to the physician who is supposed to have restored Cardinal Consalvi to life. Nobody knew what was wrong. The Duchess while in Naples had written perpetual letters to him and he to her. The wits said 'Qu'il était malade d'une correspondence rentrée'.†[4]

---

*The duc de la Val, French ambassador in Rome and a friend of Consalvi and the duchess.
†'An illness of a reciprocated correspondence.'

By the end of March, Consalvi seemed fully recovered, and was out and about again. He was able to take part in the traditional ceremonies at Easter, and to entertain a party of English visitors including the Kinnairds, some Cavendishes and the Ellices. The duchess recorded that 'He is wonderfully recovered, but much thinner and requires great care and attention to his health.'[5] She continued to badger her friends and relations in London with questions about the best way to treat the cardinal and prevent a recurrence of his illness. Her stepson sent the opinion of his own physician. The duchess was very grateful and replied: 'I have received your letter with Baillie's opinion, it is a most real comfort to find them agree in the opinion of there being no disease of the heart and in foreseeing the possibility of water forming, seemed [sic] confident of relief from the medicines prescribed – I have just sent it to the Cardinal – one prescription he can't follow, the absence from business, it would be the ruin of this country, and he answers "Il faut mourir à son poste."'[6]

With the fine weather of early summer 1823, Consalvi seemed fully restored and was back to his old routine, holding audiences all morning and even through his dinner, and dictating drafts, letters and proclamations all afternoon and evening. In accordance with Italian custom, he had to devote several hours a day to audiences, not bespoken beforehand, to anybody who wanted to call on him. He dealt first with those of position or responsibility and gave them individual interviews in his audience chamber. When he had finished with them, he sallied forth into the ante-room and walked among the humbler suppliants, having a word with each and listening patiently to their complaints, accepting their written petitions, naming a day when they could expect a reply.[7] As well as these petitioners, many others thronged his rooms: distinguished visitors and foreign ambassadors, especially the duc de la Val and Artaud de Montor, the French contingent, Count Lebzeltern, the Austrian, and Baron Franz von Reden of Hanover, and, of course, there were personal friends like the Duchess of Devonshire. They all mounted the staircase and processed through the sequence of state rooms on the *piano nobile* of his official residence as secretary of briefs in the Palazzo della Consulta adjoining the Quirinal. They passed through the ante-rooms hung with different coloured brocades and furnished with gilded chairs and marble-topped side tables in Empire style, the walls covered with Roman *seicento* pictures, the pier tables and chimneypieces crowded with *objets d'art*, recalling Consalvi's personal friends and his European-wide travels and connections, many being presents from distinguished statesmen and visitors. There were French ormolu clocks and Sèvres porcelain, English crystal chandeliers and lamps, marble obelisks, classical bronzes and marble busts from Canova's studio of Cimarosa, the Marchese Andrea Consalvi, the Perseus and the Paris. Four ante-chambers led to the cardinal's reception room hung with cream damask, the grand saloon with a pair of eight-branch English chandeliers and splendid views from the windows across to the Castel S. Angelo, and the state bedroom with a French-style *lit en bateau*. Consalvi's private suite of living rooms was situated on the mezzanine floor below the *piano nobile* and was less richly decorated and furnished. It included a music room with the German piano on which Cimarosa had played, and engravings of George IV and Viscount Castlereagh; his study, with a writing desk, folios of maps and an English briefcase; and his own bed-sitter containing a simple iron bedstead, but crowded with innumerable little tables and cabinets displaying a rich miscellany of objects: little bronzes, gold, silver, *pietra dura* and ormolu boxes, medals, and miniatures including portraits of Pius VII, Talleyrand, Canova, Louis XVIII, the Emperor of Austria, and Consalvi's own brother Andrea. Many of these objects were presents. Other fruits of his diplomatic career were displayed in other rooms or stored in the china and silver rooms. The latter contained the set of fifteen gold snuff boxes from the Congress of Vienna, and two magnificent Sèvres dessert services, one in the Etruscan style and the other decorated with gold heads of emperors and philosophers on a lapis blue ground. His everyday china, however, was simple Wedgwood cream ware. Despite the Empire magnificence of his rooms and the splendid receptions and dinner parties which he

gave from time to time for distinguished foreign visitors to
Rome, Consalvi, when on his own, followed a simple routine
without luxury, spending very little on himself and living mainly
on poached eggs and glasses of water, while walking to his office.
He had a good stable, however, with several carriages and six
horses; and his well-stocked wine cellar contained seventy-five
bottles of pink champagne.[8]

It was amidst this mixture of frugality and splendour that the
secretary of state recuperated and spent his last summer in the
company of his friends, surrounded by the mementos of a
lifetime, while carrying on the relentless business of government.
But the end was near. At the beginning of July he had a return of
the stabbing pains in his chest, though not the breathlessness or
the swelling of his legs. Far worse, the pope fell and broke his leg
and took to his bed in a semi-delirious state. The dramatic
sequence of events is captured in Lebzeltern's letters to Metternich.

> I am losing not an instant to inform Your Highness of an
> event of great importance. The death of the Pope is
> approaching and is inevitable. The sixth of this month he
> was working with his secretary, called here the auditor. He
> wished to get out of his chair to look for something else and
> fell to the ground on the left between the chair and the desk.
> He hit his head and remained unmoving without the
> strength to get up . . .

The pope was carried to his bed and the best surgeons of Rome
were called to examine him. It was found that he had broken his
femur. He spent a restless and feverish night, the delirium
coming and going in waves. The fever continued through the
following days and it became clear that the pope would not
recover. The cardinals pretended to be sad, but were secretly
pleased by the prospect of a new regime and began to talk openly
of the conclave. 'The Cardinal Secretary of State is perhaps the
only one whose affliction is immense and true.'[9]

On 19 July the basilica of St Paul's-Outside-the-Walls, the
least altered and most magnificent of the ancient churches of

Rome, 'unique in that it had preserved its primitive form intact', was destroyed by fire. Immediately, Consalvi had driven out to inspect the ruins and within twenty-four hours had given instructions that it should be restored as 'a noble monument to its former self'. He commissioned a report from the architects Pasquale Belli and Andrea Alippi showing how it could be reconstructed and the surviving ancient mosaics and marble columns salvaged and re-incorporated.[10] Consalvi took it on himself to spare the dying pope knowledge of the fire. Pius was especially fond of St Paul's as he had spent some time there as a Benedictine novice when young and Consalvi was determined that the old man's last moments should not be made miserable by bad news.

Consalvi was in such dejected spirits that he could not disguise his misery. His own illness had so consumed him that he was left without the strength to cope with sudden tragedy or to face up to the *zelanti* cardinals openly gloating at the prospect of his imminent fall from power. The pope grew steadily feebler, the surgeons' purgings and bleedings contributing to his weakness. A month after the burning of St Paul's, on 19 August, Pius received the Last Sacraments. He died at six in the morning on 20 August. Consalvi had attended on the pope all through his illness, 'like a parent on its child', and sat up with him for the last two nights. He alone was able to persuade the pope to take the medicines prescribed by the doctors. In his own weakened state, the fatigue and grief made him ill again himself and it was as an automaton that he carried on with his duties at all. On 21 August, Consalvi wrote to all the foreign ministers of Europe announcing his resignation as secretary of state 'in consequence of the sad event of the death of the Sovereign Pontiff', and asking them to send all diplomatic communications to the secretary of the Sacred College, Monsignor Mazio, during the interregnum.

'Poor Rome! What a blow to its prosperity.'[11] Even at this sombre moment, the end of his political career, overcome with grief at the loss of his sovereign and friend of twenty-three years' standing, Consalvi must have been gratified by the response to his resignation. From all the ministers accredited to the Holy See,

from Naples, from Bavaria, from France, from Spain, from
Austria, from Prussia, from Hanover, from the monarchs and
foreign ministers of all of Europe poured in sincere letters of
condolence which went far beyond the diplomatic formalities to
be expected on such an occasion. Baron Bunsen, the Prussian
minister, was not alone in regretting the 'qualities of heart and
spirit that marked every action of His Eminence'.[12] Despite the
hurtful glee of the *zelanti* at his resignation, and the seeming
indifference of the Romans, the last months of Consalvi's life
were warmed by the European-wide appreciation of his character and achievements. The English Foreign Secretary, George
Canning, wrote:

> Let me add my own [regrets] that established custom has
> removed your Eminence from a post which you filled with
> talent, wisdom and moderation. These regrets are shared by
> all my countrymen who have the honour of knowing your
> Eminence and for that reason have on occasion benefited
> from your goodness. They are shared, I have to say, by the
> King my master. Accept, my dear Cardinal, the assurance of
> my profound respect . . .[13]

The cardinals immediately started to plan the conclave, which
it was decided to hold at the Quirinal rather than the Vatican
because of the hot summer weather. Before entering the conclave, Consalvi went to say goodbye for the time being to the
Duchess of Devonshire. 'Cardinal Consalvi came to see me to
take leave of me, he had some oppression on the chest, and has I
believe met with much ingratitude, but strong in conscience,
noble and disinterested in his conduct, lov'd and esteemed as you
know by all whose opinion he cares about, he is indifferent to the
stings of *the reptiles* and I never saw him more full of life and
energy than he was this evening; still, it is an anxious time to
know him shut up there for months perhaps with a swarm of
wasps, all men with the exception of some very few, would put
things back to where they were one hundred years ago.'[14] She
consoled herself with the thought that her friend had a room in
the Quirinal with a beautiful view of the Alban Hills.

Consalvi had still not given up hope entirely. If one of his few protégés among the cardinals were to be elected pope he might still be able to direct the temporal policy of the Holy See and so prevent the *zelanti* from overturning everything he had been trying to achieve. And indeed the first ballots made it seem likely that his secret supporter Francis Xavier Castiglione might be elected. But Cardinal Castiglione* was defeated at the second round. An English visitor to Rome recorded why. The *zelanti* were determined to elect a new pope who would not continue Consalvi's policies. When Castiglione looked the likely candidate they decided to test his political views and sent one of their number, Cardinal Vidoni, to discover what he thought of Consalvi's conduct of the government. Vidoni called on Castiglione in his cell and congratulated him on the seeming certainty of his election from the way the ballot had gone so far. They talked about different subjects, and just before he left Vidoni carelessly asked Castiglione what he thought of doing as pontiff. 'The thoughtless cardinal replied that the State was going on so well that he should not be disposed to make any alteration. Vidoni took his leave with much assumed veneration and regard, hastened to betray the intentions of Castiglione, and next day he had scarcely a vote.'[15]

The conclave elected Della Genga as pope on 28 September, because of his well-known and long-standing personal antipathy to Consalvi. The new pope took the name of Leo XII in memory of the Medici pope Leo X who had established the Della Genga family fortunes in the sixteenth century. As far as Consalvi was concerned, it was the end. More dead than alive, he had already decided to leave Rome, stifling in the late summer heat, for the country and some fresh air as soon as the coronation was over. He played his part as cardinal deacon in that ceremony on 5 October. In one of those dramatic scenes, more usual in opera than in real life, Della Genga and he, who had been rivals since their youth and had disliked each other heartily for most of their lives, publicly made up their quarrel at the Kiss of Peace just

*He was elected pope, as Pius VIII, in 1829, but reigned for only a few months.

before the singing of the *Agnus Dei* in the coronation mass. Apart from that symbolic gesture, however, there was no particular mark of esteem for Consalvi from the new pope in the first weeks of his reign. Cardinal Sommaglia, an aged reactionary, was appointed secretary of state.

The autumn of 1823 must have been a profoundly depressing time for Consalvi and he was impatient to get away from the papal court. But before leaving Rome, he performed one last act of homage to the dead Pius VII. He planned a magnificent tomb for St Peter's. He set aside 20,000 scudi of his own money and commissioned the internationally renowned Danish neo-classical sculptor, Bertel Thorwaldsen, to do the work. He had intended in the first place to employ Canova, but the latter had died in 1822. Consalvi had met Thorwaldsen at the time of Prince Christian Frederik's visit to Rome in January 1821, and greatly admired his work. The fact that Thorwaldsen was a Protestant led to more outrage among the *zelanti* who saw Consalvi in retirement as still aiding and abetting heretics, but there was little they could do, since the project was privately funded. Even today, Pius VII's monument is the only work by a non-Catholic artist in St Peter's. It is an heroic design in white marble with a seated figure of the pope in vestments and triple tiara, on a classical throne supported by allegorical statues of strength and wisdom 'two qualities certainly he eminently possessed'. The epitaph, dictated by Consalvi in his will, reads simply and proudly:

Pio VII, Charamontio, Coesenati, Pontifici Maximo
Hercules, Cardinalis Consalvi, Romanus,
Ab Illo Creatus.

In settling the details of Pius VII's tomb before leaving Rome, Consalvi was putting his affairs in order. He himself was mortally ill and he knew it. He had managed to keep going as long as Pius VII lived, but the death of the pope had removed the sole reason for persisting and he gave in to his illness. He left Rome on 25 November for the mild seaside climate of Anzio. As usual before a journey, he made his way to the Palazzo Spada to take his leave of the Duchess of Devonshire.

> Dear Consalvi set out yesterday for Porto d'Anzio, far, far from well. He came to me the preceding evening. We had much and interesting conversation, never did his fine mind appear to more advantage – he has given Torwaldsen [*sic*] the order for a monument to Pius 7th wch will be erected in St Peter's – the design, expence everything he settled with Torwaldsen who came strait to me from him, saying he never should forget the goodness, affability and nobleness of his whole manner and conduct on the occasion – and 'Who', said M. Artaud who was with me, 'who is to pay the expence?' '*Il e incognito*' said Torwaldsen . . .[16]

Consalvi spent the whole of December at Porto d'Anzio, in declining health, watching the sea, and preparing himself for death. He returned to Rome for Christmas. His vacation seemed to have done him good, and the duchess, clutching at straws, convinced herself that he was fully recovered. There was to be a final rallying, and to the horror of the *zelanti*, Leo XII now turned to Consalvi for advice. On Christmas Eve, the new pope sent for the former secretary of state and spent some time in discussions with him. To the astonishment of his enemies, on 14 January 1824 Consalvi was named Prefect of the Propaganda Fidei, the congregation responsible for all the Church's missionary work. This post was particularly appropriate as the Propaganda was responsible for all relations between England and the Holy See. Consalvi remained secretary of briefs, as that appointment had been for life and he retained most of his other appointments, continuing to be a judge of the Inquisition, Apostolic Visitor of the Ospizio di S. Michele a Ripa, and Cardinal Protector of the English College. Pius VII, before he died, had had written out new copies of all the official documents confirming Consalvi's various posts, many of the original papers having been lost during the French occupation of Rome. He also retained his official residence at the Palazzo della Consulta. It all amounted to a sound base for a possible return to power. On 15

January, he spent several hours closeted with Leo XII and explained to him in detail his whole scheme of politics at home and abroad. Cardinal Sommaglia, the new secretary of state, was eighty-two years old and was not expected to live long, and the rumour spread that Leo XII intended to restore Consalvi as secretary of state. Nearly every day the pope consulted him on some aspect of policy, for, after all, Consalvi was the only cardinal in Rome with any experience of government. The Duchess of Devonshire meanwhile was plotting away on her friend's behalf. While Consalvi was at the seaside, she had got George IV to offer to send his own portrait by Lawrence to Consalvi as a mark of esteem, and, knowing that it would please her, the King had told her that she could break the news of the royal gift to Consalvi on his return to Rome. 'Nothing for a long time has given me such pleasure than the offer of the King's portrait,' she told Thomas Lawrence.[17] She saw that such a public mark of esteem from the King of England towards the ex-secretary of state would be a resounding slap in the face for the *zelanti*. On Consalvi's return to Rome, they spent a great deal of time in each other's company, visiting each other at least twice a day, and he thanked her for all her kindness to him over the years since she had come to live in Rome.

Consalvi's last flicker was short-lived, and from the middle of January his illness came back with renewed virulence. He was attended by two English doctors whom the duchess had procured for him, Dr Baillie, the Duke of Devonshire's own physician, and Henry Halford, 'Doctor to the King of England'. In addition, written instructions were sent out from England by Dr Forbes, Lord Londonderry's physician. Their treatment comprised a purgative once a week and a dose of *beaume de vie*, ('a well-known medicine on the continent and easily obtainable. Preferable to our extract of aloes') an hour before dinner every day except the purgative day. Consalvi was also given two opium pills every evening to help him sleep, made up specially strong or weak, depending on the amount of pain he was suffering in his chest. Dr Baillie wrote to Dr Forbes, 'I do not think it a heart illness, but the irregularity of the organ is occasioned by the stomach and the upper intestine which are slow in their operation.'[18]

The attentions of the doctors failed to stem the cardinal's rapid decline. On 23 January, the Duchess of Devonshire wrote to her stepson:

> We are in a state of sad anxiety about dear Consalvi, just as we thought him so much better, a violent fever and pain on the chest came on three days ago, and tho' he is rather better he might and has had some hours of sleep, yet he has still a good deal of fever. He was blooded twice yesterday and it was heart breaking to see the pain he suffered, and with such patience and kindness to all around . . .
>
> PS   How unhappy I am . . . all is over – this morning that pure and noble spirit, that kind and benevolent heart ceased to exist . . . I know how you will feel for me.[19]

Consalvi died at half past one on 24 January 1824. A post-mortem revealed that his painful illness and death had been caused by a disease of the lungs. On one side they were so inflamed and decayed that they had stuck to his ribs. The duchess sent a fuller report a few days later, when she was able to pull herself together.

> Having borne his painful illness with angelick patience and fortitude, he died in possession of his faculties with the most blessed tranquillity of mind and spirit that a pure and virtuous mind could alone inspire. He foresaw his death. His letters to me from Anzio however spared my feelings. When he returned to Rome he did not go out but his friends went to see him. His Anti-Chamber was more that of a Minister than a man in disgrace.

She added that he was no longer in disgrace but had been restored to favour by the new pope and but for his death would have been restored to secretary of state. The progress of his final illness had been mercifully rapid. He received the Last Sacraments, and the pope sent a last blessing via Cardinal Castiglione, a tactful gesture. Consalvi's last words were addressed to the pope:

> '*Dite che son tranquillo.*' With a countenance expressive of these beautiful words he expired without a struggle. All his servants were in tears around.[20]

The population of Rome poured out for the last sad ceremonies and the traditional homage. Consalvi lay in state for a week in the Caracci Gallery of the Palazzo Farnese, the most beautiful room in the world. Arrayed in his scarlet cardinal's robes, of which he had been deprived by Napoleon, his many-tasselled hat, the first to have been bestowed by Pius VII, at his feet, he lay on a catafalque surrounded by sixty-six candles, one for each year of his mortal life. His body was embalmed in accordance with the rites of the Sacred College; his face covered by a wax mask modelled by Thorwaldsen, the greatest living sculptor in Europe, who could scarcely do this work for tears. 'The crowd pressed by to contemplate and to pray beside the spectacle of the Christian apotheosis of this great man of the world.'[21]

The solemnities of the funeral itself took place in the Consalvi family church of S. Marcello in the Corso to the slow, sad cadences of Cimarosa's last requiem. The duchess herself did not attend, so overcome was she by the loss of her friend. Madame Recamier, who was in Rome at the time, came across her on the day of the funeral walking up and down on her own in an avenue of cypresses in the gardens of the Villa Borghese, while the tolling of the bells of Rome 'proclaimed the approaching obsequies of her friend'. Madame Recamier was struck by this scene of the duchess's sad soliloquy in a classical landscape: *Et in Arcadia Ego*. It reminded her of the paintings of Poussin. She persuaded the duchess to leave her lonely vigil and to return to the city. Together they drove to the Palazzo Farnese and made their way through the pious crowds to the catafalque. 'The Duchess gazed once more in the stillness and holiness of death at that face which she has seen every day for twenty years* animated with all the

---

*Madame Recamier exaggerated, the Duchess of Devonshire had known Consalvi for less than ten years.

beauty and grace which characterised his expression . . .' Overcome with grief, she fainted into the arms of Madame Recamier who took her back to her suite in the Palazzo Spada close by. Such was the posthumous farewell of the Duchess of Devonshire at the catafalque of Cardinal Consalvi.[22]

The duchess only survived Consalvi by two months, dying in Rome on 30 March 1824. Her body was taken back to England and, having lain in state in the saloon of Devonshire House in London, was buried in the Cavendish vault at Derby alongside Georgiana and 'Canis', the fifth duke, thus perpetuating in death the *ménage à trois* of their life together. Consalvi was buried in accordance with his wishes in the same tomb as his brother Andrea, beneath a white marble monument adorned with a life-size statue of Religion by Rinaldo Rinaldi, and a touching Latin epitaph explaining how the two brothers had been so close to each other in life that in death they had wished to share the same tomb.

In his will Consalvi appointed Monsignor Alexander Buttaoni his executor, and left the greater part of his property including most of the contents of his palace and his personal archives to the Propaganda Fidei, of which he had just been appointed Prefect; there were also a large number of individual bequests. He left money to pay for masses for the dead to be said each year for his mother and various of his youthful friends, including Princess Isabella Ruspoli,* the Duchessa di Ceri, Catherina Odescalchi, the Marchesa Porza Patrizi, the Duchessa Costanze Braschi, as well as Domenico Cimarosa, Alberto Parisani his erring steward, and Philippo Monti, his valet. The garden at Ponte Rotto was left to Pio Braschi, the great-nephew of Pius VI; and his jewels and works of art were divided among friends and relations including his Carandini cousins. Another cousin, Count Parisani, General of Brigade in the papal army, was left two yellow marble obelisks and a medal commemorating the victories of the Duke of Wellington. Chevalier Manno, the artist, received the portrait of 'my brother painted by him'. Capital of 3,000 scudi went to the

*Princess Isabella Ruspoli was one of the Giustiniani sisters and had died forty years earlier at the age of eighteen, to Consalvi's great sadness.

Parisani family. Cimarosa's two daughters were left his silver plate, the portraits of their father and all his music. Pope Leo XII received several paintings, including twelve landscapes by Locatelli and a religious subject by Guido Reni. Various English friends also figured. Lady Matilda Ward was left an ormolu model of Trajan's Column; the Countess of Sandwich an ormolu obelisk, and the Duchess of Devonshire a Florentine *pietradura* snuff box, which is still at Chatsworth. Perhaps the most endearing bequest was that of forty pounds of chocolate to his confessor. Of the fifteen gold-and-diamond-studded presentation snuff boxes from the Congress of Vienna, eleven were left to various religious and charitable organizations in Rome such as the Ospizio di S. Michele a Ripa in return for prayers for himself and Andrea. The remaining four boxes were to be sold to raise money for completing the façades on three unfinished Roman churches: the Aracoeli, S. Andrea delle Fratte and S. Maria della Consolazione. These were finished in 1826 under the direction of the architect Pasquale Belli except for that on the Aracoeli which was never executed, though the design still exists. The other two survive and are embellished with Latin inscriptions recording Consalvi's munificence: 'The façade of this temple was completed and ornamented according to the last will and testament of Ercole Cardinal Consalvi. 1826.'

These Roman church façades and the marble tomb by Rinaldo Rinaldi in S. Marcello are not Consalvi's only memorials. The Duchess of Devonshire, after the first shock of grief, devoted the last two months of her life to the memory of Consalvi. With the assistance of Artaud de Montor and Baron Franz von Reden, she commissioned a pair of bronze commemorative medals to be struck by Giuseppe Girometti and Giuseppe Cerbera, and opened subscriptions for them. 'The occupation pleases and soothes me,'[23] she noted in her diary. The plan was to use the proceeds from the sale of the medals to pay for a memorial to Consalvi in the Pantheon, his titular church. The duchess commissioned this from Thorwaldsen, the plinth to be embellished with a relief showing Consalvi restoring the Papal States to Pius VII after the Congress of Vienna. On top there was to be a bust of the cardinal modelled from Thorwaldsen's death mask and Lawrence's portrait drawing. The duchess ordered a second version of the bust for herself, and on her death this was acquired by the sixth Duke of Devonshire for the sculpture collection at Chatsworth. He also paid for the shortfall on the monument, having been asked to do so by the Hanoverian minister, Reden, who 'came and bored me before breakfast, he is fussed to a degree about the Consalvi medal, there is a plan approved by the Duchess for placing his bust in the Pantheon. I have offered to supply the remaining expense . . .'[24] The monument was not set up till September 1824, the carved relief being added in the spring of 1825. As a gesture of thanks, Artaud, Reden and the Duke of Devonshire gave Thorwaldsen a silver cup by Pietro Belli decorated with a medallion of Consalvi.[25]

George IV's portrait by Lawrence only arrived after Consalvi's death, so the King decided to give it to the duchess instead, thinking that Consalvi would probably have left it to her, but she too was dead before it was delivered, and it ended by being given to the sixth Duke of Devonshire, and now hangs at Chatsworth. A last letter from George IV to Consalvi also arrived after the cardinal was dead, but it would have given him great pleasure had he lived to read it. As it was, it was printed verbatim in his *Elogio* published by the Roman Academy of Archaeology:

> I am anxious to inform Your Eminence of the great pleasure which your letter of 15 December, forwarded by the Earl of Munster, has given me. I attach a very high price to the sentiments and good wishes which you express towards me and I reciprocate them most sincerely.
>
> The friendship and special esteem which I hold for Your Eminence is based equally on your distinguished qualities and personal character, and on the wisdom and moderation which you have shown in your high position under the venerable Pope Pius VII. You have been entrusted with the most important and most critical moments of his reign.
>
> May the wise principles which you have followed during your administration always guide the Court of Rome, and

may your health permit you a long time of working to that end with your advice. These are the sentiments with which I am, My dear Cardinal, your good friend.   George R.[26]

Alas, the 'wise principles' which Consalvi had followed during his administration did not guide the court of Rome during succeeding reigns. As Consalvi and the Duchess of Devonshire had feared, the *zelanti* were determined to reverse his policies. Most of his reforms, including the councils of laymen, were abolished. The Jews were sent back to the ghetto; even the waltz was forbidden in Rome. In time the constituent parts of the Papal States, beginning with the Legations and culminating with Rome itself in 1870, were gradually absorbed into the united kingdom of Italy, but still without achieving the integration of the north and south which had eluded Consalvi. Indeed the administrative and socio-economic problems which he failed to solve in 1816–23 remain to an extent unsolved today. But much of what he achieved outlived him. The concordat system continued to flourish, and to be augmented, into the twentieth century. Catholic Emancipation was carried into law in England in 1829. Consalvi's improvements to Rome, and the restored papal museums, survive almost exactly as he left them, while his laws against the export of works are still in force.

Much has been made of Consalvi's 'liberalism' and he has been frequently represented as the only 'modern' figure in the nineteenth-century curia. In truth, however, he was more of a survivor from the eighteenth century than the harbinger of nineteenth-century liberalism. He was essentially a product of the Enlightenment. Like many of the great eighteenth-century reforming administrators he was a lawyer by training and outlook. His internal policies as secretary of state were a continuation of those of successive eighteenth-century pontificates. His architectural improvements in Rome, and the economic, social and administrative reforms of the Papal States can all be traced in origin to the reigns of Pius VI and Benedict XIV, or indeed back to Sixtus V and his predecessors in the sixteenth century. It is a mistake to judge Consalvi as a proto-nineteenth-century liberal.

He was nothing of the kind. He did not believe in freedom of the press (except in England which he saw as a special case) and had no hesitation in having rebels and brigands shot. But nor was he a reactionary; indeed the majority of Ultras among his colleagues at the curia saw him as dangerously 'Jacobin'. He was a cool, sensible conservative with a tinge of worldly scepticism. It could be argued that the zealous and ascetic rulers who succeeded him in Rome were more in tune with mainstream nineteenth-century developments; they certainly saw themselves as the leaders of the great revival of religion in Europe, and their full-blooded extremism was more in tune with the flood tide of Romanticism. Consalvi by contrast was an eighteenth-century rationalist, the ideal of the moderate statesman striving to preserve a balance between revolution and reaction and to maintain the standards of the Age of Reason in a more turbulent century. A master of diplomacy, he strove to preserve what he regarded as the essentials, such as the neutrality of the Holy See, while smoothing irritating sharp edges and avoiding the burden of lost causes. He was always willing to give way on minor points in order to win support for the larger issues. He was brilliant, dedicated and charming. His career, however, remains a paradox; he was much loved but lonely; supported and admired by all the courts of Europe, but loathed by most of the cardinals in Rome; he was spectacularly successful, but also a failure. The last word should perhaps be left to the French ambassador in Rome, the duc de la Val, in a letter to Chateaubriand:

> Today it is necessary to do nothing but praise his memory, honoured by the tears of Leo XII, by the silence of enemies, finally by the profound sorrow with which the city is filled, and by the regrets of foreigners, and especially of those who like myself have had the good fortune to know this minister so agreeable in his political relations, and so engaging in the charm of his private acquaintance.[27]

Notes

Chapter I

1 A.P.F., Fondo 80/17, Consalvi, I. 'Nobilta della Famiglie Consalvi . . . e Brunacci.' Papers prepared as proof of nobility for Consalvi's reception into the Order of Malta, 17 December 1790.
2 Ibid. I, Fasciola 2. Certificate of matriculation and school fees.
3 J. Crétineau – Joly, Ed, *Les Mémoires du Cardinal Consalvi* (2nd ed, Paris 1866) II, 6–8.
4 Nicholas Wiseman, *The Four Last Popes* (1858) 100. The college was largely destroyed by bombing in 1943, but Cardinal York's books were rescued from the ruins.
5 *Mémoires*, op. cit., II, 8.
6 Wiseman, op. cit., 100.
7 A.P.F., III. 'Materie Scolastiche.'
8 Wiseman, op. cit., 103.
9 A.P.F., III. printed copy. The stilted but literal English translation is by Cardinal Wiseman.
10 A.P.F., II. 'Eredità Perti'.
11 *De Christi in Coelum Ascensione Oratio in Vaticano Habita MDCCLXXX Pio Sexto Pontifice Maximo A Marchione Hercule Consalvio Aca. Nob. Ecclesiastico.*
12 A.P.F., XXXI. 'Carriera e Requisiti Personali dell' Em^mo Consalvi'. His doctoral degree on parchment, bound in black leather tooled with gold.
13 Stendhal, *Voyages en Italie*, including 'Promenades dans Rome' (new edition Paris 1973) 1046, 1205.
14 Ibid. 1206–09.
15 A.P.F., XXVI. 'Specchio dell' Amministrazione di Mon. Consalvi delle Rendite d' Ospizio Apos'.
16 *Mémoires*, II, 23–5.
17 A.P.F., I. op. cit.
18 *Mémoires*, II, 47.

192 CARDINAL CONSALVI

19 A.P.F., XXXIII. Inventory of the contents of Cardinal Consalvi's palace, 30 January 1824.
20 A.P.F., V. 'Musica'.
21 V.A.S. Bologna 397–402.
22 Windsor Castle, R.A., SP Add MSS 1.
23 *Mémoires*, II, 37–46

Chapter II

1 Owen Chadwick, *The Popes and European Revolution* (Oxford 1981) 445–50.
2 *Mémoires*, II, 50–54.
3 Chadwick, op. cit., 462.
4 C.A. Eaton, *Rome in the Nineteenth Century*, I (1820) 190.
5 A.P.F., II. Fasciola 3. 'Eredita della Marchesa Carandini Consalvi'. In his *Mémoires* Consalvi says his mother died in 1797, but the funeral expenses in the above record the date as 5 April 1796 which is more likely to be the correct date.
6 *Mémoires*, II, 57–8.
7 Ibid.
8 *Mémoires*, II, 64.
9 E.E.Y. Hales, *Revolution And The Papacy* (1960), 113–115.
10 A.P.F., XXXIII. 'Peripezie, Lettere Autografe di Sovrani e Particolari Corrispondenze'.
11 Chadwick, 466.
12 *Mémoires*, II, 74.
13 A.P.F., XXXIII. op. cit.
14 *Mémoires*, II, 78–84.
15 A.P.F., XXXIII. op. cit.; *Mémoires*, II, 88–9. Consalvi in his *Mémoires* says he spent twenty-five days at Terracina, but his papers give the time there as twenty-two days. The dates in the *Mémoires* often do not quite tally, because he was writing in exile without any papers to refer to.
16 A.P.F., XXXIII. op. cit.
17 *Mémoires*, II, 91–5.
18 Chadwick, op. cit., 467–70.
19 Windsor Castle, R.A., S.P. Add. MSS. 1; B.L., Egerton MS 2401, ff 132, 136.
20 *Mémoires*, II, 97–109.
21 E. Celani, 'I Preliminari del Conclave di Venezia', *Archivio Della Società Romana di Storia Patrie*, XXXVII (1913); *Mémoires*, II, 238–89.

Chapter III

1 *Mémoires*, II, 104–9, 230.
2 A.P.F., XXXIV. 'Conti diversi de denari amministrati', Ojatti's travel expenses.
3 Horace, *Epistles*, Book II, lines 22–3. I am most grateful to Peter Howell for identifying this quotation for me.

4 A.P.F., XXXI. 'Carriera e Requisisti Personali dell' Em^{mo} Consalvi'. Copies made in 1823 of the original Latin parchments of his appointments which were lost when the papal archives were taken to France in 1810.

5 *Bullarii Romani Continuatio*, XI (Rome 1846), 18–72.

6 *Mémoires*, II, 257.

7 *Mémoires*, II, 268. This passage has sometimes been quoted out of context to suggest that it was the ancient abuses that were 'immovable as a rock' in the face of the reforms, but the text is unambiguous in its statement of the opposite.

8 *Mémoires*, II, 253. Consalvi's Noble Guard survived in Grecian helmets down to the reign of Pope Paul VI.

9 A.P.F., XVII. 'Agricoltura e Pubblici Edifici', report on the condition of the Colosseum by Giulio Camporese and Rafael Stern.

10 G. Paranello, *L'Opera Completa del Canova* (Milan 1975) 85–6.

11 A.P.F., XXIX. 'Conti particolari', copy of Cimarosa's death certificate and accounts for 1801.

12 A.P.F., XXXII. 'Provviste Ecclesiastiche di Sua Em^{za} Consalvi'.

13 *Mémoires*, II, 273–6.

14 *Mémoires*, II, 351.

15 V.A.S., Nunziatura di Francia Vols. 586, 587, Spina's dispatches from Paris; Vols 584, 598–602, Consalvi's replies.

16 Vincent Cronin, *Napoleon* (1971), 214.

17 Consalvi wrote two versions of the story of his visit to Paris for the Concordat, *Mémoires*, I, 312–436 and II, 352–90. The relevant documents from both the French and Roman archives have been published in various volumes including Boulay de la Meurthe, *Documents Sur la Négociation du Concordat* (Paris 1891).

18 *Mémoires*, I, 353.

19 In Horace Walpole's memorable phrase.

20 *Mémoires*, I, 387.

21 The French text of the Concordat reads:

Le gouvernement de la République reconnaît que la religion catholique, apostolique et romaine, est la religion de la grande majorité des citoyens français.

Sa Sainteté reconnaît également que cette même religion a retiré et attend encore, en ce moment, le plus grand bien et le plus grand éclat de l'établissement du culte catholique en France et de la profession particulière qu'en font les consuls de la République.

En conséquence, d'après cette reconnaissance mutuelle, tant pour le bien de la religion que pour le maintien de la tranquillité intérieure, ils sont convenus de ce qui suit.

Art. 1. La religion catholique, apostolique et romaine sera librement exercée en France. Son culte sera public, en se conformant aux règlements de police que le gouvernement jugera nécessaires pour la tranquillité publique.

Art. 2. Il sera fait par le Saint-Siège, de concert avec le gouvernement, une nouvelle circonscription des diocèses français.

Art. 3. Sa Sainteté déclarera aux titulaires des évêchés français qu'elle attend d'eux, avec une ferme confiance, pour le bien de la paix et de l'unité, toute espèce de sacrifices, même celui de leurs sièges.

Après cette exhortation, s'ils se refusaient à ce sacrifice commandé par le bien de l'Église (refus néanmoins auquel Sa Sainteté ne s'attend pas), il sera pourvu par de nouveaux titulaires au gouvernement des évêchés de la circonscription nouvelle, de la manière suivante:

Art. 4. Le Premier consul de la République nommera, dans les trois mois qui suivront la publication de la bulle de Sa Sainteté, aux archévêchěs et évêchés de la circonscription nouvelle. Sa Sainteté conferera l'institution canonique suivant les formes établies par rapport à la France avant la changement de gouvernement.

Art. 5. Les nominations aux évêchés qui vaqueront dans la suite, seront également faites par le Premier consul; et l'institution canonique sera donnée par le Saint-Siège, en conformité de l'article précédent.

Art. 6. Les évêques, avant d'entrer en fonctions, prêteront directement, entre les mains du Premier Consul, le serment de fidélité qui était en usage avant le changement de gouvernement, exprimé dans les termes suivants:

'Je jure et promets à Dieu, sur les Saints Évangiles, de garder obéissance et fidélité au gouvernement établi par la constitution de la République française. Je promets aussi de n'avoir aucune intelligence, de n'assister à aucun conseil, de n'entretenir aucune ligue, soit au dedans, soit au dehors, qui soit contraire à la tranquillité publique; et si, dans mon diocèse ou ailleurs, j'apprends qu'il se trame quelque chose au préjudice de l'État, je le ferai savoir au gouvernement.'

Art. 7. Les ecclésiastiques du second ordre prêteront le même serment entre les mains des autorités civiles designées par le gouvernement.

Art. 8. La formule de prière suivante sera récitée à la fin de l'office divin dans toutes les églises catholiques de France:

'Domine, salvam fac Republicam;
'Domine, salvos fac Consules.'

Art. 9. Les évêques feront une nouvelle circonscription des paroisses de leurs diocèses, qui n'aura d'effet que d'après le consentement du gouvernement.

Art. 10. Les évêques nommeront aux cures. Leur choix ne pourra tomber que sur des personnes agrées par le gouvernement.

Art. 11. Les évêques pourront avoir un chapitre dans leur cathédrale, et un seminaire pour leur diocèse, sans que le gouvernement s'oblige à les doter.

Art. 12. Toutes les églises métropolitaines, cathédrales, paroissiales et autres, non aliénées, nécessaires au culte, seront mises à la disposition des évêques.

Art. 13. Sa Sainteté, pour le bien de la paix et l'heureux rétablissement de la religion catholique, déclare qui ni elle, ni ses successeurs, ne troubleront, en aucune manière, les acquéreurs des biens ecclésiastiques aliénés; et qu'en conséquence, la propriété de ces mêmes biens, les droits et revenus y attachés, demeureront incommutables entre leurs mains ou celles de leurs ayants cause.

Art. 14. Le gouvernement assurera un traitement convenable aux évêques et aux curés dont les diocèses et les curés seront compris dans la circonscription nouvelle.

Art. 15. Le gouvernement prendra également des mesures pour que les catholiques français puissent, s'ils le veulent, faire en faveur des églises, des fondations.

Art. 16. Sa Sainteté reconnaît dans le Premier Consul de la République française les mêmes droits et prérogatives dont jouissait près d'elle l'ancien gouvernement.

Art. 17. Il est convenu entre les parties contractantes que, dans le cas où quelqu'un des successeurs du Premier Consul actuel ne serait pas catholique, les droits et prérogatives mentionnés dans l'article ci-dessus, et la nomination aux évêchés, seront réglés, par rapport à lui, par une nouvelle convention.

22 Hales, op. cit. 57–8; Chadwick, op. cit., 491.
23 *Mémoires*, II, 125.
24 A.P.F., I. Fasciola 3, 'Concordia con Parisani'; Fasciola 4, 'Conti di Alberto Parisani'; Fasciola 6, Toscanella estate etc.
25 Hales, op. cit., 160.
26 A. Latreille, *Napoleon et le Saint-Siege* (1801–1808); *l'Ambassade du Cardinal Fesch à Rome* (Paris 1935).
27 *Mémoires*, II, 397.
28 *Mémoires*, II, 425.
29 *Mémoires*, II, 424; Paolo Marconi, *Giuseppe Valadier* (Rome 1964).

Chapter IV

 1 B.M., Add. MSS. 34949, ff 11–22, Consalvi to Thomas Jackson, January 1804.
 2 Artaud de Montor, *Pius VII*, (Paris 1837), II, 103.
 3 *Mémoires*, I, 436.
 4 Ibid, I, 426.
 5 Hales, op. cit. 174.
 6 *Mémoires*, I, 447.
 7 Artaud de Montor, op. cit. II, 135.
 8 A.P.F., XXXIII. 'Peripezie, Lettere Autografe di Sovrani e Particolari Corrispondenze'. Consalvi to French Commandant of Rome, 20 June 1809.
 9 A.P.F., XXXIV. 'Conti diversi di denari amministrati.'
10 *Mémoires*, II, 182–3.
11 *Mémoires*, I, 452–4.
12 *Mémoires*, I, 460.
13 Hales, op. cit., 145–86; Chadwick, op. cit., 211–33.
14 Ilario Rinieri (Trans. J.B. Verdie), *La Diplomatie Pontificale* (Paris 1903), IV, 663.
15 D.M. Stuart, *Dearest Bess* (1955), 213.

Chapter V

 1 Duke of Wellington, *Supplementary Sketches*, IX 492.
 2 Ilario Rinieri, *Il Congresso di Vienna* (Rome 1904).

196 CARDINAL CONSALVI

3 A.P.F., XXV. 'Materie Legislative' etc.

4 The passport is printed in *Mémoires* I, 20, note i.

5 The Duchess of Devonshire, *Anecdotes and Biographical Sketches* (1863).

6 V.A.S., S.S., R242. Busta 391. Copy of letter addressed to the allied ministers in London, 14 June 1814.

7 *Mémoires*, I, 82.

8 Rinieri, *Il Congresso*, op. cit., 131–40; Consalvi to Cardinal Pacca, 5 July 1814; Windsor Castle, R.A. 215378; Viscount Castlereagh to the Prince Regent, 20 October 1814; D.M. Stuart, *Dearest Bess* (1955) 227.

9 Rinieri, *Il Congresso*, op. cit., 151–63; Consalvi to Pacca; A.P.F., IV. 'Produzioni letterarie e letteratura'; the copy of Wilberforce's pamphlet which Consalvi carefully kept.

10 A.P.F., V. 'Musica'.

11 H.M. Colvin, *Ed, Kings Works* VI (1973) 317–19.

12 A.P.F., XXXVI. 'Catalogio dei Libri posseduti del Cardinal Consalvi'.

13 Durham County Record Office, Londonderry Papers, D/LO/C11, Memo by Viscount Castlereagh of a conversation with Cardinal Consalvi in Vienna, 11 October 1814.

14 John O'Connell, *Ed., The Life and Speeches of Daniel O'Connell M.P.*, II (Dublin 1846) 209.

15 Edited and published in a rather unsatisfactory manner by Ilario Rinieri in 1903–1904. A new, more accurate series is currently being prepared, Alessandro Roveri, *Ed., La Missione Consalvi e il Congresso di Vienna* (Rome 1970–).

16 Consalvi to Pacca, 8 September 1814.

17 Consalvi to Pacca, 17 September 1814.

18 Consalvi to Pacca, 1 November 1814.

19 Consalvi to Pacca, 16 November 1814.

20 Consalvi to Pacca, 1 November 1814.

21 Consalvi to Pacca, 18 November 1814.

22 Consalvi to Pacca, 11 February 1815.

23 Consalvi to Pacca, 25 February 1815.

24 Consalvi to Pacca, 12 June 1815.

25 Harold Nicolson, *The Congress of Vienna* (1946) 219.

26 J.T. Ellis, *Cardinal Consalvi and Anglo-Papal Relations 1814–1824* (Washington 1942) 40.

27 V.A.S., IV, 11(1) Regestum Clementis Papae V. Annus Primus CCCI–CCCXV.

28 Ibid, Consalvi to Marini, 11 January 1815.

29 Ibid, Consalvi to Marini, 12 August 1815; *Mémoires*, I, 99, Canova to Consalvi, 15 September 1815.

30 Ibid, I, 101; Canova to Consalvi, 2 October 1815.

31 Annibale Campari, 'Sull' Opera di Antonio Canova del ricupero dei Monumenti d'Arte Italiani a Parigi', *Archivio Storico dell'Arte*, V (1892); Alessandro Farrajoli, *Ed., Letters inedite di Antonio Canova al Cardinale Ercole Consalvi* (Rome 1888).

32 Consalvi to Pacca, 18 January 1815.

33 Consalvi to Pacca, 12 June 1815.

34 A.P.F., XXV. 'Materie Legislative. Giurisdizioni Controverzi, Orazioni Funebri, Pastorali, Allocuzioni Consistoriali, Congregazione Cerimoniale.' Copy of Consalvi's protest at Vienna, 14 June 1815 and copy of Pius VII's address to the Consistory on 4 September 1815.

Chapter VI

1 V.A.S., Ep. Nap. It. Busta VIII, Fasc. 14.
2 *Mémoires*, I, 39.
3 Mrs C.A. Eaton, op. cit., II (1820) 308.
4 *Mémoires*, I, 150, 182–3.
5 Mrs C.A. Eaton, op. cit., II (1820) 328.
5 A.P.F., XVIII. 'Pubblica Amministrazione', memorials on State Finance, Mortgages, Land Holding, Pasture, the Economic System of the Provinces Re-acquired in 1815; A.P.F. XVII 'Agricoltura e Pubblici Edifici'.
7 *Bullarii Romani Continuatio*, XIV, (Rome 1849) 47–49; *Motu Proprio*, 'Reformatio Publicae Administrationis et Tribunalium ditionis Pontifidae'.
8 A.P.F., XXVII. 'Polizia, Milizia e Commissione Militare', copy of letter of Duke of Campochiaro, minister at Naples, 1820.
9 Stendhal, op. cit., 60–61, 16 March 1817.
10 Charles Abbot, Ed., *Diary . . . of Lord Colchester*, III (1861) 4 January 1821.
11 Royal Academy Archives, Lawrence MSS, 3/111, Duchess of Devonshire to Sir Thomas Lawrence, 20 April 1820.
12 Stendhal, op. cit., 1001.
13 Ibid, 24.
14 A.P.F., XVIII. 'Collezione di Pubbliche Disposizioni emanate in Sequito del Motu proprio di N.S./Papa Pio Settimo.' Published by E. Card./ Consalvi 6 July 1816.
15 M. Petrocchi, *La Restaurazione Romana 1815–23* (Florence 1943).
16 A.P.F., XVII. 'Agricoltura e Pubblici Edifici', Giuseppe Mancini, *Nuovo Proggetto di Agricoltura e Commercio da porsi in esecuzione nello Stato Pontificio e specialmente nell' Agro Romano* (Rome 1816).
17 G. Cassi, *Il Cordinale Consalvi ed i primi anni della restaurazione pontificia 1815–1819* (Milan 1931) 66–148.
18 A.P.F., XXVII. 'Polizia, Milizia e Commissione Militare'.
19 The numbers and distribution of the papal army in 1820 were as follows:
Rome

Noble Guard	120
Guardia al Campidoglio	170
Assigliera	100
Veterani	50
Troops of the line	1750
Soldati di Finanza	100
Provinces	
Troops of the line	1620
Civitavecchia	
Veterani	50

Troops of the line	200
Assigliera	80
Soldati di Finanza	30
Guardieralle	50
Customs	11
Marines	30
S. Leo	
Troops of the line	50
Ancona	
Troops of the line	700
Veterani	60
Assigliera	60
Soldati di Finanza	50
Marines	18
Legations	
Bologna	
Gendarmes (foot soldiers and cavalry)	250
Dragoons	60
Troops of the line	1000
Forli	
Gendarmes	100
Dragoons	40
Troops of the line	1000
Ravenna	
Gendarmes	100
Dragoons	20
Troops of the line	30

(NB Ferrara was garrisoned by Austria)

The Marches

Ascoli		500
Fermo }	Troops of the line	100
Macerata	Gendarmes	
Pesaro		250
Sinigaglia }	Troops of the line	120
Urbino	Gendarmes	

Total

Veterans	500
1st Regiment of the line	1700
2nd Regiment of the line	1700
3rd Regiment	2000
Assigliera	600
Dragoons	800
Gendarmes, cavalry	600
foot soldiers	1400
Soldati di Finanza	1000
Total of troops	10,750

20 A.P.F., XXVII, op. cit., 'Ufficiali Reduci, 1816, Repertorio dei sudditi

Pontifici rientrati negli stato di Nostro Signore Qualificatisi Ufficiali reduci da diversi eserciti con note sullo loro condotta politica e morale'.

21 Stendhal, op. cit., 1102, 1223.
22 Ibid, 1248.
23 C. van Duerm, *Correspondence du Cardinal Hercule Consalvi avec le Prince Clément de Metternich*, (Louvain 1899) 396.
24 Stendhal, op. cit., 62.
25 *Diary of Lord Colchester*, op. cit., III, 192.
26 Consalvi to Pacca, 25 July 1814.
27 Martin Haile and Edwin Bonney, *Life and Letters of John Lingard* 1771–1851 (1911) 154.
28 D.E. Williams, *The Life and Correspondence of Sir Thomas Lawrence*, II (1831) 165, Thomas Lawrence to John Julius Angerstein, 23 Mary 1819; Royal Academy Archives, Lawrence MSS, Sir Thomas Lawrence to Joseph Farington, 2 July 1819.
29 Stendhal, op. cit., 1080–81.
30 *Mémoires*, I, 151.
31 Duchess of Devonshire, op. cit., 28–9, 'Copied 21 May 1817 in Cardinal Consalvi's garden.' The first quotation is from Ovid, *Epistulae ex Ponto*, Book I, Poem 9, lines 7–8. The second is an adaptation by Consalvi of Orpheus's lament for Eurydice from Virgil, *Georgics*, Book IV, lines 465–6: 'Te, dulcis coniunx, te solo in litore secum, te veniente die, te decedente canebat.' I am most grateful to Peter Howell for identifying these quotations for me, and for the elegant translations.
32 Ferrajoli, op. cit., Consalvi to Canova, 26 October 1815.
33 Haile and Bonney, op. cit., 152.
34 Royal Academy Archives, Lawrence MSS, 3/39, Sir Thomas Lawrence to – 14 May 1819.
35 Hon. F.L. Leveson-Gower, *Letters of Harriet, Countess Granville*, I (1894) 110.
36 Stendhal, op. cit., 573.
37 Royal Academy Archives, Lawrence MSS, 2/334, Duchess of Devonshire to Sir Thomas Lawrence, 18 November 1818.
38 John Kenworthy-Browne, 'A Patroness of the Arts', *Country Life* 25 April 1975.
39 In the possession of Lady Maureen Fellowes.
40 Consalvi to Duchess of Devonshire, 29 December 1819.
41 Ibid. 25 December 1819.
42 Ibid, 30 August 1822.
43 Lady Maureen Fellowes, Diaries of the Duchess of Devonshire.
44 Windsor Castle, RA Misc. Vol. 66.
45 Chatsworth Mss, 403, Duchess of Devonshire to 6th Duke of Devonshire, 11 December 1819.
46 Ibid, 424, 18 February 1820.

Chapter VII

1 D.E. Williams, *The Life and Correspondence of Sir Thomas Lawrence*, II (1831), 155–62. Sir Thomas Lawrence to Lysons, 27 June 1819.

2 Siegfried Giedion, *Space, Time and Architecture* (Cambridge, Massachusetts, 1949) 150–55; Paolo Marconi, *Giuseppe Valadier*, (Rome 1964) 88–92, 177–80.

3 Giuseppe Valadier, *Narrazione Artistica dell' operato finora nel restauro dell' arco di Tito* (Rome 1822); Michael Pfanner, *Der Titusbogen* (Mainz 1983).

4 Michael Grant, *The Roman Forum* (1970) 197.

5 The copy on 'imperial paper' which she presented to the 6th Duke of Devonshire is still in the library at Chatsworth – just!

6 C.A. Eaton, op. cit., I, 282.

7 Royal Academy Archives, Lawrence MSS 3/23A, Duchess of Devonshire to Sir Thomas Lawrence, 16 December 1820.

8 Ibid, 4/104, 15 March 1823.

9 Chatsworth MSS, 510, Duchess of Devonshire to the Duke of Devonshire, 16 February 1821.

10 Ibid, 641, 3 June 1822.

11 Ulrich Hiesinger, 'Canova and the Frescoes of the Galleria Chiaramonti.' *Burlington Magazine*, CXX (1978), 654–65.

12 Carroll Meeks, *Italian Architecture 1750–1940* (1979) 74.

13 Valentino Martinelli e Carlo Pietrangeli, *La Protomoteca Capitolina* (Rome 1955) 10–12.

14 C.A. Eaton, op. cit., I, 79–80.

15 Alan Reinerman, 'The Austrian Policy of Cardinal Consalvi 1815–1823.' (PhD Thesis, Loyola University, Chicago, 1964).

16 Williams, op. cit., Sir Thomas Lawrence to Lysons, 27 June 1819.

17 Ibid, 196, Lawrence to Joseph Farington, 2 July 1819.

18 C.A. Eaton, op. cit., III, 169, 163.

19 Durham Record Office, Londonderry MSS, D/LO/C27 (1)–(6).

20 Windsor Castle, R.A., 22102–3, Duchess of Devonshire to the Prince Regent, 23 November 1817.

21 James Brougham to Henry Brougham, 1819.

22 B.M., Add MSS 41536, Consalvi to William A'Court, 15 February 1820.

23 Rome, Venerable English College Archives, 57; 58 1.2, 3.5, 3.8, 4.4, 4.5, 4.10; 59.5; 15; 60.5, 10; 61. 8–11; 64. 5–7; 68. 1–10; 83. 9–2; 93.15; 31.1.

24 Royal Academy Archives, Lawrence MSS 2/334, Duchess of Devonshire to Sir Thomas Lawrence, 18 November 1818.

25 Ibid, 3/39, Lawrence to – , 14 May 1819.

26 Williams, op. cit., Lawrence to Farington, 2 July 1819.

27 Royal Academy Archives, Lawrence MSS 3/55, Duchess of Devonshire to Sir Thomas Lawrence, 6 July 1819.

28 B.M., Add MSS 41535/172/3, Duchess of Devonshire to William A'Court 1818.

29 Joseph Brady, *Rome and the Neapolitan Revolution of 1820–1821* (New York 1937) 9–15.

30 V.A.S., S.S., R204, The Delegate of Civita Vecchia to Consalvi, 30 September 1820.

31 V.A.S., S.S., R242, *Notificazione*, 8 February 1821.

32 Chatsworth MSS, Duchess of Devonshire to Duke of Devonshire, 16 February 1821.

33 Brady, op. cit., 107–145.
34 A.P.F., XXVII, op. cit., Count Lebzeltern 'Coup d'oeil Impartial sur l'attitude de Rome', 26 January 1821.
35 Van Duerm, op. cit., 311, 326.
36 V.A.S., S.S., R165, Consalvi's Edict against the Carbonari, 10 April 1821.
37 Alan Reinerman, 'Metternich and the Papal Condemnation of the Carbonari, 1821', *Catholic Historical Review*, LIV (Chicago 1968), 63–5.
38 *Bullarii Romani Continuatio*, XV (Rome 1835–55) 446–8.

Chapter VIII

1 Royal Academy Archives, Lawrence MSS 3/64, Duchess of Devonshire to Thomas Lawrence, 19 August 1819.
2 Chatsworth MSS, 766, Duchess of Devonshire to the 6th Duke of Devonshire, 16 February 1823.
3 Royal Academy Archives, Lawrence MSS 4/104, Duchess of Devonshire to Thomas Lawrence, 15 March 1823.
4 Earl of Ilchester, ed, *Journal of The Hon. Henry Edward Fox* (1923) 159–60.
5 Chatsworth MSS, 791, Duchess of Devonshire to the 6th Duke of Devonshire, 31 March 1823.
6 Ibid, 803, 26 May 1823.
7 Wiseman, op. cit., 119–20.
8 A.P.F., XXXIII, 'Peripezie, Lettere Autografe' 'Description of the Good Inheritance of Cardinal Consalvi, 30 January 1824'. Inventory of the contents of his palace.
9 A.P.F., XXXIV, 'Malattia e Morte di Pio VII'. Count Lebzeltern to Prince Metternich, 8 July 1823.
10 A.P.F., XVII, 'Agricoltura e Pubblici Edifici', Report by Pasquale Belli and Andrea Alippi on the ruins of St. Paul's-Outside-The-Walls.
11 Chatsworth MSS, 831, Duchess of Devonshire to 6th Duke of Devonshire, 19 August 1823.
12 A.P.F., XXXIV, op. cit. Diplomatic letters, August 1823.
13 A.P.F., XXXV, Notizie Istoriche . . . Malattia dell' Em^mo Consalvi . . . George Canning to Cardinal Consalvi, 25 November 1823.
14 Chatsworth MSS, 840, Duchess of Devonshire to 6th Duke of Devonshire, 4 September 1823.
15 *Journal of Henry Edward Fox*, op. cit., 346–7.
16 Chatsworth MSS, 867, Duchess of Devonshire to the 6th Duke of Devonshire, 26 November 1823.
17 Royal Academy Archives, Lawrence MSS 4/175, Duchess of Devonshire to Thomas Lawrence, 4 December 1823.
18 A.P.F., XXXV, op. cit.
19 Chatsworth MSS, 898, Duchess of Devonshire to 6th Duke of Devonshire, 23 January, 1824.
20 Royal Academy Archives, Lawrence MSS, 4/195, Duchess of Devonshire to Thomas Lawrence, 3 February 1824.
21 Alphonse de Lamartine, *Souvenirs et Portraits* II (Paris 1872) 226.
22 Ibid, 227.

23 Lady Maureen Fellowes, Diary of Duchess of Devonshire.
24 Chatsworth MSS, The 6th Duke of Devonshire's Diary, 20 April 1824.
25 Else Kai Sass, *Thorvaldsens Portraetbuster*, II (Copenhagen 1963) 90–111. I
    am grateful to Mrs Dyveke Helsted for information about Thorwaldsen.
    Mrs Diana Scarisbrick drew my attention to the Consalvi Cup. It is now in
    the National Historiske Museum at Frederiksborg. See Jörgen Birkedal
    Hartmann, 'Coppa Consalvi', *Strenna dei Romanisti* (1964).
26 *Elogio detto alla Memoria di Ercole Consalvi*, 6 May 1824.
27 Duc de la Val to Chateaubriand, 24 January 1824, quoted in Ellis, op. cit.,
    191.

Index